SHANE RICHIE

Rags to Richie

First published 2003 by Contender Books
Contender Books is a division of
The Contender Entertainment Group
48 Margaret Street
London
W1W 8SE

This edition published 2003

1 3 5 7 9 10 8 6 4 2

ISBN 1 84357 099 8

Printed in the UK by Butler & Tanner Ltd, Frome and London
Cover and text design by Button One-to-One
Typesetting by E-Type
Edited by Emily Gale
Production by Sasha Morton

Front cover photography by Colin Thomas
Plate section photographs supplied by Alpha Press / Rex Photos /
BBC Photographic Library / Shane Richie's family collection.

Lyric from 'That's Life' (Kelly Gordon & Dean Kay) reproduced by
kind permission of Universal Music Publishers.

Lyric from 'Town Called Malice' (Paul Weller) reproduced by kind
permission of Notting Hill Music/Stylist Music.

SHANE RICHIE

Rags to Richie

the story so far

RAGS TO RICHIE

contents

	Acknowledgements	9
	Prologue	11
1.	'Hello, Mister, my name's Shane'	15
2.	'People like us can't afford to have dreams'	31
3.	'You do know he's only 16, don't you?'	47
4.	The Noddy train is out of control	59
5.	'You too cheeky, English boy'	75
6.	Hanging up the Blue Coat	85
7.	'Four topless birds and I can't mention 'em?'	97
8.	'This is Bobby Ball, my hero, and he's threatening to break my legs'	111
9.	A tattoo for Colin	125
10.	'Mummy, I've got glitter in my eyes'	141
11.	'That's for you, Danny Zuko!'	157
12.	'Tell me the fucking numbers'	167
13.	'Would you like some Pringles, Mr Richie?'	185
14.	'Shane, she knows'	195
15.	'You've let down the general public'	203
16.	Cracking up	215
17.	'Didn't you used to be Shane Richie?'	225
18.	Easy Rider	237
19.	Labour of love	251
20.	Love, happiness and Alfie Moon	265
	Index	285

This book is for my boys. Anything I have achieved is meaningless without them. There is no love greater than ours. Pure, unconditional love. Shane and Jake, without you guys I am nothing.

Acknowledgements

There are several folk I need to thank. First and foremost, Chris Gosling (Goz). Can you believe he's kept a diary since he was 12? Boy, did that come in handy, especially the Pontins years. Without those little black books you've kept in a cardboard box all these years, this book wouldn't have been possible. We have a relationship that goes beyond friendship. I love you, mate.

Coleen, for her continuing support, both professionally and personally. Wherever our lives take us, we were then and we always will be there for each other.

Stan Dallas, my former personal manager: what can I say about you, Colonel, that you don't already know? Had you not been in my life I might still be driving the Noddy train on my way to another Donkey Derby. Thanks for your guidance and wisdom.

Jon Conway and everyone at Qdos – thanks for sticking by me and putting me back on track. Jon, thanks for being there when I needed you.

Barry Dye and Paul Wagner, for giving a chance to a young naïve lad who didn't know his arse from his elbow and helping him get to where you always thought he should be.

Julia Crampsie at EastEnders for helping me get my foot in the door and Louise Berridge for letting me in.

Michèle Brown, Sasha Morton, Alison Parker and Lydia Drukarz at Contender Books, for all your enthusiasm and support.

Phil Dale, my personal manager, for believing in me when no one else would take a chance. I owe you so much for your determination, your drive and your commitment to me. Here's to the future, pal.

To my mum and dad – thanks for hours of searching the cupboards for them 'feckin' photos'. I love you both so much,

Finally, to Christie, thanks for listening to me re-live my past 24/7 for the last few months. The good times and the bad. It can't have been easy for you, but you never once complained. Without you constantly pushing me to do it, this book would never have happened. I love you so much.

Prologue

As a little boy I loved to sit on the top deck of the number 18 bus from Harlesden to Wembley and gaze out of the window into people's houses. My mum once asked what I was doing.

'One day, Mum, I want all these people to know who I am.'

'Well, who knows son, maybe one day they will.'

As I sit in my BBC dressingroom or look out over the EastEnders set – Albert Square and the Queen Vic – I have to pinch myself to believe this really has happened. They say a leopard can't change his spots, but I changed mine a long time ago and if I muck up now I know what the consequences are. Through my own stupidity I've gone from rags to riches and then back to rags again. I owe the bank and I drive a rented car – but I'm in a better place now than I've been for years.

Most people are lucky to get a second chance. With Alfie Moon I've been given a third. Come on, Sexiest Male at the British Soap Awards – I'm 39, slightly out of shape and divorced with two kids … there's hope for us all!

Yet if it all goes pear-shaped tomorrow I won't complain. Because all I wanted to be was a Pontins Bluecoat, nothing else.

My chalet was my home and as I stepped out of the door people wanted my autograph, they wanted their picture taken with me, they wanted to be with me and talk to me. I made them happy and I made them smile.

That's no different to what I'm doing now, only the country has become my holiday camp and I've got a better chalet. But I guess I'm still a Bluecoat at heart and whatever happens in my life I suspect I always will be.

Shane Richie
August 2003

I've been a puppet, a pauper, a pirate, a poet, a pawn and a king,
I've been up and down and over and out and I know one thing:
Each time I find myself flat on my face,
I pick myself up and get back in the race.

'That's Life', performed by Frank Sinatra, 1966

To blag: To obtain or achieve by persuasive talk or plausible deception; to bluff, to dupe or deceive by bluffing; to scrounge, esp. by clever or deceitful talk. Freq. in to blag one's way into (or out of): to talk one's way into (or out of).

Blagger: A person who seeks to obtain or achieve something by persuasive talk or plausible deception; a bluffer, a scrounger, a cadger.

Oxford English Dictionary, Ed. John Simpson, 3rd. ed, OED Online. Draft Mar. 2000. By permission of Oxford University Press.

CHAPTER ONE

'Hello, Mister, my name's Shane'

We all pretty much know where we were born, but have you ever wondered where you were conceived? I always had a lovely vision of my dad romancing my mum. She was very young at the time. Many times I've asked how young, but she's always laughed and changed the subject. So this is a pure guess, but I reckon she was close to 16. Which side of 16 I don't think I'll ever know.

But my vision was that they were truly, madly, deeply in love. It was a hot, beautiful summer in Dublin, the fair city, where, trust me, the girls are so pretty (there I go and I'm not even born yet)! Picture the scene, June or July 1963. My dad had enjoyed a cold light beer, perhaps with a lemonade top; my mum a chilled glass of Chablis. Gazing into each other's eyes, they both knew that tonight was going to be a special night – the special night they would try for a baby.

They spent the evening chatting by the banks of the River Liffey about their future. Then, as the sun set over O'Connell Street, they walked hand in hand to a nearby five-star hotel, where my dad swept my mum up into his arms and made his way to the penthouse suite. The room was dimly lit with a hundred flickering candles; the queen-size mahogany four-poster bed was covered in rose petals, and on the radio Elvis was singing 'Love Me Tender', especially for Harry and Lily. He told her how much he loved her, before gently laying her down on the bed. He stroked her hair and tenderly kissed her neck, slowly undressing her before making beautiful lo... *Whoa!* I told it there, folks. That's the fantasy.

The reality was that the two of them knocked back a few drinks in a scruffy backstreet boozer and then nipped behind the local cinema. And that was my conception. A knee-trembler in a back alley in Dublin.

I was born Shane Patrick Roche on 11 March, 1964 in St Mary Abbott's Hospital in Kensington, London and I was helped into the world by nuns. My mum said she never understood why, because it had hardly been the immaculate conception. According to my mum, when I was in the womb I would lay there with a finger either side of my right eye. Nowadays my kids tell me that when I fall asleep I still do the same thing. Mum reckons that was me giving two fingers to the world. She told me that I was a blue baby and I never quite knew what that meant as a child, but apparently I was born with the umbilical cord wrapped around my neck and I was a horrible blue colour when I came out. But I recovered quickly and after a couple of days my dad came to take us home. Straightaway I had a taste of what life was going to be like in the Roche household. The nuns insisted all newborn babies go home by car, so when they escorted us outside to wave goodbye, with a few Hail Marys and a set of rosary beads tucked into my nappy, my dad plonked me and my mum in a taxi and waited for the nuns to go. At which point we got out the other side of the cab and walked to the nearest bus stop for the number 18 to take us home. My dad was a great blagger.

'Is Shane your real name?' I'm often asked. My mum says they chose the name because she and my dad were obsessed with Alan Ladd and when he had a premiere for his movie *Shane* in Dublin the whole family went along. I just thank God they weren't mad about *Chitty Chitty Bang Bang*…

I was one of two children. I say two children but I actually mean three – I just didn't know about the third until some years later, so I grew up thinking it was just my younger brother Dean and me.

My mum, Elizabeth – known by everyone as Lily, and my dad, Harry – Paddy to his friends, were both from very poor families in Dublin. My dad was making a name for himself on the amateur boxing circuit, but he had to knock it on the head when they found out my mum was pregnant. Jobs were few and far between in Dublin, so they came over to London. My dad arrived in Britain with just £10 in his back pocket, but with the promise of a job as a labourer on building sites. They found a place to live in Harlesden in north-west London, an area populated by Irish families. It was a rough area – there's a waiting-list to get mugged round there – and three of us lived in a bedsit in Fairlight Avenue. There was a sign on the door that said 'No Blacks, No Dogs, No Irish', but somehow they managed to blag their way in.

The room was so tiny there was no space for a cot, so my mum piled up blankets and anything else she could find to make me comfortable and put me in the top drawer of an old chest. My dad managed to pick up a bit of labouring work, but they found it impossible to make ends meet, so my mum went to our priest at the local Catholic church to ask for help – money, clothes, food vouchers – whatever they could spare. She was desperate, but they turned her away. It was at that point that my mum gave up on the church, but never her faith. When I was a young boy she always encouraged me to go to church, but from that day onwards she would only go herself for christenings, weddings and funerals.

Round about the age of two we moved a few streets away, to 19 Craven Park, where I spent the next nine years of my life. It was a huge dilapidated detached house, with paint peeling off the windows, but to me it seemed like a fairy-tale castle. I loved it. It was always full of families; some would stay for a couple of days, others would be there for months on end. As a young child I couldn't understand why no one would stay longer than six months. By the time I was eight I realised the grim truth – we were living in a home for battered wives. My mum helped run the place and we lived in the top flat.

The four of us lived in three rooms – a bedroom, a living room and a kitchen. There was a second bedroom, but it had no roof. By the time Dean was two we were sharing a single put-you-up bed in our mum and dad's room, which Dean, like most little kids, would wet most nights. He was so embarrassed about it and would plead with me: 'Please don't tell Mummy and Daddy,' and I never did. I'd lie in this wet bed for hours rather than tell them and if they ever did notice I'd say it was me, just to protect him. The toilet was actually a flight of stairs away with a huge gaping hole in the wall, so we had a bucket under the bed, which we used at night. Not that I dared get out of bed much – the whole house was infested with mice and I'd lie there in the dark listening to them scurrying up and down the stairs. The whole house shared a single bathroom, but when the place was full there was never enough hot water to go round, so my mum would boil a kettle and bath me in the sink instead. It wasn't the cleanest of places either. Because it was a council refuge, neighbours would dump their rubbish in our back garden. Constantly women would ask why there were so many rabbits running around in there.

'Rabbits?' Mum would say. 'They're not rabbits, they're feckin' great rats.'

So there we were, this Irish family stuck in a tiny flat at the top of someone else's house with half a roof over our heads, yet I was having the best time. There was always so much to do. There were kids around and we'd all become best of mates for a few weeks. Then they'd suddenly disappear and a few weeks later they'd be back again. I never really understood why at the time, but of course the truth was the abuse would start all over again once they were at home and they'd end up back with us. Yet despite the awful things these families must have been going through there was always a happy atmosphere at Craven Park. I'd see these mothers gather strength while they were with us – my mum would sit with them for hours and just listen.

My mum had a heart as big as a number 18 bus. She would do anything for anybody and I adored her. She could never refuse a waif or a stray and several times I'd come home from school and see a tramp sitting on the doorstep with a doorstop sandwich on his lap. Like most mums in the area she loved the bingo and if she didn't turn up the other women would be really disappointed. 'Ah, it's not the same unless your mum's there,' they'd tell me. She had a huge personality and could liven up any bingo hall on a wet Thursday evening. I'm told I take after her in many ways. She can be the life and soul of the party, but at the same time she has a really shy, insecure side. She's one of those people who puts up a façade and tries to be what people want her to be at any particular moment.

My mum was a real grafter. She'd take on cleaning jobs as well as taking care of 19 Craven Park, and she'd never miss a trick. Craven

Park made up part of Harrow Road, which was the main route from the West End to Wembley, and one year, just before a big England versus Scotland football match, my mum managed to get her hands on several crates of tiny cans of Panda Cola. We set up a table outside the house and sold them to all the drunken football fans on their way to the game. When the football coaches got caught up in the traffic, I'd flash my big smile and get them to open the doors, then I'd go up and down the coach flogging these warm cans of Panda Cola. Someone would give me 50p. 'Don't worry, Mister, I'll be back with your change.' By the time I'd taken a slow walk back to the house the coach was two miles nearer Wembley and five miles further from me. My first blag!

School was Stonebridge Junior and Infants, which was famous at the time for film locations. Whenever they wanted to make a gritty working-class drama they would come to Stonebridge. It was Harlesden's concrete jungle, full of one-parent families, and black and Irish immigrants. They just threw us all in there and left us to get on with it. It was where the 1970s sitcom *Please Sir* was filmed and in the opening credits you can see a load of six- and seven-year-olds dangling their feet through the school railings – that was my first television appearance, a pair of those feet were mine. I remember being fascinated by the cameras and the fact that everyone at school was in awe of all the actors because they saw them every week on that little box in the corner of the room. I never saw the programme myself because we didn't have a television, but that's where my interest started.

And yes, predictably, I was the school joker. My first school play was *Toad of Toad Hall* when I was eight years old. I was desperate to be in it. Not the rat, not the mole, not the badger, but the toad. I pleaded with my teacher and told her I could do a better toad than anyone else in the school. She finally gave in. We all had to make our own masks – all the other kids made masks that covered their whole face but I was having none of it. I just wanted a little bit of paint on my forehead and chin so everyone could see my face and know it was me playing the toad. Even back then I had to stand out from the crowd. Our local paper, the *Willesden & Brent Chronicle*, took a cast picture on the opening night and printed it. I was so proud I showed the cutting to everyone.

Following that I was asked to perform a recital of ''Twas the Night Before Christmas' on stage at the Christmas carol concert in front of all the other children and the mums and dads. *Some Mothers Do 'Ave 'Em*, starring Michael Crawford, was one of the big television shows at the time and when I did the recital I broke into an impression of his character, Frank Spencer. Having no television at home I had no idea who he really was but I'd seen people do impressions of this guy who wore a beret and said 'Mmm, Betty', so I copied them. I got huge laughs; it was pure instinct.

My mum totally understood me from the off. Occasionally she would round up some of the families from the other rooms and I'd do shows for them in our living room. Dean would pretend to do a roll on the drums and Mum, in her great Irish accent, would sit there and compère: 'Laydeez and fellas, would'ya please welcome, all de way from Harlesden, de one an' only, de star, Shane Roche.' I'd come out and sing 'Puppy Love' like Donny Osmond, or put make-up and glitter on my face and pretend to be the camp guitarist in The Sweet and then throw in a bit of Frank Spencer for good measure. My mum got a great kick out of it.

By the time I was eight I'd found music and in particular Donny Osmond. I liked him then and I still do now. Don't get me wrong – I didn't put posters on my wall and scream at the radio every time I heard him. I wasn't that sort of fan. But as soon as I saw him and his brothers on television at a friend's house I knew what all the euphoria was about. They were slick, professional and entertaining and they did everything so right. I badly wanted to be up there with them. It wasn't just the girls; it was the adulation and the fact that they were loved. All my friends were running around dreaming of being footballers, train drivers and astronauts. I just wanted to be an Osmond.

Two years later I was to discover some home-grown talent – none other than the Bay City Rollers. Not only did they sing great tunes, but also they had their own TV show, *Shang A Lang*. I used to read *Look In* and *Disco 45*, which listed all the latest chart lyrics, and I'd memorise all my favourite Rollers' songs – 'Give a Little Love', 'Bye Bye Baby', 'Shang-A-Lang' – and sing them to my friends. It was mainly girls who liked them, but that didn't put me off. I'd see kids at school dressed as their favourite Roller, but like everything else we couldn't afford new clothes, so my mum bought some cheap white trousers and a tartan scarf and sowed the tartan up the side and along the turn-up. She put some tartan into my denim shirt and I teamed it up with striped socks and baseball boots.

I don't know what to say about my dad at this stage, because I didn't really know him. He was just the bloke who would leave the house in the early hours of the morning and come back around five o'clock. My mum always made sure his dinner was waiting on the table. He'd eat it and then be out an hour later to join his mates for a few pints at the local working men's club. Most of the time it felt like he didn't even know that Dean and I were there.

An early memory is of an explosion at a bar not far from where we were living and my dad being dragged out of Craven Park by the police. He was held in cells for two days and questioned as to his whereabouts at the time. They'd picked him up simply because he was Irish. When he came home he was angry and embarrassed that people could even think he had any connections with terrorism, just because he was Irish.

A big influence on my life in those early days was my Aunty Mary. She was my mum's youngest sister and she came over from Ireland and moved in with us. Any time I couldn't get to spend with my mum because she was working, I'd be with my Aunty Mary. She adored Dean and me, and she was forever taking us to the pictures or the local swimming pool. She was like a second mum.

It was in 1974 that we got that little magical box in the corner of our room. It was only a small portable black and white, but for me it was pure escapism. For years I'd had to bluff, but now I could finally join in the conversations at school about the latest TV shows. One in particular I remember was *Planet of the Apes*. I was hooked. Several of my friends got the small figurines for their birthdays. I don't think I ever asked my mum if I could have one, because I knew what the answer would be. Or worse than that she'd have offered to make me one, a bit like she did with the Bay City Rollers kit.

When I was ten the council finally washed their hands of 10 Craven

Park and the house was sold to a Greek bloke. He was a bald, fat, nasty piece of work who, with his slimeball teenage sons, set about turfing out these poor families who were trying to make a fresh start. At one point we were the only family left in this huge house. He wanted us out, too – he wanted to do up the place and sell it off as luxury flats – and he made our life hell. For days on end we'd go without hot water because he'd turned it off and several times we came home to find the locks had been changed on the front door. They even left an Alsatian roaming around the house to try to intimidate us, but it didn't work – after a couple of days of attention from Dean and me it ended up becoming our family pet.

Things got so bad that one afternoon when my mum, Dean and I came back from the shops, one of the sons stopped my mum in the hallway, held her against the wall and threatened her. My mum swore at him and he slapped her across the face. I remember thinking, 'You're dead, mate. My dad's gonna kill ya.' That same night a group of my dad's Irish mates turned up at the house and Dean and I were sent to bed early. I never did find out what happened, but suffice to say we never got any more trouble from the landlord or his sons.

Mum decided she'd had enough of living like that and took us off one day to the council offices in Willesden. We arrived just as they were opening up and Mum told them she wasn't going to leave until they found us somewhere better to live. We stayed until five o'clock, but no one would see her, so we went home and the next day we were back there again at nine o'clock in the morning. At lunchtime she'd go out and get Dean and me a bag of chips, and then we'd sit there all afternoon. This went on for a week until her dogged determination won them over and we were finally given new accommodation – 6 Tavistock Road, Harlesden. It wasn't fantastic, but it was semi-detached on a one-way street that linked the two main roads in and out of Harlesden. I didn't care where it was, all that mattered was that Dean and I had a bedroom each.

As well as changing homes I also changed schools. When I was 11 my parents hoped I'd go to Cardinal Hinsley School in Harlesden. It was the local boys' Catholic school and quite prestigious, but they wouldn't let me in because they thought I wasn't a practising Catholic. I don't know how they defined it, I can only think it was because I wasn't at

Saturday School. I did go for a few weeks, but I was asked to leave after upsetting the priest. We had a whole lesson about Jesus and how he'd died for our sins and at the end we were shown a picture of Jesus on the Cross and asked to write a caption about what he might have said. I couldn't resist and wrote: 'Here lads, I can see my house from here,' because I'd heard a comic crack the same gag at my dad's club. For some reason they didn't see the funny side. They asked me not to come anymore, but what we didn't know at the time was that it was the priest who decided who could go to the Catholic school. My mum and dad were really disappointed that I didn't get in. Me, I couldn't care less. It was an all boys' school and at that age I thought boys' schools were for boys who didn't like girls, so I was quite happy to go to the local comprehensive instead.

To say Willesden High was rough is an understatement. The head called an assembly one day for the whole school and announced that due to the school's terrible reputation and the behaviour of certain individuals, he had been forced to employ security staff to patrol the corridors – the first school, not only in Brent, but the whole country, to resort to such desperate measures. To top it all, John Craven's *Newsround* would be coming to the school to do a report on it. Now *that* got my attention. From the moment he arrived I wouldn't leave his side. C'mon, it was John Craven for God's sake! As far as I was concerned this was going to be my second TV appearance. When the report went out on BBC1 that teatime, you could clearly make me out mugging at the camera. Sorry, John.

I soon settled into Willesden High and by the time I was 12 I'd made enough friends to last me a lifetime. The school was predominantly black. There were 33 kids in my class and three of us were white. I never gave it a second thought, until on the way home when I'd pass Cardinal Hinsley and the lads there would shout, 'Oi, nigger lover!' – and these were the Catholic boys. I've hated that word ever since. Even now, if someone tells a joke where that word is used I have to say something or walk away. The colour of our skin at Willesden High was very rarely an issue. If there was ever any trouble it was over which music you liked or which football team you supported.

It was easy for me because I was growing up with different national-ities at school and I could see people for what they were, but my parents had come from Ireland and were thrust into this racial mix in London and at times they found it hard to cope. I had a big row with my dad about it when I was 12. My mum had recently been mugged for the second time, both times by black men, and I took home a black girl called Lorraine. I really liked her, but after she'd gone home my dad said to me: 'How dare ya bring a black girl into dis house after what's happened to ya mother?'

'Jesus, Dad, listen to yourself.' I tried to get through to him that if all blacks were muggers then all Irish were terrorists – that's how logical his argument was. But I'd backed him into a corner and he reacted the only way he knew how – with the back of his hand.

My dad was from the old school. He was an unfulfilled, unhappy man who had briefly worked on the building sites before finding a job in a factory as a sheet metal worker. When he was made redundant when I was 12 it changed him. He became angry and bitter and although he managed to find work, first as a labourer working from site to site and then finally as a street-sweeper, he was never the same again. I think he was embarrassed by the job and I'm ashamed to say I was, too. He cleaned the streets near my school and I'd always hope none of mates would spot him.

My dad was a real charmer with the ladies, with a thick black mop of curly hair. I looked just like him as a young man. Everyone respected him, but he was a hard man – big with huge hands and a boxer's broken nose – and as a small boy I was really frightened of him. He'd row with my mum a lot and he'd often get angry with me. On a good day he'd joke around with us and call Dean and me Second-hand Paddies – to this day he still does – but most of the time he thought I was nothing but a daydreamer and he was quick to use his fists. If I annoyed him he'd slap me round the head. It was usually only a clout, or perhaps a couple of punches if he'd been drinking, which at the time seemed to be quite often. And when it's a six-foot Irishman whacking you, you do feel it. I always felt there was a bit of resentment and envy in him. He was on the verge of being a professional boxer when my mum fell pregnant and I always sensed that he felt if it hadn't been for me he could have made it.

Dad never had much time for my performing. I think he saw it as my way of looking for attention. When I was 12 my school sent me along to the Barbara Speaks Stage School. It was a place that turned out a lot of young actors and I thought it was great. I used to go in the evenings, but they said I should really be there full-time. When I told my parents this, Dad hit the roof.

'You're not going to a feckin' poof's school,' he yelled. 'How on God's earth do you think I can afford f'ya to do that?'

The council certainly wouldn't pay for it, so I just had to settle for going after school. But even in those few short hours I was getting a taste of what I wanted to do.

6 Tavistock Road was right next door to a community hall predominantly used by the local black community, and that's where I got my first job. I was only 12 and I'd help put up the table tennis tables or they'd give me a few quid to set up the speakers when they had a band on. I learnt very quickly about black music and could soon quote Bob Marley and Peter Tosh chapter and verse.

1977 was a big year for me. Punk was born and the King died. But more important than any of that – I finally did it. Now I know there's been a lot of speculation and newspaper stories over the years about how and when I lost my virginity. The truth is that I lost it when I was almost 13, but you must remember I was almost 13, going on 18. The lucky lady (or unlucky) was my brother's babysitter, a lovely girl called Kim Broad. My mum always used to say that Kim was the daughter she'd never had and the sister I should have had. And you're right, I had her, or should I say, she had me.

Although I was only 12 and three-quarters I wasn't far off 6ft tall and used to go to a pub on Harlesden High Street called The Crown. The barmen in there knew I was under age, but they knew my dad so they would never refuse me a lager top. On this particular night I knew my mum and dad were out and wouldn't be back until the small hours of the morning. It only took a couple of pints for me to get completely mullered and I was home just after closing time. Dean was in bed and

Kim was sitting in the dark watching a horror film. I even remember the film she was watching – *The Creature From the Black Lagoon*. When I walked in she said: 'I'm a little bit scared, Shane, will you come and sit next to me?' I knew exactly what was going on. There she was pretending to be scared and there I was with two pints inside me and a bit of Dutch courage. So I sat down next to her on our tiny one-seater sofa in front of the television and all of a sudden her arm was around me and she was asking if I'd ever done it before.

' 'Course I've done it before,' I bragged.

I had no bloody idea what she was on about. She started kissing me and the next thing I knew, I was naked and so was she. Boy was I frightened – although I made out I wasn't – and it was all over in minutes. Not that I cared. I went to bed that night with a stupid big grin on my face and lay there for hours feeling a mixture of excitement and fear. I wasn't really sure what had happened, but I still couldn't wait to get to school the next day and tell my mates I'd actually had sex. The next day at break I took them through it like a military procedure that had gone on for hours. 'First I did this and then I did that and then she moved here and then I moved there…' Of course, I hadn't done anything. I'd just lain there while she did what she had to do.

Once I discovered sex, school became far more interesting. My mates would talk about it – the difference was I'd talk about it and want to do it. I started to go out with girls who were older than me and I went out of my way to impress them. Until then all I'd been interested in was showing off to my mates. I was the first one in our school to wear his tie around his head and teachers were always pulling me up over it. They'd say: 'The rules say you've got to wear your tie,' and I'd say 'Yes, sir, but they don't say where.' I was always like that. There was a maverick in me and I'd do anything to get a laugh or to make the day go quicker. But once I started going out with the older girls I started to wear my tie around my neck instead, because that was what you did when you were a little bit older and trying to pull the birds.

For as long as I can remember, the Harlesden Working Men's Club was our second home. It was nicknamed The Steps because of the steep steps leading up to the large wooden door. Lots of Irish families went and from the age of six I can remember being in there almost every night. We all felt at home there. At weekends the club would host cabarets and I'd sit there, wide-eyed, watching comedians and singers and bands on this tiny stage. It can't have been more than 10ft by 10ft, yet they'd still find room for the drummer, the keyboard player and their pint pots. I'd get there early so I could go to see them in the dressing room.

I'd knock on the door and say, 'Hello, Mister, my name's Shane, can I help you with anything?' I was always obsessed by the glamour of it. I loved the fact that these guys would be at our club one day and then they'd leave and play somewhere completely different the following night. When the cabaret had been and gone and just before the band packed up, it didn't take much for my mum to coax me into getting up on stage and belting out a song. I'd do 'Puppy Love' or 'Oh Carol' by Neil Sedaka. I loved it. Any chance I got I'd help call the bingo, too. Anything to be up there.

The older I got the more I could see that my dad had a drink problem. When he worked in the factory he wasn't home until late after-noon, but his job as a street-sweeper meant his working day was over by midday, giving him more time to drink. I'm not saying he was always drunk, but if he wasn't at home he'd be in The Steps, where he'd now become a committee member. The place was everything to him and he seemed to do everything there, from booking the cabarets, to running the doors and calling the bingo. He even ran a loan club in there. He'd look for any excuse to be at The Steps. I started to resent the place after a while because it was driving a wedge between my mum and dad.

That year, along with 1001 other kids, I persuaded my mum to take me along to the London Palladium to audition for *Oliver* to play the Artful Dodger. I sang 'Consider Yourself' and they seemed really interested in me. At the end of the day they asked me for a phone number so they could get in touch. Of course, we didn't have a phone and the only number I knew off by heart was the number of the Harlesden Working Men's Club. To this day I don't know if they phoned. If they did they'd have ended up speaking to a drunken Paddy. 'Oh Jayzus, artful dodger? What? There's no feckin' artful dodger here.' I never did find out who got to play the Artful Dodger, but I later found out that one of Fagin's gang was a young lad called Perry Fenwick who, many years later, went on to play Billy Mitchell in *EastEnders*.

In the summer of 1977, Dean and I were sent to Dublin. We were never told why – I can only assume it was to give my mum and dad some quality time together to sort out their problems. We stayed with my mum's sister, Aunty Kathleen, her husband, Uncle Tom, and my grandad. I had the best time ever. My aunty and uncle lived in a nice house in a cul-de-sac in a place called Whitehall, which I loved. There were no main roads and everyone left their doors open. There was such a community spirit that suddenly I realised where my mum's warmth came from. I was this Cockney boy with his arse hanging out of his trousers and all the other children who lived there had never heard a London accent before, so I was king of the hill and for the first time I felt I belonged. At home mum and dad were always rowing, they worked so hard I hardly saw them and Dad spent what spare time he had in the club. Here I was part of a carefree, extended family with aunties and uncles and more cousins than I knew existed. There was always someone at home and always lots of laughter. I felt I was around my own and it broke my heart to go home. I'd always thought there had to be more to life than Harlesden. And now I knew there was.

Although I used my daydreams to avoid some of what was happening at home, there were times when it was impossible to escape. Christmas was one of them. Most people look back with fond memories of their childhood Christmases, but our festive season was always centred around The Steps, so it never really felt that special. Maybe it was because Christmas was always a good excuse for my dad to drink, or maybe it was because I never believed in Father Christmas. From as early as I could remember my dad would come home in December, the worse for wear, put some parcels on top of the wardrobe and tell us: 'Don't ya go looking up dere kids, they're ya presents from Father Christmas.'

I always knew my one present was hidden up there on the wardrobe and I always knew it was a board game. One particular Christmas one of my mates was given every single toy from his Christmas list but I never moaned to my mum and dad because I knew there was no point.

I knew they couldn't afford all that stuff, but my mum could see I was bitterly disappointed and she put her arm around me and said: 'One day, son, you'll be able to have what you want.' Those words stayed with me for a long time.

Although Christmas wasn't great I always looked forward to the last week of July and the first week of August because that was holiday time and every year would be the same – Pontins. Whether it was Pontins Blackpool, Pontins Jersey, or Pontins on the Isle of Wight, better known as Little Canada, they were always fun, right from the off. Every time we went to the Isle of Wight my dad would make out he'd forgotten our passports and that he'd have to blag his way on to the ferry, and I believed him. When he wasn't drinking he was the best dad in the world. I relished every bit of those holidays, from getting on the ferry, to being met by the Bluecoats and travelling on the coach with 'Pontins' written on the front. The Bluecoats were my heroes and I'd follow them around all day like a devoted puppy. I'd enter every competition – the fancy dress, 'It's a Knockout', the swimming gala – just to be with them. I'd tell them that one day I'd be just like them and they never once doubted me. They thought I was a funny little kid with bundles of energy and they took me seriously, which was fantastic at that age.

When I was ten we went to Pontins at Plemont Bay in Jersey and it was there that I entered my very first talent competition. The Bluecoats teamed me up with an 11-year-old boy who was a good singer and said we'd make a great double act. The other boy went out first, singing: 'Daniel is travelling tonight on a plane...' and then I'd interrupt with a joke. I'd pick a woman in the audience and say to her: 'Excuse me, do you know what's got eight legs, is hairy all over and if it was to bite you it would kill you?' She'd say she didn't know and I'd reply: 'I don't know either but there's one crawling up your leg.' I was full of silly jokes like that. The other boy would say: 'Shane, do you mind?' and carry on singing and then I'd interrupt him again. Then I'd wander out into the audience and sit on old ladies' knees and kiss them. All the grannies and mums loved us and we ended up winning the whole competition. I was so proud that I'd actually won something through telling jokes and making people laugh.

I used to have a great time with my mum on those holidays. My dad would be off drinking in some bar, making new friends and talking about Manchester United, but my mum would take Dean and me dancing, or I'd go with her to bingo and sit close by her side. As the Bluecoat called out the numbers she'd look at me proudly and say: 'That'll be you up there one day, son.' She knew how much I wanted to be a Bluecoat. Nothing else mattered to me, so hearing her say that was fantastic. No one else believed in my dream, but my mum always knew.

CHAPTER TWO

'People like us can't afford to have dreams'

I couldn't believe my luck. I was only 14 years old, yet one of our gang had managed to get hold of an air pistol. That night we all met up for a bit of target practice. We'd seen how Dirty Harry held his gun and we wanted a bit of that. Around the back of the community hall there was a tiny alleyway with a little ledge, which looked out on to Harlesden High Street. One by one we took it in turns to crawl out on the ledge and take pot shots at the bus shelter. We were having a real laugh, but apparently someone complained that they'd heard gunshots and before we knew it there were police cars everywhere and even a police helicopter overhead. We legged it and the gun ended up being thrown into our front garden. My mum saw this, dragged me into the house and tore into me. She screamed at me and I saw a side of her that I'd never seen before.

'Ya feckin' eejit, what de feck ya playing at?'

When the screaming finally subsided she became upset.

'After all we've talked about Shane, about ya wantin' to make something better of ya life and get away from here. Is this de route ya really want to go down, playing around wid guns?'

Like a lot of teenage lads I was running with the pack and could easily have gone off the rails. I'd bunk off school any chance I got and get caught up in whatever trouble was going on. My dad was up and out of the house at five in the morning to start clearing the crap off the streets and my mum would shout upstairs at eight o'clock: 'C'mon now, Shane, time for school.' She was always in a rush and never came up to check, so I'd put my feet out of the bed, stomp around a bit to make it sound like I was getting ready and then she'd leave for work and I'd have the day to myself. Often I'd catch the 18 bus to the West End and just walk around all day on my own – I ended up knowing the place like the back of my hand. Sometimes I'd tell my mum that I was staying overnight at a friend's house and go up to Willesden bus depot, slipping underneath the fence. We'd prise open the bus doors and then wander through looking for loose change that had fallen down the seats. It wasn't long before I progressed to nicking bikes. People would leave them chained to railings in the hope that they'd be safe, but they were easy enough to take off. We couldn't afford bikes of our own so we never really felt it was so wrong.

Shortly after the incident with the gun I was suspended from school for two weeks for fighting. During that time I did a lot of thinking and realised my mum was right. Although I was a bit of a tearaway, I knew what I wanted from an early age. I wanted to be in showbusiness and I wanted out of Harlesden and that wasn't going to happen unless I sorted myself out and stayed away from trouble.

I'd had my first taste of real drama at Willesden High aged 11 when the English teacher made us read out Shakespeare in class. I was bored out of my brains. I didn't understand Shakespeare and I didn't want to. He'd tell us that it was the purest form of the English language, but I couldn't care less. It wasn't until I was 14 and started drama lessons that my life began to change. By then I had a fabulous English teacher, Diane Marcus, and a wonderful drama teacher, Pauline Rowlands, and they felt like the only two people in the world who cared what I was up to. I remember Diane Marcus getting a really hard time from our class once. She sent everyone out and it was the first time I'd seen a teacher cry. I stayed behind and said: 'I'm really sorry,' and she took hold of my hand and said: 'Shane, you don't need to be part of what's going on here. You can be so much better. You have wit, you're sharp, you listen and you have a twinkle in your eye. Don't be a follower, be a leader.' After that she made me stay behind after class and read plays with her and try out different accents. She taught me how important it was to listen. She knew I wasn't interested in geography and maths, but she told me to use my mind as a filter. She'd say: 'There might be one thing you learn that you'll need. You might not want to know about algebra or arable farming in the Pennines, but learn about percentages.'

I didn't understand. 'What do you mean?' I asked.

'If you get an agent you'll have to pay him 15 per cent; learn what 15 per cent is!' she'd laugh. She could see what I wanted to do.

Pauline Rowlands was another big influence on my life. She was a fabulous Welsh lady who looked like she'd stepped right out of Woodstock, with flowery skirts and her hair in beads. She'd re-do Shakespeare – the Montagues and the Capulets became black and white families, or English and Irish, and all of a sudden I knew what Shakespeare was about. All my mates at school thought drama was for 'poofs' and used to bunk off, but I spent my whole week waiting for Friday afternoons to come round. One week she asked me if I'd like to take a class of 11-year-olds for drama. A couple of teachers looked down their noses, but Pauline didn't care and it meant a lot to me that a teacher would trust me enough to do that.

It was around this time that I joined the Moonshine Youth Theatre. It was a community theatre on the Harrow Road and I heard about it from a girl at school called Angela Lumb, who'd mentioned in passing that her older brother Mick went there. I told Pauline Rowlands and she said she'd heard of it and would make a phone call. She found out that in the summer holidays they were running drama workshops and booked me in. I was really scared. Not only was I one of the youngest there, but also many of them were professional actors – they'd either toured in rep or had bit-parts on TV. Yet to my surprise they really took an interest in taking 14-year-old oiks from council estates and getting them interested in the arts.

Predictably, my obsession with acting wasn't going down well with my dad. Moonshine was booked to do a series of plays touring around the local parks in Brent. My dad, however, had got me a summer job, clearing up at a local factory. He said it would be good for me to make some money and when I said that I didn't need money he went mad.

'What the feck d'ya mean? I'm not going to keep giving ya money,' he shouted.

'But Dad, I've got a chance to do these plays,' I explained.

He went mad. 'Nobody feckin' does that in our family.'

Years later when I wrote my musical *Boogie Nights*, which was semi-autobiographical, I used the line – 'People like us can't afford to have dreams.'

And that was exactly what my dad said to me that day.

'That's my dream, Dad,' I said to him, trying to explain why the plays meant more to me than a few quid in my back pocket.

'People like us can't afford to have feckin' dreams.'

I did the tour anyway. In one of the plays we had to improvise around a favourite song. I'd choose early Jam stuff or songs like 'Working for the Yankee Dollar' by the Skids. My mates from school would come along and shout: 'Oi, Shane, you big poof, what you doing up there?' But I couldn't care less; I was in my element.

At Moonshine we had an inspirational teacher called Liz Armour. When the summer came to an end she asked me if I'd like to continue with the workshops in the evenings after school. A lot of the time I wasn't doing anything more than making the actors cups of tea and stapling scripts together, but I loved just watching them rehearse and listening to their fabulous stories about tours, digs and theatres. I had no idea what they were on about, but I'd sit there and nod because it all sounded so wonderful. I loved it so much that I even bunked off school to hang around there in the day. After a while the school noticed and got in touch with my mum, who asked me what was going on. I explained to her that I didn't want to go to school; I just wanted to be at Moonshine all the time. My mum contacted the school and explained this and to their credit they said they would turn a blind eye and let me go down there a few mornings a week.

Some of the professional actors were involved with a project called TIE – Theatre in Education – where they toured schools around London and put on a series of plays about safety. I was allowed out of school for two weeks and we appeared at three schools each day. Of course, I thought this was going to be my big professional acting debut. Little did I know that my role was to stand there dressed up as either the Belisha beacon, the Green Cross Code Man or a traffic light, while the professional actors performed their plays around me. Not that it put me off. Let me tell you now, no one has ever played a traffic cone with as much enthusiasm as me!

I also managed to chalk up my third TV appearance that year. Following my feet's debut in *Please Sir* and my face pulling behind John Craven, I managed a day as a schoolboy extra on *Grange Hill* – blink and you missed me.

Growing up in Harlesden I was well aware of the drugs scene, but the first time I tried a joint myself was at a Moonshine Christmas party in 1978, when I was 14. I was sitting chatting to some actors and listening to Jimi Hendrix and they were talking about how good he was. Of course, you only know how good he is when you're stoned. A joint was being passed around nonchalantly and eventually it came to me. I took a drag and for a minute I thought I was going to lose all control of my bodily functions. My head was floating so high that I couldn't work out if I was enjoying it or whether I was going to die. Was this what showbusiness was really about? It was the last time I smoked a joint for a very long time. I hated the feeling of being so out of control, but Jimi Hendrix did sound good…

It was during my time at Moonshine that I tried LSD for the first time. In the spring of 1979 I went to a party in a flat above a carpet store and I was given a tab of the stuff by a friend of one of the actors. Some of the carpets were stored in the spare room and I remember unravelling one and opening the window, thinking I'd got myself a flying carpet. Luckily someone dragged me back from the window ledge and I never touched the stuff again. Of course, people had told me not to do it and warned me it could have that effect, but warnings weren't enough for me. I needed to know for myself what it was like. I needed to put my hand into the fire.

It was around this time that I first saw two men kiss. I'd been invited to another Moonshine party and gone along on my own, as usual. This was a new life I was making for myself and I wanted to keep it separate from what was going on at school and, more importantly, at home. Besides, none of my mates from school would have understood why I liked it. Their attitude would have been: 'This is just a load of nobheads talking bollocks.' Which it probably was, but I liked it. That night I was making my way though the crowd into the kitchen to get myself another can of beer when I saw two blokes snogging each other. I just froze. It wasn't until they pulled apart that I realised one of the guys was an actor called Matt. He was 21 and I'd always been in awe of him. Now here he was with another fella. Shocked is an understatement.

Of course, once I got used to the idea, my attitude changed. There was a bit of gay bashing at the time and I hated it. I remember it was when the Pink Triangle gay rights thing started and some of the gay guys at Moonshine would wear these pink triangles on their lapels. I put one on too and naïvely thought that because I was a straight guy it would stop my friends getting beaten up. Obviously a 15-year-old schoolboy from Harlesden wasn't going to change anything. Wearing the Pink Triangle, meanwhile, just confirmed my dad's worst fears – by now he thought I was gay anyway.

In one of the plays at Moonshine I played a drugged-up musician. I wanted to get it right so I put on lots of mascara and lipstick and a feather earring. I went home like that without even thinking about it.

My mum found it funny: 'Jayzus, what's with de mascara and de shite around ya eyes!' she laughed.

But when my dad walked in and saw my face he grabbed me by the hair. 'What de feckin' hell have ya got on ya face?' he yelled. Then he turned to my mum. 'Lily, he's a feckin' poof. He's hanging around with a load of gays. He's a feckin' poof.' And then, inevitably, I felt the back of his hand.

I said very little because I was frightened he'd take it out on my mum, but afterwards I went back to the theatre and thought: 'Right, I'll put more make-up on.' I was very stubborn. I came home the next night and he shouted again and each night I went back to the theatre and put on even more lipstick, even darker mascara and even thicker eyeliner, until eventually he ignored me. To wind him up even more I'd talk in a really camp voice to my mum and his friends. They'd find it hilarious, but when they'd gone he'd say: 'I know your game, don't try and embarrass me, ya little bastard, ya.'

The more time I spent with Moonshine, the less time I was spending with Dean. Four years is a big age gap in boys and I don't think I was there for him when he needed me. At times he was a tortured soul and seemed to live in my shadow. Sadly, I never realised. I was a teenage boy and had other things on my mind.

When I was 15 I got a Saturday job at Liptons supermarket, the biggest supermarket on Harlesden High Street, with convent girls on the till and a store manager who could have doubled for Captain Peacock in *Are You Being Served*? One of my jobs was to wander around the store and spot shoplifters. Of course I'd see my mates, sidle up to them and whisper a warning out of the corner of my mouth.

'Right lads, be careful 'cos you're being watched. Go round to aisle two and get a load of Curly Wurlys and pocket them in aisle four.'

And why was it that old ladies would come in and try to nick cat food? Instead of grassing them up I'd meet them round the back of the store and give them the dented tins we couldn't sell. My favourite part of the day was when the manager, Mr Day, went on his lunch break. As soon as he'd left the shop I'd go on the microphone and read out the special offers in the accent of an American radio DJ.

'Howdie folks, have we gotta cotton-picking deal for y'all today! We're taking two pence off the dee-licious bacon and three pence off the creeee-am crackers. And if you order chicken and eggs, you can make up your own mind about who comes first. Y'all have a nice day now!'

The convent girls would be in stitches and the shoppers would know it was Lily's daft son Shane, but someone would always tell Mr Day when he came back. I only got away with it because he fancied the pants off my mum. She would come in to the store and he'd said very sternly: 'Your son Shane, he is a handful, Lily.' My mum would flirt with him and he'd promise to give me another chance.

I'd use the money I earned at Liptons to pay for nights out in the West End. I used to go to a club called The Sundown, which was just opposite the Dominion Theatre in Tottenham Court Road and was really trendy at the time. I used to go with a mate, a judo instructor called John

Woods, who was a couple of years older than me. They played great music like 'Ain't No Stopping Us Now' and 'Oops Up Side Your Head' and everyone did the same dances, it was almost like line-dancing. I used to drink vodka and tonic. I hated the taste but I thought it was really cool to walk up to the barman and say: 'Another VAT when you're ready, mate.'

But even with my Liptons money the prices were too much for us and from the moment we got into the club we had to start thinking about how we'd afford to get home. I always stayed at John's place, so we couldn't split up. If one of us fancied a girl, she had to have a friend for the other one. She also had to have a car. Taxis didn't like going out to Harlesden in those days because it was a no-go area, and even if they would go we couldn't afford them.

This was my challenge most Saturday nights. I needed to pull a girl who had her own car, lived out my way, fancied me and had a mate who fancied John. Not as easy as it sounds. I think I got two out of four a couple of times but we often ended up having to get a cab, most of the time with no money. When the cab reached a street in Harlesden called Furness Road we'd say to the driver: 'Pull over here, mate, because it's one-way and you'll never be able to get up there.' As soon as he stopped I'd shout: 'Leg it!' and of course they'd never catch us, despite my flares flapping in the wind and the lingering smell of Hai Karate.

Aside from acting, my other big ambition was still to work at a holiday camp. To me that was fame and success. Forget Butlins, forget Warners. It had to be Pontins, because the Bluecoats were the ones I'd idolised on family holidays for as long as I could remember. I got my chance in September 1979. Reading a copy of *The Stage* newspaper, which the drama teacher had brought to school, I noticed a Pontins advert, which said they were holding auditions for Bluecoats. They were looking for all-round entertainers with the ability to sing, dance and generally have a good time. It said applicants must be 18 or over, but I wasn't going to let that put me off and I sent off my form. A week later I received a letter saying that I'd got an audition the following Tuesday morning at 11 o'clock at Pontins head office just off Oxford Circus. I told no one about it, but my mum was surprised to see me up and about before her. She thought my hair looked smart, but put it down to a new girlfriend at school. I was the first in registration and the first out. I was supposed to be sitting a maths exam, but that could wait: I had an audition to go to. Not for one minute did it occur to me that I would ever get the job, but I knew I had to try. I walked out of the school gates, took off my school uniform and trainers and stuffed them in a Liptons' carrier bag, put on a pair of shoes and a smart jacket and caught the number 18 into the West End. When I think about it now I can still feel the butterflies in my stomach as I walked in. I wasn't scared that I'd mess up the audition, it was more that they'd say: 'Get out of here, kid.' That they'd see through me and realise I was only 15.

When my time came I was called up by the Pontins Entertainments Booker, Bridie Read, who told me to sit down, and then asked what I'd been up to since I left school. That totally threw me. I had thought I'd just get up, sing a song and leave, so I began to reel off some daft stories. Where they came from, to this day, I don't know.

'Well, I've done lots of compèring at various clubs around London,' I bluffed.

Actually, all I'd done was get up and fool around a bit at my dad's club.

'Anything else?'

'Well, I've called bingo.'

'Really?'

'Absolutely.'

Again, I'd just got up as a kid at my dad's club and messed around in front of eight people.

'Anything else?'

'Well, I can dance.'

In the kitchen to Radio 1, when no one was watching.

'And of course I've done some theatre.'

I'd been a Belisha beacon, and remember – no one does a traffic cone like me.

'So, have you ever been on holiday to Pontins?'

At last we were on safe territory and I opened right up. I told her all about my family holidays there as a child, how I sat in the wings and watched the Bluecoats for hours on end, how I entered every show going, how I knew all the Bluecoats by name and loved the Donkey Derby. She sounded impressed that I loved the camps so much, so by the time I got up to sing my song I was feeling a bit more confident.

I'd chosen Michael Jackson's 'She's Out of My Life' because it sounded so beautiful when I sang along to my tape at home. Now, any singer with only the tiniest bit of experience will tell you that a song doesn't sound anything like the original when it's bashed out on a wonky old piano by an eighty-year-old who's never even heard of The Jacksons, let alone their younger brother Michael. That's what I found myself up against. Within seconds I realised that one of us, or more likely both of us, was out of key. Purely out of panic I started to fool around.

'Listen, mate, if you don't know it then don't play it,' I ad-libbed to the pianist. He started again.

'C'mon, try using more than two fingers, pal.'

The song started up once more and this time I joined in deliberately out of tune.

'C'mon mate, any key – the door key will do,' I told him.

They were all jokes I'd heard the comics use at my dad's club as an eight-year-old, but to my amazement when I looked across at Bridie she was laughing.

'OK, very good, you're obviously a funny man, Mr Roche. Anything you'd like to sing for us now?'

I was on a roll now and started singing 'Teddy Bear' by Elvis Presley. I got so carried away that I started throwing the microphone from hand to hand like I'd seen singers do at my dad's club, when suddenly I missed and the mike hit the floor. The feedback from the speakers was awful, but I looked across at Bridie and she was laughing again, so I picked the mike up and started to sing like Norman Wisdom. At the end of the song she called me over, told me she was impressed and that they'd be in touch. I walked out of that place on such a high.

Autumn and Christmas 1979 came and passed with the usual mixture of The Steps, family rows and boring school lessons and I never heard anything from Pontins. I was a bit disappointed, but meanwhile I had other distractions in the form of love. Scunthorpe Youth Theatre had come down to spend a week at our theatre earlier that year and the plan was that they would sleep in the theatre and we'd do workshops together. It was there that I met Lisa Cross. Without doubt she was the first love of my life. It was that amazing thing that only happens once or twice in a lifetime, if you're lucky – you see someone for the first time and your eyes meet and your heart skips a beat. She had dark hair and beautiful dark eyes and she nicknamed me Shaneypegs. This was the first time that nothing else mattered, the first time I wanted someone so much that I felt sick. It was love. I know it was. I was 15 and she was 14, yet even to this day – nearly a quarter of a century on – we still keep in touch and she still calls me Shaneypegs. When I told her I was writing this book she asked me if I was going to write about her. I couldn't even think about writing a book about my life without talking about her, she meant so much to me.

Lisa and I spent every second we could together and when the theatre group went back to Scunthorpe we started visiting each other. Of course, we had to have separate rooms – she'd have my brother's room and my brother would come in with me – but like any teenagers in love we'd wait until everyone was asleep and meet in the middle of the night. In February 1980 I went to stay with Lisa for a long weekend. We'd go out for long walks in the day and plan our future together – marriage, children, the works. I'd forgotten all about Pontins, when my mum called one morning to say that a letter had arrived for me with the Pontins logo on the front. I told her to open it and to my amazement it said that I'd been accepted to start in March at Pontins in Pakefield, near Lowestoft on the east coast, as the Sports Organiser. Organise sports? I couldn't organise a packed lunch. But that was the least of my worries; what concerned me more was that the letter said I would need to take along my birth certificate, P45 and National Insurance number when I turned up for training.

When I got home I had some serious explaining to do. Not surprisingly, Mum had assumed I'd been offered a summer holiday job. Now I had to sit down and tell her that this was a proper job, so not only would I be leaving school before taking my CSEs, but also I'd need a week off in March – two weeks before my 16th birthday – to go to the Pontins training week at Bracklesham Bay in Sussex. This was where we would be fitted for our uniforms and taught the rules of bingo, how to plug in a microphone, how to run a Donkey Derby and how to do the three main dances – the quickstep, the waltz and the hokey-cokey – all the essentials you'll ever need for life as a Bluecoat, basically.

The great thing about my mum was that she knew this was some-thing I simply had to do. The careers office at school would tell me to work in a bank or a building society or an office. That wasn't what I wanted and Mum understood that. She understood enough to let me take the week off school and cover for me, and enough to lend me the money for my train fare. The fact that I'd lied about my age, however, was something I was going to have to sort out myself.

To this day I can remember arriving at Chichester station and hearing the coach driver shouting: 'All trainee Bluecoats this way.' I could have cried with happiness. This was my childhood dream come true. All I had to do now was keep my head down, keep my bottle and blag my way through. The following day 150 nervous-looking new recruits were called into the ballroom. We took our seats and politely applauded as Bridie Read came out on stage to address us. After welcoming us and wishing us luck, Bridie explained the Pontins Code of Conduct and how important it was to live by it at all times. She told us that people looked to us to help them forget their worries and it was our job to entertain them as best we could. I hung on her every word and from that day on the Code of Conduct was like a bible to me. I believed in it so much and I still do to this day. Even when people have stopped me to ask for autographs at the most awkward times, or when my life has been at rock bottom, I've always tried to keep a smile on my face. Pontins taught me that no matter how frustrated, angry, tired, upset or bored you are, you are getting paid to make other people happy – that's your job.

After Bridie's talk we were given our uniforms – white polyester trousers, white trainers and slip-on shoes, a white shirt, the Pontins blue and gold tie and the blue blazer with the Pontins logo on the pocket. When I put that jacket on for the first time I felt like all my childhood heroes rolled into one. This was what I'd always wanted to be and nothing that I've worn since has ever felt as important.

But although I was bursting with pride I was determined not to draw attention to myself. If I stayed in the background then I might just get away with it. For once I would keep my mouth shut, I'd stop playing the joker and if they ever asked for a volunteer for anything then it most definitely wouldn't be me. Unfortunately, things didn't go quite as planned. On the second day, after a bingo demonstration, Bridie asked for a volunteer to come up on stage and have a go. There was silence. No one was feeling confident enough to be put on the spot like that.

'Come on, there must be someone,' Bridie persisted. Again, silence.

'Shane Roche, are you out there?' Bugger. I'd been rumbled. I was mortified. Why had she picked me out of the 150 people there?

'Shane, come on, I know you're out there, darling.'

This is it, it's all over, I thought. I stood up, made my way through the sea of faces and slunk on stage in total fear. I was convinced that Bridie had sussed me and was going to humiliate me in front of everyone by telling them that I was only 15.

'Come on, Shane, we know you've been lying to us. We've just had a phone call from your school – you're not 18 at all. Off you go, silly little boy, and stop wasting our time.'

Even to this day Bridie reminds me of that afternoon in Bracklesham Bay and still insists she always suspected.

If she did, she wasn't letting on that afternoon and instead, to my amazement, she proceeded to tell everyone how funny I'd been at my audition and then asked me to call the bingo. There I was, 150 faces looking to me for inspiration and all I'd ever done before was call bingo at my dad's club and warble my way through 'Puppy Love' in front of a load of drunken Paddies.

I sat down, cleared my throat and began.

'Right, you lucky people, eyes down, looking for a line.'

Everyone cheered and I was off. I was on stage in front of my peers and I couldn't have been happier. I remembered all the jokes and the lines and the more they clapped the better I got. I was in my element. After that there was no point trying to lie low; everyone knew who I was and as I was clearly the youngest trainee I was given the nickname Baby Blue.

The sad thing about that week was that I completely forgot about Lisa, my first love. It was something I would end up doing to girlfriends again and again over the years, but I was so wrapped up in my new life that I didn't remember to call her. I finally phoned her on the Thursday and luckily she was incredibly understanding. I called my Mum the same night to tell her how well I was doing, but all she could do was panic about my age.

'Jayzus, does anyone know? Has anyone found out yet?'

'No Mum, they haven't.'

Not yet, anyway. That night we were told that the following morning we had to turn up with our documents – our birth certificates, P45s, National Insurance numbers and bank details. Bank details? What details? And what the hell was a National Insurance number? My career was over before it had begun. I was a nervous wreck. Was there any way I could blag my way through?

The next day in the administration office, inspiration struck. 'I am so sorry, I've been away working and asked my mum to post my documents but she forgot,' I blagged. I made such a fuss that they told me not to worry. We'd be meeting up again in May and I could hand them over then, they told me. It felt like a weight had been lifted off my shoulders. Now it was just a problem that I'd deal with another day. That was me all over – stick my head in the sand and worry about it later.

That night was the farewell party and they put on a disco for us. The DJ was a guy called Micky Salmon, who would end up becoming one of my closest mates. He'd been a Bluecoat the previous year. Everyone seemed to look up to him – I just wanted to be him. There was a great atmosphere and when they played the party dances –'March of the Mods', 'The Hokey Cokey' – everyone got up on the floor. It was then that I noticed that the Entertainments Manager from one of the other camps, whose nickname was Angel, couldn't keep his eyes off me. This middle-aged man, who was slightly balding and had a bit of a paunch, was eyeing me up. Now I might have been 15, but I knew what was going on. Sure enough after a few minutes Angel brazenly walked out onto the dance floor and joined our group. He ignored the others and while he was still dancing, took hold of my hand, quietly slipped me his chalet key and whispered: 'That's where I'll be later.'

It was one thing him giving me a wink and a wave, it was another entirely to suggest I go to his room. I knew his game and, typical me, I played along. I could see Angel sitting at the bar with his camp mates and I could see they were giggling and whispering about me, so I left the dance floor, walked over and dropped Angel's key into his lap. He went to retrieve it and I said: 'No, no, Angel, let me get it.'

All his friends were shrieking: 'Ooh, we've got a young catch here, haven't we?'

I ignored them and, as I bent down to get the key, I put my hand between Angel's legs and grabbed hold. Then, without his friends hearing, I said: 'You try and embarrass me one more time and I'll rip these sad old nuts off and shove them down the back of your throat.' Without anybody noticing he just whispered in my ear: 'Sorry.' I picked up the key, put it back in his hand, smiled and walked off without another word. I'm glad to say Angel later saw the funny side and we went on to become great mates.

Later that night I managed to hook up with a girl called Lucy. She was in her early twenties and she was obviously getting quite a kick out of getting off with what she thought was an 18-year-old lad, because she was going round telling everyone: 'I'm going off with Baby Blue.' I remember thinking: 'Love, if *you're* getting a kick out of it, think how *I* feel.' We went back to her chalet, where she threw me around like an empty crisp bag in a storm. It was over in minutes. I still had a lot to learn.

After experiences like that it was with great reluctance that I went back to school. I just didn't feel like I belonged there anymore. I confided in a couple of trusted teachers, who were very understanding. One of them was quite a funky guy and I used to see him in the local pub. One night he introduced me to a friend of his and we hit it off, so when I met her again at a party the following week we ended up in the bathroom having a snog and a fumble.

Back at school the following Monday I was sauntering along the corridor, late as usual, listening to my best mate Andrew Sheward harp on about how fit one of the new teachers was. Imagine my shock when I walked in and there was the girl from the weekend standing at the blackboard, asking why I was late. For the next half hour she stood at the front shouting and trying to teach us grid references, when a week earlier she'd had me up against the bathroom wall and we were snogging the face off each other. I had the dirtiest big grin on my face, but her secret was safe with me – and six of my mates.

When May came round I knew I had to sort out the problem with my ID. The administrative staff at Pontins wouldn't forget they hadn't seen my documents, so there was only one way round it – I had to fake my birth certificate. In the end it was simpler than I thought – I just gently rubbed away at the four in 1964 with my finger so I could get it to look like a two. If only every problem in life were that easy to sort out.

Things at home were going from bad to worse. Although my mum understood why I was going to Pontins, she was still upset that I'd be missing my CSEs. Meanwhile, my dad and I ended up falling out yet again, this time because he'd set me up with work on a building site for the summer. My mum was totally on my side. Every time my dad started to have a go, she'd pick up my hands and laugh: 'These hands were not made to pick up feckin' bricks and stones, these hands were made to be on da television.' My dad was having none of it.

'What the feck are ya wanting to be working on a feckin' holiday camp for?' he'd yell every time he'd had a few drinks. 'What kind of job is that?' I think he wanted to say that he was going to miss me and that he was frightened for me, but being the stubborn Irishman he was, there was no way he could do it.

CHAPTER THREE

'You do know he's only 16, don't you?'

As my mates were sitting down to start their exams in May 1980, I was on the train to Lowestoft ready to start my new life as a Pontins Bluecoat. While my mates were going home to tea with their mums and dads, I was settling into my own wooden chalet on the side of a cliff overlooking the North Sea. Welcome to Pakefield.

I soon made myself at home and even laid out a razor in the bathroom to convince any visiting ladies that I was actually old enough to shave. Little did they know that I should have been sitting in a classroom, in my school uniform, taking my CSEs. Not that the school seemed to know or care whether I was there or not, although they didn't miss the opportunity to fine my mum a few quid for every exam I missed.

Being the Sports Organiser I had to be up at eight o'clock to take the early morning keep-fit classes in the ballroom. Then we'd have to stand by the door welcoming the punters into breakfast. Around ten o'clock there'd be a bowls competition on the lawn, followed by rounders on the playing field. After lunch with the punters it would be the swimming gala or a couple of games of tennis, a round of bingo, and if they were really lucky, the Donkey Derby. It wasn't exactly Ascot; I'm sure these were the same donkeys that carried Mary and Joseph into Bethlehem.

You name it, I'd have to do it – and what's more I'd have to pretend I knew what I was doing, too. I'd only held a tennis racquet once in my life before Pontins, and that was for pretending to be the guitarist from Sweet in front of my mirror at home. But luckily it never really seemed to matter. That was one of the great things about Pontins – the punters didn't seem to notice how crap you were at things as long as you were laughing and joking and making sure they had a good time. We never stopped. After dinner there'd be more bingo and of course in the evenings I'd be at the discos or dances or working the doors of the Embassy bar as security. There I was, this 16-year-old bouncer with the power to turn away lads older than myself! I was in heaven that summer.

The nickname Baby Blue had stuck with me from Bracklesham Bay. After me the youngest Bluecoat there was 22, so there was quite an age gap. Most of them were in their mid twenties or thirties. Being the youngest and cheekiest there had its advantages and usually singled me out for special attention.

It was a quiet start because the first few weeks at Pontins are always for the families with pre-school children and the pensioners. The poor pensioners… More than once during the hokey cokey I'd see an OAP put his left leg in, his left leg out and never again get the chance to shake it all about. What did they expect? These were folk who sat in their chairs in front of the telly for 50 weeks a year, then they'd come to Pontins and in two weeks ride a donkey, jump off the diving board, join the end of the conga and take part in the wheelbarrow race.

Once we got into July and August things really picked up though.

Girls, girls, girls, girls, girls.

There's always been a lot of debate about how many women I slept with at Pontins. It came about as a gag, which ended up backfiring on me. Someone once asked me if I'd slept with a couple of hundred women and I said: 'Shut up, a thousand women more like.' It wasn't a thousand, but the funny thing is, it could have been…

I don't know whether it was the sunshine, the holiday atmosphere or the cheap booze, but when the girls came away on holiday the Bluecoats were always their first target. Being 16 years old I couldn't believe my luck. There were times, at the height of the summer, where, if I wanted to, I could sleep with a different girl every day. Sadly, there was never enough time; there was always a Donkey Derby or another game of bleeding bingo to organise.

Back then I didn't really have a type. I've always loved a woman with beautiful eyes and something to say but, if I'm honest, when I was 16, I didn't really care much about what they had to say, other than 'alright then'. Maybe that gave me a reputation I could have done without, but in those days it didn't occur to me to say no.

One week in July a group of six girls came down from Chelmsford. They called themselves the Sexy Six and in my memory they were all blonde. They must have been aged around 19 or 20 and obviously they thought I was 18. We were always laughing and joking together and one night they invited me out to a club in Great Yarmouth. I said I'd bring some mates along, but they told me I should come on my own and I remember thinking: 'I'll have some of that!' At the club they offered me a tab of what I assumed was speed. I'd never taken it before but I knew it was supposed to give you energy and make you high. In my case it did neither – it just ended up making me incredibly horny.

We left the club and went back to their chalet. I'd had my eye on one of the girls all night, so we went off into one of the rooms on our own. We were kissing and cuddling when suddenly I realised there was another girl on the bed. I thought, 'this is good, my first time with two girls!'

All the Bluecoats used to talk about it and I'd lied and pretended I had too, but now it was really happening. I was quite happily taking it in turn to kiss these two girls when one of them said: 'My friend wants you to kiss her, too.' I couldn't believe it – three! Just wait until I tell my mates. I walked into the other room to kiss her friend and couldn't believe my eyes – all four of them were sitting there, naked. They were smoking a joint, a bottle of wine had been opened, one of the girls was singing and two were kissing each other. I wasn't quite naked, but I was getting there and the next thing I knew I was being passed around from girl to girl. I'd go off into one room with one girl and the girls in the other room would shout: 'No, come back in here.' It was like an X-rated tag match. Of course it stopped being horny when there were six – there was no way I was going to please six women – but it didn't stop us all having a fantastic night. I think had another bloke been there it could have been crude, but all I remember is this constant giggling from the girls – nobody was embarrassed. Gradually they dropped off one by one and fell asleep until it was just down to two of us. We eventually passed out and the next morning I woke up and realised I'd been used and abused and spat out the other end. But guess what? I'd loved every minute of it!

Of course, at 16 you think you know everything there is to know about women, particularly after a night like that. The truth is I actually knew next to nothing. What brought it home to me was when I became friends with a well-to-do local businesswoman called Sandra, who used to pop in to one of the Pontins bars for a drink every week. She was in her late thirties and she became like a big sister to me. I remember her telling me that only a woman knows what a woman wants. I was a bit young and naïve in those days and asked her what she meant – the next week she brought in a pile of lesbian porn films. Wow! I could have died and gone to heaven. What I learnt in two hours watching them, the average man couldn't hope to learn in a lifetime. It was through Sandra that I ended up becoming a gigolo. I use the term gigolo loosely and only because it sounds far more romantic than 'horny little devil with his brains in his boxers'.

Sandra commented one night that she'd noticed I didn't get out of the camp very much and didn't seem to have much of a social life. She told me she had two older friends who were great fun. Now don't forget that when you're 16, someone in their thirties seems old and these ladies were in their fifties. So although they were very glamorous and beautiful, it didn't cross my mind that there might ever be anything in it. One was divorced and a property tycoon and the other one was a widow whose husband had died and left her a stable full of race-horses. Sandra told me she was going to the races with them in Great Yarmouth and invited me along. The lady with the property took a liking to me, but I really didn't think much of it and it wasn't until the second time we all went out that I realised Sandra was setting me up. This lady invited me out on my own to dinner and a fashion show on a boat. Being young and game for a laugh I thought, why not? She asked if I would pick her up in my car. She had no idea I had no car and wasn't old enough to drive one anyway! I made some excuse and she ended up sending a chauffeur-driven Mercedes to pick me up. It was fantastic. The last time I'd been in a Mercedes it had been nicked by one of my mates. I went along, drank champagne, ate caviar and pretended I knew what I was doing. At the end of the night she asked to see me again and added: 'Shane, I understand you won't want to do this for nothing'. I was gobsmacked. I had no idea what she was going on about until I next saw Sandra. She explained and to my amazement she said the other woman wanted to see me as well.

'You mean I'm going to make money just by going out to dinner with them?' I couldn't believe my luck.

'Not exactly, they'll expect you to spend the night with them, too,' Sandra replied.

'You're 'aving a larf, ain't cha, Sandra? These birds are older than my mum.'

'But they'll pay you,' she reminded me.

'Well, how much?'

'I'm not sure, about £20.'

'Twenty quid just to have a bit of how's-your-father? Yes please!' Bear in mind I was earning about £22 a week and sending as much as I could to my mum. Now here I was going out in lovely cars, to smart restaurants – anything else was the icing on the cake, the truth is I'd have quite happily done it for nothing. So that's how it started. I'd go out to dinner with them and then go back to their homes and in return they'd buy me clothes and give me money. The first lady never actually wanted to do very much in the end. We'd have a kiss and a cuddle and end up starkers in the bath, drinking expensive champagne, with me massaging her shoulders. That's as far as it went. I think she wanted the companionship more than anything else. After our bath she'd ask me to go to bed and stay there with her until she was asleep before I left.

I did do the rumpy pumpy with the other lady, maybe five or six times during the summer. It would always be after a night out and lots of champagne and it never lasted very long. It never felt strange or sleazy, though; these were lonely ladies who simply wanted company. I enjoyed it, they enjoyed it, so what's the harm in that? I have fond memories of those nights and I hope they do, too. They'll be pensioners now and I often giggle my nuts off wondering if they realise who I am.

Pontins wasn't all about sex though. It was also about mates. Most people went around in little groups, but not me, I'd be friends with everyone. As well as the other Bluecoats I'd spend time with the catering staff, the bar staff, but most of all the punters. It was like no other job on earth.

My love for dancing began at Pontins. Graham Henry, the Entertainments Manager, was a big influence on my early career and he asked me to host the weekly Disco Dancing Competition. To kick off the evening I had to go out and do a dance display first. I used to wear black tails and a baseball cap back to front and do routines to Michael Jackson. I wasn't trained, but I wasn't a bad mover. Then, after dancing, I'd get on the mike and do a few jokes. We weren't really encouraged to do gags because the funny one was Graham and he frowned on anyone else who got laughs, but because I was Baby Blue I could get away with it a bit.

I loved hearing the laughter, but I soon realised that getting laughs on a holiday camp didn't necessarily mean you were funny, because punters would come on holiday and laugh simply because you were a Bluecoat. You'd drop your trousers and they'd laugh. You'd pull a funny face and they'd laugh. You try and do that in the clubs up North or on television and you'd be booed off or switched off.

We also had Black and White Minstrel Shows that year. I had to black up my face, paint on red lips and white eyes, wear an Afro wig and sing Al Johnson songs. This was in the days when these shows were hugely popular, long before people worried much about racism and political correctness, but I didn't like it. A lot of the other Bluecoats seemed to come from well-to-do areas. Now I don't know if it was because of my background – growing up in a black area with black friends – but I felt it was taking the piss and only did the show a couple of times before making some excuse about why I didn't want to be in it. I didn't tell anybody the real reason because I couldn't put it in words at the time. It just didn't feel right. It didn't feel like entertainment to me.

During that first season I met a guy called Colin who was the resident DJ. He was crazy – he reminded me a bit of Micky Salmon – and he really knew how to work an audience. I'd help him out sometimes and we decided to get a little act together called The Fun Funkyteers.

We'd sing along with the records, get people up dancing and organise little competitions. We convinced ourselves that we were so good that we should take this show out of the camps and into the clubs once the season ended.

Lisa came down to see me a few times during that summer. We were still boyfriend and girlfriend in name, but she knew things weren't the same. I felt sorry for her because I'd changed. I wasn't the same guy she'd fallen in love with, but she was trying to make it as an actress so she had her dreams too and I think she understood. I didn't have the heart to end things with her because I still really liked her, but it didn't stop me seeing other girls. There was one girl in particular that I adored. She was called Caron and she was 22 and from Penge. She'd come on holiday with some of her friends and was meant to be going on somewhere else afterwards, but she stayed on for another week to be with me.

When the Pontins season ended in September I was distraught. I'd made so many friends and I couldn't bear the thought of being apart from them. What I should have done was go home and leave everything behind – all the phone numbers, all the lies, all the stories, all the memories – but Caron had got to me and I invited her to come and stay with me in London for a few days. We got home and dropped off our bags. Everyone was out so we went to the pub for the evening and by the time we returned they were all in bed. The next morning I got up and went downstairs. I remember my granddad from Dublin was staying with us at the time and he jumped up and gave me a big hug, and then my mum threw her arms around me, but the atmosphere went distinctly chilly when this girl appeared behind me wearing nothing but a towel.

'Who de feck is that?' said my mum.

'Mum, Grandad, this is Caron,' I replied, trying to bluff it out.

My Mum was having none of it. 'Jayzus, what de hell are ya doing bringing a girl home at your age in front of ya grandad?'

After a whole summer pretending, I'd made the fatal mistake of actually beginning to believe I was 18. Mum and Grandad were horrified. As far as they were concerned I was little more than a schoolboy and there was no way on earth I should be having girls stay over in my bedroom.

Caron was really embarrassed and set off up the stairs to get dressed. As if the situation weren't bad enough my mum couldn't resist shouting after her: 'Ya do know he's only 16, don't ya?' Not surprisingly, I never saw Caron again.

After all the freedom I'd had on the camp I knew I couldn't start to live as a schoolboy again, explaining my whereabouts and being forced to live by my parents' rules. I'd changed and I'd started to notice a change in Dean, too. He was turning into an angry lad and his temper was getting the better of him. My Mum told me the police had been round several times about his fighting or stealing. But I knew it was a phase he was going through and that it would just be a matter of time before he found what he wanted to do in life.

After a few days I got in touch with my mate Colin and we decided to take The Fun Funkyteers out on the road. We had no equipment, but Colin had a box of records and we had the clothes – tailcoats, crazy trousers, loud T-shirts, baseball boots and baseball caps and more important than that – the attitude. We got ourselves some publicity photos and sent them out to clubs and agents all over the country. Colin lived in Bournemouth and I spent a week with him in his bedroom rehearsing our jokes and dance routines; at one point I was even practising back-flips. Colin had a mate who was an agent and to our delight he managed to get us the promise of a residency at a club in Plymouth every Thursday to Sunday. We arrived there at the end of September and found digs in a rough-looking place called Stonehouse, which was right next door to an army barracks. The plan was to stay there for a couple of weeks until we found our feet, then we'd rent a nice apartment overlooking the harbour.

That's one of the downsides of working at Pontins. It gives you a false air of confidence – you think you can walk on water – but when you come out of the holiday camp the truth is you're no one.

We turned up at the club on the Monday before our first Thursday booking and met the manager, who told us that unfortunately there'd been some confusion over the dates. He wanted us to come back the following week instead. We weren't too worried and vowed to enjoy our freedom for ten days. We had a few quid and we decided to check out the local nightlife and make a bit of a holiday of it. But when we turned up on the appointed Thursday and the manager said the same thing again we began to panic. By now we were running out of money. We argued with him but he wouldn't budge. Dejected, we went back to the digs and explained we couldn't pay the rent. Not surprisingly we were asked to leave immediately. I wasn't too worried because the place stank and was actually a brothel used by the local squaddies and I thought they were doing dance classes in the room above me!

So Colin contacted a friend who lived locally, who told us of a squat on the other side of town. It was a big house on the edge of a council estate with the front door hanging off and floorboards missing in the rooms. It was a bit clichéd, with flea-bitten mattresses on the floor and pictures of Che Guevara and Bruce Lee on the walls alongside the famous poster of Bob Marley smoking a spliff.

Reluctantly we moved in there and turned up again at the club the following week. Again there was no work. By now we were beginning to look a bit shabby and we had no money at all, but my pride kicked in and I was determined not to call my mum and dad to ask for help. We went back to the club the following week and it eventually emerged that there had never been a job for us. What had happened was that a friend of a friend of Colin's friend had said: 'Oh well, if they're about we might use them one night,' but in the nightclub world managers move on quickly and when we arrived the place had changed hands. I learnt a big lesson that day – don't commit yourself to anything until you've signed the contract.

Things were about to get worse. To get by, we decided to sell our records, but we ended up falling out because Colin said they were his so he should keep the cash, while I reckoned we were a double act so we should split it. Then I fell out with one of the girls at the squat. I can't remember what it was over, something or nothing, but it meant I had to leave. With no money and no place to go I had no option but to find a park bench. The funny thing is I didn't really feel homeless – at that stage it felt more like an adventure. I had my jeans, a shirt and jumper and an old parka jacket, and I stayed for a couple of weeks on this bench under a tree. During the day I'd beg at the railway station, although I never got very far. I'd ask for five pence for a cup of tea but I'd always do it with a smile on my face and the combination of that and my London accent meant people thought I was taking the mick. Luckily I got quite friendly with a guy who ran a dilapidated old burger van by the station and at night he'd call me over and give me something to eat.

As the days passed, being homeless started to get to me. What had started out as a laugh was no longer funny. I was cold, hungry, dirty, tired and starting to smell; it was becoming harder and harder to stay cheerful. I began to feel more and more sorry for myself and more and more lonely. My only real friend by then was a shaven-headed Scouse nutter called Tats (I can only assume because he had so many tattoos). I'd met him in the squat and he had this theory that the more drunk you got the less you felt the cold. It seemed to work for him.

Tats was very unpopular, but I liked him because he wouldn't take any shit from anybody. He'd come over and talk to me in the park some evenings. One night he ended up somehow talking me into robbing a post office. I must have been so desperate and low, because I went with him to a hill that overlooked the place. He'd nicked a bottle of Pomagne, which he told me was the most expensive champagne you could get. Who was I to argue? We sat there at two in the morning, smoking roll-ups and drinking this Pomagne. He had it all planned and I was completely up for it, talking through the details again and again, until suddenly, from nowhere, he pulled out a gun.

To this day I don't know if it was real or not, I just remember panicking and Tats calming me down, telling me he didn't plan to use it, it was just to show that we meant business. We talked and talked about it until the sun came up, but by this time I was in a mess. I was scared – I'd realised I couldn't do it – but what frightened me most was telling him I'd changed my mind. Eventually I took a deep breath, turned to him and simply said: 'I can't do this, Tats.' Very few people said no to Tats and from that moment I knew why. I'd never seen someone so angry. He punched me hard in the side of the face and called me a wuss and a chickenshit, but I was so relieved that it was all over that I didn't care.

The following day I did my best to avoid him. I went back to the railway station and started begging again. It seemed a safer way to make money, but then, out of nowhere, two policemen appeared and arrested me. Apparently someone had called and reported that I was being a nuisance. They took me back to the station and I was charged with vagrancy. Luckily the cops were a decent pair. They gave me a hot meal and a nice cup of tea and said: 'Right, young man, you can get yourself back to London.' They drove me to the edge of town and left me at the M5 where I hitched a lift home.

It was years later before I went back to Plymouth, but I often think back to that night on the hill and how differently my life could have turned out. If I had held up the post office and been caught I'd have ended up in jail and my career in showbusiness would have been finished before it had even started. But what's most frightening of all is the realisation that the only reason I backed out was because I panicked. It had never crossed my mind that what I was planning was actually wrong, illegal or dangerous in any way. I learnt a big lesson that day: you're capable of anything when you've got nothing.

I arrived back in London in the early hours of the morning and knocked on the door. My mum answered and didn't recognise me because I'd lost so much weight. The last time she'd seen me had been when I'd returned from the holiday camp with a big smile on my face. Now here I was with my clothes in a carrier bag. She was upset and made a huge fuss of me, and for a while I was glad to be back, but things had changed. My mates had left school and got jobs by now – one was working for the gas board, one was working for the post office, another was in a bank and several were in prison. They'd changed and I'd changed, too.

On top of that I still didn't feel I'd achieved much in my life. It was the end of 1980 and all I'd come home with was a load of memories, a book full of phone numbers, a few love bites and a bruise on the side of my face from a bloke whose tattoos weren't even spelt right. I'd had a great time at Pontins and learnt a lot in Plymouth, but I didn't think I'd moved forward.

December came and Pontins invited me back. My mum was upset that I was going to be away from home for Christmas for the first time. What neither of us knew was that I would never actually go back home for Christmas again. This time I ended up at Brean Sands in Burnham-on-Sea, Somerset. I was put in a chalet with a guy called Chris Gosling, who I straightaway nicknamed Goz. I remembered him from the training week in Bracklesham Bay because he had long blonde hair, always wore a tracksuit and looked like the sort of guy who did 300 sit-ups a day. I'd no idea then, of course, that he was going to become my closest friend for the next 20 years and that we would go through so much together, but I knew straightaway that I liked him. We both loved a laugh and boy did we tear it up that Christmas! With Goz by my side I seemed to pack in more in those few weeks than I did in the whole summer. After the Christmas season was over I reluctantly went back home again. I had no job but to pass the time until the next season at Pontins I rejoined the Moonshine Theatre. In January 1981 I dyed my hair blonde for a play called *Class Enemy*. I had a great time doing it, but it wasn't the same. My mind was elsewhere. I was itching to get back to Pontins. I'd had the time of my life and I just didn't want it to end.

CHAPTER FOUR

The Noddy train is out of control

Have you ever seen the film *One Flew Over the Cuckoo's Nest*? That's the only way I can describe the team of Bluecoats I worked with at Brean Sands in 1981. They were crazy inmates.

Let's start at the top. Firstly there was our Entertainments Manager, Alan 'I know a good horse, put your money on it' Phillips. Then there was the Assistant Manager, Trevor Gray, who did all the jobs on camp and was full of energy. Frank Lewis, who sounded like a Scottish Roger Moore, was as suave as Prince Charles and owned every aftershave going. Jack, the Children's Uncle, who dressed as a clown called Weedy and looked after the kids every day. They loved him, but behind the make-up he always seemed on the verge of suicide. He hated kids, which didn't help. Then there was Ian Robinson, nicknamed Blockhead; to this day I have no idea why. Only two seasons earlier he had been a kitchen porter, but he made such an impression on the punters they decided to make him a Bluecoat. He had no talent other than a great personality. Denise, a round girl from Birmingham with an unbelievable voice, was probably the only one out of the lot of us with any real talent, but she would sulk for days on end if she wasn't allowed to sing. Sally, a real dizzy Essex girl, fell in love week in week out with a different fella, and dozy Rosie, who was a great bundle of fun, giggled from morning to night. Then there was Debbie, who got great pleasure from telling us all about her sexual adventures from the night before. Finally there was Pete, who wasn't the best looking guy. He had a mole on his face with hairs coming out of it, which looked like a spider. One day we heard a small child call him Pider, because she couldn't say spider, so the nickname stuck.

Then of course there was me and Goz. He was the sports organiser this year and was much more suited to it than me. We quickly had it sussed. I'd always had an eye for a blag, but this was the year that I really started to get into it and realised I could easily make a few quid on the side. Pontins had a weekly event called 'cine racing'. It was horse-racing from America on film, which we'd show on a projector in the bar. The films were sealed in tape and I'd get a punter to choose one from a huge box to show it wasn't rigged. The horses would be numbered one to eight and there'd be a tote table where the punters could place their bets. What they didn't know was that we'd already seen these films. We'd then re-sealed them and scratched a little code on the side of the packet that would tell us which number horse was going to win. I'd see which tape it was and then say to Goz at the back of the room: 'Goz, get me a couple of bags of crisps will you?' That was my way of telling him the number of the winning horse was two. Goz would then pull a likely looking family to one side and tell them to put £20 on that horse. The horse would win; the family would make a few quid and slip Goz and I a few quid. We made bundles. Well, it seemed like bundles at the time. Enough to buy condoms and a bottle of Hai Karate anyway.

Another great blag was chair bingo, which we'd do when it was raining and everyone had congregated in the ballroom. We'd get 90 people to bring their chairs into the middle of the floor and pay a pound each. They'd all be given a number, 1–90, and when their number was called out they had to sit down. We'd say: 'Don't forget, whoever's left sitting in the middle of the floor at the end, wins £50!' They'd all gasp and there'd be lots of applause and 'oohs' and 'aahs'. They never once thought to ask what happened to the other £40. What a great blag!

Goz and I shared a chalet that season, as well as the odd girl. In fact my reputation as a ladies' man really came from 1981 at Brean Sands. We had a running competition throughout the season to see how many girls we could sleep with. It didn't matter what you looked like – I'm not trying to make out I was the best-looking bloke there – it was just the power of that blue jacket.

We were careful never to get a love bite – that would kill it for the next girl. To make sure we didn't interrupt each other, we had a signal: if the curtain was sticking out of the louvre window it meant the room was occupied. We'd collect knickers as souvenirs and pin them on the ceiling – it became competitive to the point that we nearly fell out about it. I remember if you scored on a Saturday night you got 50 points, Sunday 40, Monday 30, and so on. If you copped off with two girls at the same time you got 70 points, if they were sisters you were off the scale – you'd won the FA Cup! Forget fantasy football, this was fantasy sex. One week, at the height of the summer, the fantasy came true. One of the most popular jobs amongst the Bluecoats was wandering around the tables listening for people calling 'house' at the opening night bingo, because it was a great chance to check out the new talent that had arrived that day. This particular week I spotted two stunning blondes. They looked very alike and I assumed they were sisters. I chatted the youngest one up; she was about 20 and told me her name was Diane. I guessed her older sister must have been in her mid-thirties. At the end of the night I walked Diane back to her chalet. The chalet was empty and we started kissing and cuddling on the couch, when all of a sudden we heard the door go.

'Bloody hell, who's that?' I said in a panic.

'Don't worry,' she replied. She didn't seem concerned. Her sister came in and I sat there, nervously, waiting for her to go to bed. We all chatted politely and after a while Diane said she was going to the bathroom. To my total amazement the second she disappeared her sister moved up next to me on the couch and started kissing me. Wow! I've pulled two sisters. I'm off the scale! I've won the FA Cup! Wait until I tell Goz and the lads, I thought.

At this point Diane opened the bathroom door and saw exactly what was going on. I started to panic, thinking she would go ballistic. Instead, she coolly wandered over and sat the other side of me.

'You've met my mum then.'

He shoots, he scores! Forget the FA Cup. A mum and a daughter? I'd just won the World Cup!

Before I had a chance to say anything it was a free-for-all. The funny thing was, rather than enjoy it, I just wanted it to finish really quickly so I could go and tell Goz. And I did. It was two in the morning, but I still woke him up and paraded around the chalet with a big grin on my face. Top that, Goz!

At the beginning of every Pontins season we had speciality weeks. There was Gingerbread Week for single mothers and divorcees – you can imagine. During Country and Western Week there were plenty of squaws and the odd cowgirl. Majorettes' week? Enough said. Less popular was Model Makers' Week, when people would turn up and fly model planes on the sports field, take over the swimming pool with their toy submarines and boats and cover the ballroom floor with the latest remote-control cars. During weeks like that we'd turn our attentions to the staff – one of the cleaners or cooks, or a barmaid if we were lucky.

It didn't always go according to plan though. Just a few weeks into the season Pider was fired. It happened to coincide with a huge party in some girls' chalet. We were having a great time, but suddenly, in the early hours, there was a banging on the door. Our hearts sank; we'd been caught. You weren't supposed to go to the punters' chalets, but as there were four of us we knew we weren't going to get the sack. Written warning, slap on the wrist, dock your wages – we didn't care, it was worth it for the girls. But instead of security guards, standing at the chalet door was the manager of the camp. He'd had a phone call from the police saying that one of the Bluecoats – Pider – had just threatened to drown himself and he wanted us all to go straight to the beach to stop him. It was a fifteen-minute walk down there and when we arrived there were police with torches everywhere. Bear in mind, it was now three o'clock in the morning and we'd missed out on a night of passion with four beautiful girls to search for a guy we didn't even particularly like. So we're scrambling through the bushes and the sand-dunes screaming, 'You dopey tosser, when we find you we are going to kill you!'

Then all of a sudden we heard this pitiful cry of 'Help, help!' and out in the distance we saw a figure waving. Apparently Brean has one of the longest tides in the country, it goes out for miles, and Pider had clearly decided to wade out to sea, not realising how far he'd have to go, and sunk up to his waist in mud. We had to get the tractor from the Noddy train down on to the beach, wade out in the mud in our white uniforms with a rope and drag him out. For his own safety it was probably a good job he left the camp that night.

The Noddy train ended up being the bane of my life. One wet Wednesday afternoon I was asked to drive the Noddy train around the camp. It was basically a tractor painted in funny colours and covered with stickers of Noddy and Big Ears, pulling along four brightly covered open carriages. I'd done this many times before, but never in the rain. First mistake.

Our first station stop was the ballroom, where I picked up close to 30 kids.

'Sorry, no adults. Are you ready, kids?'

Thirty screaming kids yelled back, 'Yes!'

We made our way along the side of the chalets on an old dirt track to the car park. By now the rain was torrential and the tyres were picking up mud and leaves. I decided to get the kids back as quickly as possible and took a short cut across the football pitch, around the back of the swimming pool, past the crazy golf and down the hill, back to the ballroom. Second mistake.

This wasn't any old hill. It was a bloody steep one. We started to make our way down slowly and I soon realised we were picking up too much speed. I tapped my foot on the brake. Nothing. The mud and the leaves had clogged up the break pads.

The Noddy train was out of control.

Thirty kids were screaming from the back, 'Faster, Shane! Faster!' They were having the time of their lives. All I could think was that this could be the end of their poor little lives. We were gathering more and more speed. By now some of the kids at the back were beginning to panic. Meanwhile I could see my career flashing before me. Please don't let it finish here on a Noddy train! The ballroom wall was getting closer and closer. In desperation I kicked the gears and managed to slam it into first. The train came to an abrupt halt, I banged my head on the steering-wheel and the four carriages swung round to the right and ended up in front of me. The kids were fine. I said if they didn't tell their mums and dads what had happened, we might even do it again. Do it again? As far as I was concerned, I never wanted to see the Noddy train again in my life.

I've been asked many times: ''Ere, Shane, how did you get that scar on your head?' I like to blame Goz. One night he managed to get his hands on a blue movie. We'd arranged to meet some girls in their chalet to watch it and he went on ahead and asked me to lock up the ballroom and meet him there. As I picked up the video and turned off the lights I heard a voice.

'Oi, Bluecoat, come here you tosser.'

I knew who it was. I'd made the fatal mistake of chatting up this guy's girlfriend earlier in the evening and now he wanted to have a chat with me. I decided to brazen it out.

'Come on then, let's have it. You and me, now.'

What I didn't see were his three mates standing in the shadows behind him.

Suddenly I remembered my mum's old saying: 'Better to be a live coward, than a dead hero.' Without waiting to be introduced to his friends, I legged it at top speed, keeping one hand on the video. But when I reached the glass double-doors of the ballroom, one of the guys had caught up with me and before I could push them open he shoved me in the back, sending me flying headfirst through the glass. It split my forehead open and I fell to the floor, where the lads gave me a good kicking. But you know what? I never let go of the video. Goz was proud of me.

As the season came to a close the thrill of the chase became enough for me a lot of the time. I'd talk a good game, but once I knew I could end up in bed with someone I'd walk away. And I was like that for years afterwards. I'd just want to know that I could, and that was enough.

If I did seriously fall for a girl I'd often end up getting hurt, particularly with the older ones. They'd tell me they loved me left, right and centre 100 times a day, but then after we'd made love and I'd be cuddling up for the night they'd say: ''Ere love, switch the light off on your way out, will you?' That summer I started seeing a stunning blonde called Mary

Me and my Mum. The park we are sitting in
is now a block of flats in Stonebridge, London.

Me *(back left)* and Dean *(front left)*. Kids would
come and go at 19 Craven Park.

Me and my Dad outside our first home.
"No blacks, no Irish, no dogs." That's what
it said on the door!

Dean & me at Craven Park.
It wasn't long after this picture was
taken he ate rat poison and was
rushed to hospital.

Once we got a TV there was no way you could get me out of the chair!

Me and Dean. Happy times together at Pontins.

Ten years of age and onstage at Pontins in the Junior Talent Show, hogging the mic.

Me and my Mum at Pontins taking over the dance floor. It was around about this time my Mum taught me to jive. Little did I know that 20 years later those lessons would come in handy!

Me and Kim *(back left)*. My first 'ssssh you know what'… I certainly wasn't hers!

Aged 15, Pontins here I come!

1981, Brean Sands Bluecoats: The Dream Team!
Sally *(second row, first left)*, Debbie *(second row, second left)*, Trevor *(second row, fourth left)*, Blockhead *(back row)*, Rosle *(second row, fourth right)*, Weedy *(the clown)*, Frank *(front row, right)*, Me *(front row, second right)*, Goz *(front row, centre)*, Pider (Peter) *(front row, left)*.

Me, Mick Walker and Craig at Pontins, Torremolinos. Another night, another show.

Alright, alright, it wasn't always donkey derby and bingo at Pontins! That's me with the blonde hair by the way!

My first season as a professional comic, Jersey 1984 (the photo was taken in a hotel dining room).

Early publicity photo of me, aged 18 as Shane Skywalker. What a knobhead!

Another early publicity photo, aged 17 (Duran Duran would've been proud).

SHANE RICHIE
DYNAMIC YOUNG COMEDIAN/VOCALIST

Personal Manager:-
BARRY DYE,
BARRY DYE ENTS.,
9 COYTES GARDENS,
IPSWICH, SUFFOLK.
Tel:- (0473) 216677

I had this photo taken at Puerto Banus in Spain while I was working at Torremolinos. Skywalker or Richie, I couldn't make up my mind – every comic then was dynamic!!

Me and Stan Dallas. Without Stan all my dreams wouldn't have been possible. He was like a father to me and his integrity and honesty were priceless.

With Barry Dye, my first manager. He took a chance on me when I was 19 and kickstarted my career.

It took four years from leaving Pontins to appearing at the Palladium and another 15 before they'd let me back in again.

Me and Collen. When we met in Bournemouth people thought we looked like brother and sister.

Our wedding in Orlando... it was so personal and perfect. Oh yeah, she sat on the car because her shoes were killing her!

Micky Salmon, me and Goz;
we were inseparable. I so wanted
to be like Micky.

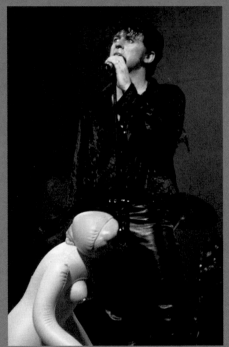

About this time I realised my stage
act wouldn't be right for TV...

On *Jameson Tonight*, Sky TV. This particular
night, I dressed up as a drag queen and
appeared as a guest on the show and I swear
for at least ten minutes Derek Jameson didn't
know it was me!!! (I knew all the years working
with drag acts would one day come in handy)

Cassidy, who worked at a camp called Sand Bay, which was about ten miles along the coast from Brean Sands. At the end of the season Mary got a job singing at a club in London and I turned up with Goz to watch her, but she sent a message out that she didn't want to see me. It turned out she was seeing David Essex instead!

Experiences like that toughened me up and made me feel that everyone was out for what they could get. Of course, I'd not exactly been an angel myself, but I suppose I'd always assumed that if a girl said she cared for me then she meant it. For a long time after that I wouldn't trust what a woman told me unless I knew all the facts.

When the Pontins season ended in October I went home again, but this time was different to the previous year. Back then I'd gone home feeling down because I didn't really know what to do with my life. This time I did. I wanted to be an entertainer. I still had the acting in my blood, that's how I'd started, but most of all I enjoyed just being up there on my own. I didn't want to be in a double act and I didn't want to be in a band. I suppose it was selfishness but I wanted all the applause and the accolades for myself. There was no better feeling than being on stage hearing 2,000 people cheering and clapping and shouting my name. That's what I was beginning to experience at Pontins and I didn't want to share it with anyone else.

I've spent a lot of my life paying for my mistakes, but the first time I realised the significance of karma was the Christmas of 1981. I'd gone back to work at Pontins and while I was there I started seeing the hairdresser. I'd fancied her all summer but I knew she was going out with one of the other Bluecoats so I stayed away, but at Christmas she seemed to be single so I steamed in. Like I said, you always tried to get a regular – a waitress, a barmaid, one of the kitchen porters or a cleaner – but this time I thought, no, I'm going upmarket, I'm going to have the hairdresser. She'd close down the shop early and we'd end up round the back in the hairdresser's chair. It was the first time I'd done it in a hairdressers' chair – they go up, down, backwards – it was fantastic! I really liked her and to be honest I may have been falling in love with her, so when one of the wrestlers started telling me that he was seeing her too, I ignored him and just assumed it was a wind-up. Unfortunately it turned out he was telling the truth. He was getting more than a short back and sides in the hairdresser's chair, too – and so was Goz, so was Blockhead and so was Frank. In fact half the bloody camp were having short back and sides in the hairdresser's chair. She was taking us all for a ride. Literally.

I suppose it was only what I'd done to a few girls myself that year. That was when I realised it's true what people say – what goes around comes around, and has a nasty habit of biting you on the bum.

I've never been one to sit at home and twiddle my thumbs and in January 1982, with the Pontins Christmas season over, Goz, Frank and I literally decided overnight that we would go to Los Angeles. I loved living like that. I loved acting on impulse and even to this day I'll get up in the morning and decide I want to be somewhere else. Goz and Frank were staying with me at the time and my mum and dad had gone to work so I left a note for my mum: 'Gone to LA, call you later, love Shane.' We managed to get standby tickets for a midday flight and at six o'clock in the evening we were in Los Angeles.

The air stewardesses took a bit of a shine to us and moved us up to Club Class. We were knocking back the champagne and acting the big shots when all of a sudden Goz put his hand up to attract attention. One of the stewardesses came over and Goz asked if he could go and sit in the cockpit of the plane and get the pilot's autograph. It turned out that he was a keen plane-spotter. Well, my credibility went right out of the window. There we were, acting the big shots, trying to impress these girls, chat them up and arrange to meet them for a drink later and I'm sitting there with a plane-spotter. I was mortified.

By that time we had a phone at home, so when we landed I thought I'd better face the fire and phone my mum. The row started the minute she picked up the phone.

'Mum...'

'Where the feck are ya? Ya dinner's on the table.'

'Mum, didn't you get my note? I'm in Los Angeles.'

'I don't care where y'are, your dinner's waiting f'ya on the table.'

'Mum, you don't understand, I'm in America.'

Well, once the penny dropped she could have died.

'What in Jayzus' name a'ya doing there? And what am I going to do about your feckin' dinner?'

That was the great thing about my mum. It didn't matter how far around the world I was, what difficulties I was in or how well I was doing. If I didn't make it home for my dinner, there was trouble.

The adventure started before we even left the airport when we were ripped off, ironically not by an American but by a guy from Northern Ireland. He must have spotted us a mile off and he came up and asked if we had somewhere to stay. When we said we hadn't he told us that because we were British he was going to do us a favour and show us to somewhere that cost 'next to nothing'. He took us to a place called the Breakers Inn in Santa Monica and when we'd checked into our rooms it turned out it was going to cost us $30 each, which was a lot of money to us. He was obviously getting a little tickle from this place. We were ready to have a row, but he got angry and as we didn't know where we were we paid up and stayed. I learnt something that day – never trust anyone who offers to do you a favour out of the goodness of their heart. A blagger is a blagger. I should know that.

Secretly, the real reason for me going to America was that I wanted to try to crack it. I know it's laughable, how naïve I was, but when you're 17 you really believe it's that simple. I thought I could turn up in Hollywood and impress them. In the meantime I thought I'd do some acting classes until I got my big break. I'd read about method acting before and didn't really know what it was, but I somehow sensed it was important, so when I saw an advert for method classes I decided to sign up. Of course I didn't bother to read it properly so I didn't realise you had to book an appointment to audition, and when I turned up they told me my name wasn't on the list.

'Well, my name's Shane Roche and I called from England, there must be some confusion,' I said, with as much confidence and conviction as I could muster.

'Er, really sir, let me go away and see what we can do.'

Another blag. They let me in and I did a monologue from *Class Enemy*, the play I'd done with the Moonshine Theatre the year before. They must have liked it because at the end of the morning they called me over, congratulated me and said they'd like to enrol me in the 12-week course. I was horrified. I wasn't supposed to be staying in America for 12 days, let alone 12 weeks. What would my mum say? Then I caught sight of the disappointed faces of the actors who had been rejected and realised how lucky I was. It didn't matter how awkward this was going to be, I was going to have to make it work.

At this point the blag got a bit out of hand. At registration, they asked for all my documents – proof of address and stuff like that – so off the top of my head I came up with a whopper that floored them.

'Unfortunately my parents are entertainers on a world cruise and they have all my paperwork with them. I'm not sure when they'll be back.'

If only they'd known the truth they'd have realised how good an actor I really was. And so there I was, 17 years old, in Los Angeles, studying method with experienced actors many years older than myself. Not surprisingly I felt a little bit out of my depth. I'd acted at Moonshine, of course, but never anything like this.

'Pretend to be a piece of meat,' one teacher told us in the first class. I chose a pork chop I think.

'OK, but *be* the pork chop. Are you being grilled? Are you being fried? Let me see the pain. Is it pain? Are you suffering?'

I thought: 'Bloody hell, this man's crazy,' But I looked around and everyone else was nodding at him with appreciation. They were serious actors who'd done this sort of stuff before and there was me, a holiday camp entertainer more used to calling the bingo.

Now everyone's interpretation of method is different, but in Los Angeles I quickly realised that acting, at the end of the day, is blagging. You're pretending to be something you're not, you're saying words that don't belong to you and the actions you make are not your own. It's all about pretending and if you do something with enough confidence you can pull it off. Acting, I discovered that summer, is really just about confidence. If you believe in what you do then it isn't that difficult to make others believe. And that was a big lesson.

By now the three of us had made friends with a couple of girls called Cherelle and Ronita and we'd moved in with Ronita and her mum till we could find something a bit more permanent. Goz and Frank were spending all their time out clubbing with Cherelle and Ronita, but because I was underage and didn't have ID I had to stay at home. Luckily Ronita's mum – a wonderful, large lady who loved to smoke dope – had taken me under her wing. We were getting by financially because Goz and Frank were having money sent out to them from their families, so one night we decided to rent an open-top car to go cruising along Sunset Boulevard, just like they do in the movies. Goz had been into an off-licence and bought a six-pack of beer and just for the crack we thought we'd go and find a 'lady of the night'. I think you know what I mean. We'd seen all the films and being daft kids we thought this was a really cool thing to do. We managed to scrape $100 between us and we pulled up alongside a beautiful black lady. She had the look – the little red mini-skirt, the red lipstick, the high heels, the low-cut top and the attitude – and she started chatting to us. She seemed quite nice and asked us about our accents and where we were from, and eventually Goz finally plucked up the courage to ask how much she charged.

He actually said: 'How much for a good time tonight, love?' He'd obviously picked it up straight from a Hollywood film and thought it sounded really grown-up, but to Frank and I it sounded hilarious and we burst out in fits of giggles. The lady scowled at us and continued talking to Goz, explaining that it would cost 100 bucks. He nodded knowingly and she was about to climb in when I piped up from the back seat: 'What, for the three of us?'

Suddenly we saw her eyes turn red. And from being this nice, gentle, attractive lady she turned into a raging monster, punching us and hitting the car with her bag.

'You bastards, what do you think I am? Some cheap hooker? You want a cheap hooker you go further down Sunset Boulevard,' she yelled. We froze, but she hadn't finished with us and started rummaging in her bag. To this day I don't know if it was for a knife or a gun, but we didn't hang around to find out.

I went up for a few acting jobs while I was there. I may get in trouble for saying this but I realised in LA that had I been gay my career would have taken off a lot quicker. I lost count of the number of times I was propositioned by directors and producers who asked me to spend the weekend at their beach house in Malibu. Probably it was my own fault – I was a flirt be it with women or men. Unfortunately, every time I auditioned they asked me if I had a Green Card. Of course I didn't, so I forged my passport in the hopes that would do instead. I found a guy and paid him $10 to burn the passport to pretend it had been in a fire and then change the date of birth. Sadly it looked like a three-year-old kid had done it, so wherever I turned up they'd soon send me on my way.

After my acting lessons finished I ran out of money and ended up having to get the British Consulate to bail me out and get me home. I only knew of the British Consulate because of the movies. Any time there was a problem with a Brit abroad in a film they'd go to the British Consulate. When I told them what had happened – that I'd totally run out of money – they called my mum. Of course she immediately panicked. She'd no idea who the British Consulate were and automatically assumed I was in jail. Of course she'd send over money, whatever I needed to get me home. She sent enough for a plane ticket and when I walked in the door with my tail firmly between my legs, guess what? My mum still said: 'Where the hell have ya been, ya dinner's on the table?'

That summer I went to work at Little Canada Pontins on the Isle of Wight, where I'd been promoted to Assistant Entertainments Manager, and Goz went off to Camber Sands in Sussex. I didn't realise how much I was going to miss him. I had fond memories of Little Canada, as it was where I used to go as a child. One of my duties there was to run one of the bars, which had its own little stage area. The whole camp had a Canadian wilderness theme with log cabins and a totem pole and my bar was called the Mounties Retreat, but I re-christened it Shane's Shack. It was great because I could do exactly what I wanted in there. I'd realised by now that I could spend the rest of my life working on holiday camps, but if I wanted to go any further I needed to improve my act, so I'd put on impromptu shows – Lovely Legs, Glamorous Granny, comedy nights – whatever I could think of, and try out my jokes as the compère for each event.

I was also coming up with even more ways of making a few quid. As I'd been the sports organiser two years previously, by now I'd become quite good at tennis. So I made out I had certificates, put the word about and started giving private tennis lessons. People ended up coming from all over the local area. Another of my blags was a Sunday ramble. I realised that a lot of the punters liked to leave the camp from time to time, so I started a Sunday morning walk where I'd take them down the country lanes, along the beach and through the woods. It was only a few miles, but I'd make it feel like a bit of an adventure and invent all sorts of stories about how a certain part of the forest was haunted and how in the tenth century there were pagan sacrifices going on. It was a bit of a blag, but they lapped it up. I used to have a real laugh doing it, too. I'd tell the kids that there was a magic scarecrow in a field along the way that could actually move. Then I'd run ahead, dress up in a scarecrow outfit I'd hidden in a hedge, stand in a field and nonchalantly scratch my head as they went past. Some people would see it and others wouldn't, but only the kids would believe in the magic scarecrow. One time I dressed up as a tramp with a beard and covered myself in dirt, and then I walked alongside the ramblers throwing insults and begging for money. I'd been with them all week, but none of them ever realised it was me.

Other times I'd tell stories about a lunatic asylum on the other side of the woods where some of the patients would escape naked. I'd convince the punters and get them scared and then run ahead and take all my clothes off so they'd just catch a glimpse of a man running naked through the trees. When word got out amongst the Bluecoats, Ron, the Children's Uncle, begged me to let him do it too. His job was to look after all the little kids on the camp, but really he was a frustrated actor and he insisted on making this streak more convincing by wearing a straitjacket. I reluctantly agreed, but reminded him that the key was to keep a distance, so the punters always believed it was an escaped lunatic. We set off on the ramble as usual and about 20 minutes into it we heard a loud scream from the woods and saw this mad man, naked apart from a straitjacket, charging straight towards us. I shouted at him to turn round, but by now he was completely in character and oblivious to everything. Before I could do anything he was running amongst us naked. Don't forget, this was the Children's Uncle. People were disgusted.

After a while I realised there were a few pubs and cafés on the route of the ramble and that if I took the walkers into a place they'd generally spend a few quid. The landlords and café owners were delighted and they'd give me a backhander to make sure I chose their place. Buoyed by my success with the walks, I expanded my repertoire to include mystery coach tours. To make them more interesting I'd go on the mike at the front of the bus and make up stories about the various sights of the island. I remember telling people that Ringo Starr lived there, but they should keep it quiet because Ringo didn't want people to know. Ringo Starr on the Isle of Wight? Come on. But people actually used to believe me. There was one particular big house on the top of the hill and after a few weeks I got so carried away with this story that I started telling the punters it was Ringo's home. They'd pull out their cameras and snap away and at the end I'd get even bigger tips than normal, but a few weeks later the police turned up at the camp looking for me. Apparently as a result of my coach tours, tourists had been going to this house at all times of the day and night asking for Ringo's autograph. The retired couple that lived there were getting just a bit fed up and wanted to know who was responsible.

In July of 1982 I was in trouble again, but for once it wasn't my fault. The Falklands War had just finished and we got a fax from Pontins Head Office saying that the warship *Canberra* was bringing troops home from the islands and would be passing the Isle of Wight as it returned to Southampton. I got up on the microphone in the ballroom the night before and told everyone that if they wanted to meet me outside reception at six in the morning, I'd gladly take them down to the beach where they could wave to the returning troops and welcome them home. The following morning there was a rattle on my door and it was Ken Bruce, the camp manager, asking why there were hundreds of people at reception. I struggled out of bed and went round to reception and there must have been 600 people gathered around the totem pole. How the hell they pulled this stuff out of the bag with 12 hours notice I'll never know, but they'd managed to make Union Jacks, hats, flags and bunting. It was a sea of red, white and blue and it was a wonderful sight – patriotism at its finest. I grabbed a loudspeaker, addressed them all in my jolliest voice and set off down to the beach with them trailing behind me singing 'Rule Britannia' and 'God Save the Queen'.

There was a Warners holiday camp around the back of our camp and word had got to them that people from Pontins were going to see the *Canberra* going past, so halfway down the path I suddenly had around 400 of their punters latch onto me. There was no other member of staff, so here I was, in charge of around 1,000 holidaymakers, all carrying flags and bunting and knocking back cans of lager. The end of the Falklands War was a huge event in British history, coupled with the fact that they were on holiday and wanted to make an occasion of it, so the mood was merry to say the least. When we arrived in the bay there was a low mist over the sea so we couldn't see much at all, but one guy had thought to bring a radio along and the local station were doing a live commentary.

After a while the presenter said that the ship was making its way past the Isle of Wight and he could see the troops on board. Right on cue we heard the sound of a loud foghorn and could just make out the outline of a huge ship. As it drew closer a gigantic cheer went up. People were in tears, waving their flags and singing 'Land of Hope and Glory', cheering and patting me on the back and thanking me for organising it; I was their hero. We could just make out people on board waving and we were all waving back and as it emerged through the fog I could finally read the name on the ship's side ... *Sealink*.

I couldn't believe it. It was only the car ferry from Cowes. The *Canberra* had taken a different route and we'd been waiting for the last hour in the wrong place. I've never seen so many faces drop so quickly. Within seconds the looks had gone from disappointment to disdain to disgust. They thought I'd pulled a fast one and that it was all a big wind-up. Well, not even I could get out of that one. They stormed back to the camp and besieged the manager's office. Word went round that it was a sick joke and the manager asked me to leave the island. I was only too happy to go. That afternoon I was on the first bus out of there, to stay with some friends in Portsmouth for a couple of weeks until things calmed down.

1982 was a quieter year for girls. As Assistant Entertainments Manager I thought I ought to set an example, and also it was a smaller camp and tended to attract families. But mainly I was getting a bit suspicious of these women who came away without their husbands or boyfriends and then spent a week with me. I was tired of hearing how their boyfriends didn't understand them. I could have written the script. Friday nights they'd be crying in my arms saying they wanted to be with me and I'd fall for it and ask them to keep in touch, and then they'd get home and I'd hear nothing. Or they'd give me a phone number and I'd call and it would be non-existent. I don't know if I was a challenge to them or maybe I was a stepping-stone to move on in their relationship, but it made me distrustful. Maybe it was a bit hypocritical of me – after all, I'd had my own share of one-night stands – but I still felt hurt.

I don't suppose I was as happy that year. I was missing Goz and there wasn't the same atmosphere, but on the plus side I was learning a lot and becoming much more confident on stage. As a result I'd been given much greater responsibilities, including looking after the professional acts that came in every week. One of my favourite jobs was refereeing the professional wrestling and I quickly learnt that even that was a blag. I'd sit backstage beforehand with the wrestlers and they'd say, 'Right, Shane, I'm going to pick you up and slam you on your back and the harder you slam your hands down on the canvas, the more painful it sounds.' And they'd teach me how to fall and even give me fake blood to make it more authentic when they pretended to hit me in the mouth. I loved pulling the wool over the punters' eyes and I don't think I've stopped doing it since. I've always found it hard to take life seriously. That's always been my problem.

CHAPTER FIVE

'You too cheeky, English boy'

When the Pontins '82 season ended, my plan was to go back to America and try to pick up where I'd left off. I'd got itchy feet again and felt it was time to stretch myself, but out of the blue the camp manager, Ken Bruce, asked me if I fancied spending the winter in Spain. Pontins had two hotels on the Costa del Sol and he could get me a job there on the condition that I would come back to Little Canada the following year. It was the first time in my life that I could see a bit of stability – a whole year mapped out. Ken Bruce made a call and I was put on the phone to the manager in Torremolinos to answer a few questions. Here we go, I thought; the blag was about to start all over again.

'Shane, can you speak Spanish?' the manager asked.

'Si, si, no problemo,' I scoffed.

'What are your dancing skills like?'

'Have you seen Fred Astaire?'

'And you do have a cabaret act?'

'Does my dad drink?'

I had no act. I was blagging. The manager fell for it and before I knew it my ticket was booked and I was on the plane. It was every holiday camp entertainer's dream to go to Spain for the winter and I'd landed it. I flew out in October and the second I arrived at the hotel, I grabbed the nearest barman – it was easy to spot them, they all sported Kevin Keegan perms at the time – and made him teach me the Spanish for 'Hello, how are you?' 'Two beers please' and 'Alright darling, your place or mine?' That was the Spanish lesson over; all I needed now was a dancing lesson and a cabaret act...

I was put in a hotel room on the fifth floor with a great guy called Craig who was just learning to fire-eat. I always knew when he'd been practising because of the scorch marks on the ceiling and the smell of burning flesh on his arms. Together we lived the life of Riley, joking around with the punters, drinking sangria, getting a suntan – and on top of all that getting paid. For a while I'd found another Goz. Things couldn't have been better, until the hotel manager mentioned in passing that I was only booked until Christmas. Ken had given me the impression I would be there until April, but this guy wouldn't listen. They'd already got other staff booked to fly out to take over and it wasn't possible to keep me on unless there was a demand for me, and that wasn't likely as I hadn't got a proper cabaret act.

Now the daydreaming had to stop. If I wanted to stay I had to get myself a proper act. I had some publicity photos taken of me dressed in a black catsuit and the manager made up posters advertising my show, which were put all over the hotel. As he was drawing them up he casually asked what name I wanted to work under. Until then of course I'd been Shane Roche, my real name, but the manager thought I might want to use something that sounded a bit more showbiz, so I came up with Shane Ryan. I don't know where it came from, but I thought it had kind of a ring to it.

The cabaret bar where I was performing was far from glamorous, but I loved it. It was in the basement of the Pontins hotel and looked like a little cave. There was a tiny dance floor, which must have measured 10ft by 8ft, and a small dressing room backstage, with a blocked sink, which could just about fit four people. Off that was a minute stockroom, which held all the costumes, everything from a soldier's uniform to a Blues Brothers outfit. At the other side was the DJ box.

When my first night came I went on stage with a false sense of security. Until then I'd been going up as a Bluecoat and they loved me before I even said anything, but this was just me on my own. It was a different ball game entirely. I opened with the Neil Diamond song 'Sweet Caroline'. It was a cabaret standard and I'd always laughed at people who sang it, but I thought I'd start on safe territory. I followed it with a disco version of the Elvis song 'Can't Help Falling in Love', which confused the hell out of the Spanish musicians.

'Señor Shane, why you want to sing this song so fast?' they asked in their best English.

'I just want to make it different,' I explained patiently.

'But why? It's a beautiful song. Why you want to mess with it?'

The rest of the act consisted of any old jokes I'd heard from my dad's club and my last few seasons at the camps. It seemed to go down well, but more important than that I finally had an act. Lee Carroll, the Entertainments Manager, put me on stage every chance he got and helped me fine-tune my performance. I couldn't have done it without him. Unfortunately that was all to change very suddenly. Lee was part of a professional act called Sweet and Simple and not long after Christmas he went back to Britain. In January 1983, by way of replacement, they sent us a guy called Mick Walker. Mick had been round the block and done bits and pieces of stand-up comedy. He was a Brummie, 6ft 3 with muscles in places where I didn't even have places, but I soon discovered he had an attitude and liked to throw his weight around.

Straightaway I knew we weren't going to see eye to eye for my last four months out there. If anyone was doing cabaret it was him. He was going to be the funny man and no one else was telling jokes. I tried everything I could to get friendly with him, but he wasn't interested. He'd constantly remind me that I was going nowhere and as he walked off he'd give me a dig in the arm that was just a little bit too hard. He was quite happy for me to be the DJ and keep my mouth shut, and he was forever boasting that he was on the verge of signing a big TV deal. Good luck to him, I thought.

One of the better things about working out in Spain was that we got a lot of visiting cabarets. One in particular, a young comic called Jeff Stevenson, made a big impression. I wasn't really aware of alternative comedy back then. In those days it was just taking place amongst a small elite group in London. It wasn't until a few years later that I heard of the likes of Ben Elton, Ade Edmonson, Rik Mayall and French and Saunders. Stand-up comedy to me was about dinner suits and dicky bows. That's what I'd learnt from the acts at my dad's working men's club and the holiday camps and that's how I dressed at 18 – like a middle-aged man. Yet this comic Jeff came on stage in a shell suit. Now as crass as that seems now, back then if you had a shell suit you had a few quid and were seen as a bit flash. Jeff was in his early twenties and he had such attitude, banging out jokes at a hundred miles an hour – all this observational humour. I was kind of in awe of him because I knew he was taking a chance and I admired that.

You meet certain people in your life who really make a difference, and that happened to me in Torremolinos. The guy in question was an agent and manager by the name of Barry Dye and he was on holiday from England with his wife, Cindy. Everybody got excited when an agent came out on holiday and because I'd worked on the East Coast I'd heard of Barry, that was his domain – he booked cabarets in and around clubs and holiday camps in Norfolk and Suffolk. He came along to the show one night and by pure luck I was the cabaret. It was Mick Walker's day off and they'd put me back on. Wow. There might have only been 60 people in the audience but to me it felt like I was playing the London Palladium. And for the very first time I had that feeling of having an audience in the palm of my hand. I dropped 'Sweet Caroline' and nicked a few of Jeff Stevenson's gags. His stuff was young and fresh, whereas I was still doing stuff about Grandad in the war and 'the wife'. My grandad was never in the war and I didn't even have a girlfriend, but I did these jokes with such passion that no one ever guessed.

I think I must have done something right because I ended up having a drink with Barry in the bar afterwards and he asked me what I was doing after Spain. I told him I was contracted to go back to Pontins for the summer season and he shook his head and told me I should call it a day with Pontins now; he said I was ready to move on. The thought of going out there on my own scared me, but Barry told me to keep in touch and talk to him when I was free. I couldn't believe it. Here I was, still a teenager, and already I had an agent. I knew from then on I was really going to enjoy the rest of my time in Spain, however rarely Mick Walker let me do my act. Now there was someone who believed in me and to this day I owe Barry Dye a great debt for that.

Sadly, not everyone was as decent as Barry and an incident with one of the cabaret acts that winter was to change my attitude to showbusiness and make me realise how bitter and angry and insecure it can make you, certainly comics. One week we had a visiting comedian called Lee Wilson. He was a Brummie and a bit of a name on the circuit because he'd appeared on a TV show in the mid-seventies called *The Comedians*. I've always found Brummie comics very funny; in particular Jasper Carrott, Lenny Henry and Ian 'Sludge' Lees – a great comic on the club circuit. Anyway, because Lee was well known and a fellow Brummie, he and Mick were inseparable.

One particular night Lee was doing his act and I was sitting in the DJ box cueing up the tape to play as he left the stage. It was typical cheesy cabaret play-off music. At the end of his act Lee looked over at me and said on stage:

'Are you taping my act?'

I was embarrassed and started laughing – I assumed he was having a joke.

'Oi, I said are you taping my act?' he asked again.

'No point, I've heard all your gags before, mate.'

He'd asked me a question and I'd answered him. The only thing was, my answer got a bigger laugh from the audience. Anyway, Lee took this as an insult and at the end of his spot I was called into the dressing room. The second I appeared around the door Mick started to quiz me about why I was taping Lee's act.

'What you talking about? I ain't taping no-one's act,' I protested.

But they were livid and wouldn't let it go. It was like the Spanish Inquisition! I refused to be intimidated, but afterwards I just felt sickened by the whole thing. If that was what the business did to you, I didn't want to be a part of it. When I eventually calmed down I swore that never again would anyone talk to me like that.

It was 15 years before I ran into Lee again. I'd been asked to captain a showbusiness football team at Wembley in front of the Cup Final. Jasper Carrott was one captain and I was the other. Everyone big was playing, from Rod Stewart to Chris Evans and Angus Deayton, and I was at the height of my fame at the time – I was in *Grease* with my name up in lights in the West End and I had my own Friday night TV show. As we stood in the tunnel to run out, Jasper suddenly shouted: 'Lee, you've given me the wrong boots,' and I saw running through the tunnel, like a little skivvy, Lee Wilson. This was the same guy who'd given me a hard time and there he was running along carrying Jasper Carrott's boots. It didn't get much better than that. I looked at him and introduced myself. He had no idea, he didn't remember, but I walked out onto Wembley feeling like I'd already won the FA Cup. What goes around, comes around; I've always believed that.

I ended up knowing Torremolinos and Fuengirola as well as the back of my hand. I'd become friendly with a guy called Rob from Middlesborough, who played piano in one of the hotel bars and one night we decided to hit the clubs in Fuengirola. In those days Fuengirola was the place to go, the nightlife was buzzing. We had a great evening flitting from bar to bar and towards the end of the night found ourselves in a club heaving with beautiful women. We'd had one sangria too many and after taking one look at the dance floor we thought, 'Why not?' Now, pulling in a holiday camp is easy because you're wearing the blue blazer, but when you're outside your own territory it becomes a bit of a challenge and you have to rely on your charm. Well, we immediately targeted two beautiful girls at the bar and started to give them the chat about how gorgeous they were. They were typical Spanish señoritas, dressed immaculately with slinky figures and long, shiny, dark hair.

After talking for a while we all went up for a dance. It was late by now and the lights were low so the inevitable happened and I ended up snogging one of them. I looked across and I could see Rob was doing the same with his girl. His hands were everywhere. When the girls, in broken English, asked us if we wanted to go back to their place we couldn't believe our luck. There we were, two young English lads with these two stunning Spanish girls, both of them slightly older than us, taking us back to their luxury apartment for a night of good old Costa Del Sol rumpy pumpy. We went outside the club hand in hand with them to look for a taxi and it was then that it hit me.

Please don't let it be true! In the bright glare of the street lights I discovered that something wasn't quite right about the girl I'd been kissing. For starters she had hairy knuckles and a five o'clock shadow. Bloody hell. How could I not have noticed? I'd been snogging a bloke. I ran straight round the corner of the club and threw up. Not only had I been kissing this bloke, what was worse I think I'd enjoyed it. After a few minutes I came back round the corner to find Rob still there, snogging his girl in the street. He was so drunk he still hadn't noticed.

'Rob, I seriously need a word with you.'

He ignored me and carried on.

'Rob, *now*.'

He finally broke off and in his broad Middlesborough accent said: 'Rochey, what is it now, you Southern twat?' He had a way with words.

'It's a fella.'

'You what?'

'Rob, you're kissing a bleeding bloke.'

But Rob was having none of it and neither were the girls. I couldn't believe it. There they were, standing there with Adam's apples, steadfastly denying that they were blokes. They got more and more angry and after a couple more minutes of arguing the one I'd been kissing came at me. There he was, in beautiful make-up and a lovely dress, squaring up to me like a builder. I stood in the middle of the street trying to work out what to do. If I hit him, passers-by would think I was hitting a woman; if I didn't he'd half kill me. So I did what any self-respecting man would do in those circumstances. I ran.

I did fall in love that winter though. Her name was Marie and she'd come on holiday with her two children. She told me she was divorced and I fell for her hook, line and sinker. Maybe being that far away from home I was just looking for someone to confide in, but we became really close. Her parents were quite wealthy and every few weeks she'd fly out to be with me. She was a few years older than me, but I was so serious about her that I even introduced her to my mum. I'd invited Mum and Dad out to stay for a week and offered to pay for their flights. Dad was still convinced that this was just a phase I was going through and that I'd eventually come back and start working on a building site, so he made an excuse that he couldn't leave The Steps and my mum flew out on her own with her suitcase packed with tins of tomato soup and chocolate biscuits. We had a great time together.

Marie kept coming back and when she was in England she'd send me these wonderful love letters. She was forever telling me how mad she was about me, but then one day, out of the blue, I received an anonymous letter telling me that she was actually happily married and that I was just a bit of escapism for her. I phoned her about it, but her attitude was that it had only ever been a bit of fun, so what did it matter. I was already suspicious of older women after some of my experiences at Pontins, but this really unsettled me. I thought back to all the women I'd become close to at Pontins. They'd tell me they loved me, but did they just love the thrill of the fling? Was it just for that moment or did they love me unconditionally, warts and all?

It wasn't all heartache though. A group of 150 American students came over on a cultural exchange with a Spanish school and they chose to stay at our hotel. Craig and I couldn't believe our luck. Their teachers and chaperones had the measure of us straightaway and warned the girls to stay away from us, but not all of them listened. One night a student invited me back to her room. It was a warm evening and we went out onto the balcony where we started kissing and cuddling. One thing led to another and before long we were both naked. Of course, this was Spain and there were still people out and about. Word quickly spread and lights started going on and people came out onto their balconies or gathered below by the swimming pool to watch. I was only young and a bit of an exhibitionist and this girl had had a few drinks so we decided to put on a bit of a show. We treated the audience to the Kama Sutra. I've never been able to do a cartwheel and keep a straight face since. People were clapping and cheering us on and the other Americans were whooping like cheerleaders. We only stopped when one of her teachers started banging on the door. I quickly dressed myself, took a polite bow and scaled down the hotel wall. Spiderman would have been proud. It was such a shame I didn't have time for an encore.

One of the responsibilities of the Bluecoats was to take punters on various coach trips. Once every two weeks they'd organise a trip to a

kasbah in Morocco and I could never understand why it was so unpopular with the staff. To me it was a day out and I jumped at the chance.
We took a coach to Gibraltar and then a ferry over and finally a coach
to the kasbah. It was only when I got there that I realised the catch. Not
only did I have a coach load of tourists to keep an eye on, but also,
because I was a blue-eyed, blonde teenager, I had blokes feeling my
bum every twenty yards. They literally wanted to swap four camels to
spend the night with me. 'I make you very happy young boy for the rest
of your life, you live with me.' It was a nightmare.

I was great at bartering though and the punters loved it. They'd find
a North African hand-woven rug they liked and then come and find me
and ask me to negotiate a good price for them. What they weren't
aware of was that I'd got to know half the market traders out there and
I'd done deals with them. So if a rug were on sale at £100, I'd tell the
punter I'd try to get it for them for £80. The trader would get very upset:

'No, the price is £90. No less you English pig, you go away.'

'Don't you call me an English pig.'

'You go away, you too cheeky English boy, you make trouble.'

We had this great act going and of course the punters loved it. In the
end he'd sell the rug and the punter would go away thinking they'd got
a £100 rug for £80. Of course it was only worth £50, so the market
trader would give me £30 and he'd keep £50 and everyone would go
home happy. I became particularly good friends with one old guy. I
couldn't pronounce his name so I called him Neville. After we'd done a
few deals with his carpets he'd invite me round to the back of his shop
to smoke a bong. It was a big bubbling pipe with a beautiful detailed
mosaic on it and I sat there for hours. There I was, off my face in a back
room, while 80 British tourists wandered around the place, getting lost,
accosted and ripped off.

I'd also be the first to volunteer for the coach run to the airport every
week. I liked being the first and last person the holidaymakers saw. I
loved meeting them off the plane and trying to put a smile on their faces
when they were being grumpy about the plane being late or moaning
that it looked like rain. They'd always ask what the weather was going
to be like the next day and I'd always say: '90 degrees. 45 in the

morning and 45 in the afternoon.' I was full of cheesy one-liners, but the punters loved it. Then on the way back to Malaga there'd always be someone in tears because they were going home, so I'd go on the mike and get them all singing 'We'll Meet Again'.

I couldn't resist a wind-up either. I'd find out the nervous travellers and then I'd say: 'Ladies and gentlemen, I know some of you are frightened of flying, but don't forget, whatever you do, try and sit at the back of the plane.'

'Why?' they'd ask.

'Because planes never back into mountains.'

At the end of April we packed up to come home. Craig was going to take his fire-eating act up North, Rob had a booking to play piano in a hotel and I was due to go back to Little Canada the following month. I was ready to come home. I'd learnt Spanish and I'd learnt to ride horses bareback on the beach, but professionally I was starting to get frustrated in Spain. I now had a cabaret act and I wanted to do something with it.

What's more I'd started to get a taste for drink. I was knocking back a lot of beer because of the heat and I'd also discovered Jack Daniels for the first time. I'd realised drink could change you into somebody you weren't and I quite liked that, but at the same time it worried me. My dad was a drinker and my younger brother Dean loved pub culture, but I was determined not to go down that route. Showbusiness had grabbed me, it was dragging me along and right at that moment I didn't want anything else getting in the way.

CHAPTER SIX

Hanging up the Blue Coat

It was a naked rendition of the 'Last Post' that landed me the job of Entertainments Manager at Little Canada in May 1983.

Once again I started as Assistant Entertainments Manager, answering to the Entertainments Manager, but he blew his job before the season had even started. The Bluecoats had two weeks to get to know each other before the punters arrived and during that time we had a party and ended up back in one of the chalets. Surprise, surprise.

Now, his party piece was to play the 'Last Post' on a trumpet while he slowly undressed. He was a slightly overweight guy and he looked very sombre, but on the very last note, when he was completely naked, he would turn round, pull the cheeks of his bum apart and a golf ball would fall out. He'd then do a whole routine where he'd pretend he was gardening using his willy as the garden tool and his nuts as the bulbs. I used to fall about laughing, but some of the other Bluecoats thought it was disgusting. Word got back and he was asked to leave. Shame. I'd have loved to have seen his act at the Palladium …

A guy called Jack, who was the Children's Uncle at the time, was asked to take over, but he wasn't cut out for it. It wasn't his fault, he was a good entertainer but he just wasn't suited to organising the day-to-day running of a busy holiday camp. After a couple of weeks they realised they'd made a mistake and I was called in and given the job. They assumed I was 21, of course, but even 21 would have been young for that job. Aged 19, I was actually the youngest Pontins Entertainments Manager in the country.

Who'd have thought it? I was in charge of the camp where I'd gone as a kid, organising the competitions I used to enter. I was so proud and I vowed that people who came on holiday to my camp would have the best time of their life. People can criticise me for a lot of things, but one thing they can never fault me on is enthusiasm and things were no different back then at Little Canada. Boy, did I love the challenge.

I had a great bunch of staff working for me that year. Some of them had absolutely no talent, but that didn't matter because the punters still loved them. That's what was great about Pontins and that's how holiday camps have changed. In those days if you could sing and dance it was a bonus, but personality was more important. If you could make the punters feel like a million dollars that was what counted. A lot of the Bluecoats in those days didn't even want to go on and have a career in the business, they just wanted to be with people and to feel special and they'd work around the clock to make sure everyone had a good time. Nowadays there are set hours, which is a shame – it's become just another nine-to-five job.

I was in my element and on a real high, so much so that I decided to change my name again. I wasn't that keen on Shane Ryan anymore and wanted something a bit more exciting. Barry Dye had told me about one of his acts called Micky Zany and all these other comics with wild names, so I decided to call myself, wait for it, Shane … Skywalker. Brilliant or what? What's more, my act was going to change too and I was going to be a bit crazy. Instead of wearing a nice posh suit I'd wear funny shoes, a multi-coloured dicky bow, trousers that were too big and a jacket that was too small.

The punters at Pontins seemed to love it, but I got my chance to try it out on a wider audience when, true to his word, Barry Dye got in touch to say that he'd landed me a gig. Lenny Henry was coming over to the Isle of Wight to do a show at the Sandown Pavilion and I was to support him. I was so nervous. Lenny was the face of *Tiswas* so I knew the crowd he would bring in would be wild, crazy and totally up for it. But that was OK. I was a wild and crazy cabaret act by then. I remember the posters advertising the show: 'Shane Skywalker: his comedy is out of this world.' And I really believed it. Boy, did I misjudge the situation. I went on first and died a horrible death. I bounded on stage with a light sabre and a multi-coloured jumpsuit (subtlety has never been my strong point). The band played the *Star Wars* music and in between bursts of music I told a series of stupid jokes.

'What's a Shih-tzu?'

Deadly silence in the audience.

'A zoo with no animals!'

More silence.

The band struck up again with the *Star Wars* theme.

'What would you do if a bird crapped on your car?'

Yet more silence.

'Pack her in!'

Not even a titter. I was rubbish.

When Lenny went on I stood in the wings and watched him, totally in awe. I was never a big fan of his material, but he was a funny man (still is) and the audience loved him. After the show we met up back-stage and Lenny was on the phone to his agent. I waited until he'd finished and as he got off the phone he just stared at me; he'd obviously watched my act. Before he could speak, I jumped in.

'Listen, I need to change my act Lenny,' I started to explain. There was a long silence.

'More important than that, Shane, you need to change your name.'

I was puzzled.

'What do you mean? It's a funny name; it means I'm out of this world.'

'It doesn't matter,' he explained patiently. 'If you want a career in this business you've got to think 20 years on. Do you really want to be appearing on television in 20 years' time as Shane Skywalker?'

I changed my whole attitude that night as well as my name. As Lenny advised I came up with a name I would keep for the rest of my life: Shane Richie. I'd like to say that a lot of thought went into it, but it wouldn't be true. I'd thought about going back to my real name and then I briefly considered calling myself Shane Patrick, which is my middle name, but I decided I wanted to get as far away from the Shane Roche of old as I could. The singer Lionel Richie was big at the time. I liked his name and it also sounded not a million miles from my nickname at school, which was Rochey, so I went with that. To convince myself I spent the whole night practising my new autograph, just in case.

After my bitter experience with the married woman in Spain it was becoming harder and harder for me to let my guard down with women. Don't get me wrong though, I still enjoyed ladies' company and now I was the Entertainments Manager it was even easier. But I still had to put up the façade of the happy-go-lucky, carefree bloke and that just wasn't me all the time. I'd grown tired of bed-hopping and trying to remember names. By now I needed a proper girlfriend. I thought I'd found her in Cathy, the on-site nurse. I used to make any excuse to go and see her, from a headache to a broken toenail. When we eventually got together I'd go over there for afternoon surgery, we'd lock the door and play 'Doctors and Nurses' and then I'd climb out of the window afterwards so the punters in the waiting room with their coughs and colds wouldn't see me.

That summer Lisa came to visit again, but I'd changed so much. The time I'd spent homeless and working abroad had made me a completely different person to the boy she'd fallen for. I was moving on and I didn't want to be reminded about the past. We still liked each other and had a lovely week together, but when she went home, although nothing was said, I think we both knew it was over as boyfriend and girlfriend.

Meanwhile I was getting quite serious with Cathy, to the extent that she wanted me to go and live with her in Blackpool once the summer season ended. Of course I'd no intention of settling down at that age, but rather than tell her I vaguely went along with it, thinking to myself that I'd deal with it closer to the end of the season. Head in the sand again.

I still had various blags going that year. Windsurfing was becoming popular so I had a little deal going with a local guy whereby I'd send punters down to him for lessons and get a rake-off from the profits. My country ramble was still a regular event and by now it was so famous that it even featured on one of the television holiday programmes. But if

I'm honest I was beginning to get a bit bored and restless. How many more times can I make the Donkey Derby sound exciting and compère the kids' swimming gala? I began to spend more and more time outside the camp going to watch cabaret acts, and I even managed to get a few bookings myself at various hotels. I got friendly with a lot of the acts, particularly a guy called Dave Lee, who became a great mate, and also a London comic called Barry Williams. He was sharp and witty and I'd never heard anyone ad-lib like him; he was a great influence on my career. I remember him saying to me: 'If you're going to do stand-up, talk about what you know.'

'Well, I don't really know much about anything apart from school,' I admitted to him one night.

'Right, well you talk about school. You talk about losing your virginity, about growing up, all the stuff that happened to you.'

I changed my act after that. I can't say it worked every time. In fact, when I first started out hardly any of it worked because the venues I performed at weren't used to that sort of material, but it eventually came together.

Barry's other great bit of advice was: 'Always have a song up your sleeve. If you're dying a death, give 'em a song.' I always remembered that one too and it came in very handy on many occasions, I can tell you. Barry was like a father figure to me and he understood my ambitions and my fears. He nearly made it himself and he really should have done. To this day I don't understand why some entertainers succeed and others don't. It's not just about talent; it's the lucky breaks.

As the season drew to a close, Pontins got in touch and offered me a permanent job as Entertainments Manager. It would mean I could work through the winter, touring the country hosting auditions and seminars. I'd already told them that I was going professional as a stand-up at the end of the summer and, as tempting as their offer was, I was determined to stick to my guns. I had nothing planned and nowhere to go however, so I was hugely relieved when Barry Dye called just days before I was due to leave to tell me that he'd managed to get me my first tour.

Before I went I had to sort things out with Cathy though. She was going back up North and I took her to Portsmouth station. She was pretty upset about us being apart and wanted some commitment from me. She said: 'Are you going to come with me and try to get a job up North, or are you going to chase your dreams and go on this silly tour?' It was the first time a girl had put me in that position and it felt terrible. She was in tears, but it made no difference. It's strange how you think you're in love until something else comes along and sweeps you off your feet. Right then the tour meant everything to me. It was my big chance and nothing could get in the way of that. It was hard, because I genuinely cared for Cathy, but my work had to come first. Not for the last time I put my career before a relationship and I kissed her goodbye.

The tour started in September 1983 and took in small clubs and hotels along the South Coast. It was a typical variety show, made up of magicians, singers and comics. I was bottom of the bill and my job was to warm up the audience with a couple of songs and a few jokes. It was only two weeks, but I learnt so much just from watching in the wings and sitting in the dressing room talking to the other acts. At the end of the tour Barry Dye and his wife Cindy let me stay with them. Not only was he my agent but he was also a good friend by now. I couldn't go home; there was nothing much for me there now. My dad was still drinking and my mum was still moaning about his drinking.

In the meantime Barry was busy getting me more jobs. The next booking was a big step up because I was to be paid £50 – a lot of money in those days – and for the first time in my career, it was a solo show. It was one thing having the security of the other acts around you; it was entirely different being out there alone. The booking was at Felixstowe Caravan Park and, if I say so myself, I did all right. I was never going to get the laughs I got at the holiday camps but they seemed to like me well enough. Barry continued to get me gigs up and down the East Coast for the rest of the year and in January 1984 he got me a booking for my very first hen night. Nowadays women tend to go to clubs for hen nights, but in those days they would book the back room of a pub or a suite in a hotel. They'd have a couple of dodgy strip-pers and a drag queen and I'd turn up and compère. We had some hilarious nights. There was one stripper I worked with by the name of

Billy Hot Rocks, who I swear had a todger the size of a lamp post. He was a well-built black guy and he'd do a trick where he'd put a pint glass on the ground and then do press-ups over it and his todger would touch the bottom of the glass every time. Boy, did I feel inadequate watching him do that. There was another stripper called Billy Ribbons who was as camp as Christmas. He'd do a strip in the middle of the dance floor with a big circle of girls around him and when he was completely naked you'd realise that hanging from the end of his manhood were lots of coloured ribbons. The DJ would put on Terry Wogan's *Floral Dance* and each girl would grab a ribbon and skip around him like they were dancing around a maypole. I've never been able to listen to that music with a straight face since.

I started building up a bit of a reputation and after a while Barry put together something called 'Shane Richie's Ladies' Night Out', where I'd travel up and down the East Coast playing as far afield as King's Lynn and even London and Kent sometimes. One night Barry called me and said he was short of a stripper for a Ladies' Night Out at a nurses' social club at Ipswich Hospital and could I think of anybody who would do it at short notice. I rang Goz and he said he'd do it for fifty quid. There's not much Goz wouldn't do for fifty quid, to be honest. Anyway, he came round to my mum and dad's and we put together a great montage of music from Michael Jackson to Adam Ant, rehearsed a routine and came up with the name Blue Thunder. I really built him up throughout the evening and then the moment came. I finally introduced him.

'Girls, will you please welcome, live on stage, the most sought-after stripper in the country, the one, the only, Mr King Dick himself, Blue Thunder.'

The King Dick bit was obviously a lie, but the girls went crazy. He bounded on stage like a rampant cockerel in a farmyard of hens, dressed in a ski suit. Goz stuck to his routine and within minutes he was down to his G-string. Girls were going mad, reaching out for him and he did the whole baby oil routine, turning round and inviting them up on stage to rub it into his buttocks – he was in his element. Now the whole thing about being a male stripper is being able to control yourself, because it's illegal to get too excited in public. It's all right if you're in a private room in a pub in front of 30 ladies, but not 300 nurses screaming and cheering. The other thing I'd learnt by now from watching the professional strippers was that you were only meant to tease the audience – you gave them a quick flash and then got off the stage. But not Goz. He broke every rule in the book and when I looked out from the side of the stage he was standing there starkers with his todger pointing north and a dirty big grin on his face. Next thing I know he's running between the tables with a glazed look in his eyes as if he's about to do the wild thing with each and every one of them. All I could think to do was turn the lights off and run out into the audience and grab him. Goz never forgave me – and neither did the nurses.

In March 1984 Barry put me into a big talent competition in Newmarket, where the prize money was £1,000. Professional entertainers were allowed to enter and I ended up going all the way through the heats and winning. That was my very first publicity. I even made it into the *Willesden & Brent Chronicle*, which was the paper my mum and dad read. It described me as an up-and-coming star and the interview that went with it said that I was sure to give most of the winnings to my mum. I didn't know a great deal about public relations in those days, but I knew enough to say that. Part of the prize was a contract to work at the Newmarket Cabaret Club, which was a great venue. A lot of the big acts at the time were appearing there and I ended up supporting everybody from Showaddywaddy to Bernard Manning. Bernard was a funny man, although I never understood racist humour. I could see why some comics did it, because it got laughs, but coming from an Irish family I didn't appreciate Irish or black or Pakistani gags. Anyway, Bernard was booked for two nights and I was compèring, which meant I'd get up before him, do a few songs and 20 minutes of stand-up. I only really had 20 minutes of stand-up in those days, so that suited me fine.

On the first night Bernard said to me in his gruff Mancunian accent: 'Right son, I want to see you do your material; I'm going to watch you.' I went out there and I was storming it. Then at the end of my act I introduced Bernard. Of course, as well as I'd gone down I knew Bernard Manning would wipe the floor with me. The guy had been in the business for years and I was right, the audience loved him. But I'd done better than Bernard or anyone else had expected, so I wasn't too worried. The following night Bernard said: 'Right son, I want you to put me on first, then I want you to come on and do your material after, just so you can see the difference.' I thought: 'Alright, there's a challenge.' I didn't know any better. I introduced Bernard, he went on and in his first 20 minutes he did every gag I'd done the night before. He changed them round to suit his style, but otherwise they were more or less word for word. I was mortified. At the end of it Bernard welcomed me back and I struggled through, but I got nothing like the reaction I had the night before, because I had next to nothing left to say.

Did I learn a big lesson that night? It taught me that if you only have 20 minutes to perform you should always have another 20 minutes of material spare. It also taught me how to think on my feet and ad-lib. But most important of all it taught me never to share a bill with Bernard Manning again.

By the summer of 1984 I was earning £60 or £70 per gig, which wasn't bad money. But then, like now, I still owed a lot of money to the bank. I ended up borrowing money left, right and centre in order to survive, but at the time it didn't really worry me. I was only 20, I was working and I was learning and that was all I really cared about.

Pontins were still calling me trying to tempt me back, offering me a budget and decent accommodation and saying I could pick my own staff, but by now Barry had got me some provisional bookings on a tour of Jersey in the summer. Every so often you meet someone who makes a real difference to your life. Paul Wagner was one of those people and still is. He was a tough-talking Scot who didn't suffer fools gladly. With his little goatee beard and long hair he looked just like Billy Connolly, and he shot from the hip just like him, too.

He was a singer as well as the Entertainments Manager and booker for the main hotel chain in Jersey. To get on the tour I had to audition for him. Barry Dye had set up a meeting in London. He'd booked the back room of a hotel and I went on in front of Paul and did 12 minutes. It wasn't the greatest material but he saw something there, although the fact that it was my first season as a professional comic and was therefore cheap might have had something to do with it as well.

I was excited to be going, because I knew that two years previously Paul Wagner had booked an unknown comic called Brian Conley to do exactly the same tour. It was called the Chris North Touring Show. Chris had a comedy magic double act and once again I was compère and bottom of the bill with my stand-up. But instead of once a week, this was touring six nights a week and two shows a night. We'd appear at a venue from 7.30pm–9pm, take all the equipment down, get changed, climb into a van and get to the next hotel to start again at 10pm. In some hotels you'd be appearing in the dining room where people were still eating dinner. You'd be delivering your punchline while they were wandering around hunting for more bread rolls or arguing about the bill.

When Pontins holiday camp in Jersey got wind of the fact that I was back on the island, they invited me along to head their cabaret every Saturday night. It was a great opportunity. Here was one of their own, trying to make it alone. I turned up and guess who was the Entertainments Manager? Only Angel. He welcomed me with open arms and as a joke I slipped him my chalet key and tickled his bum.

That night I was so nervous. I'm not sure if it showed, but something went wrong and I died a million deaths. I just couldn't get it together. Paul Wagner came to see me afterwards and I could tell he was disappointed.

'The problem with you, wee boy, is that you're forever apologising.'

I didn't understand what he meant at first, so he sat me down and explained.

'You're not a Bluecoat anymore, Shane. Stop acting like one. You're a professional entertainer now. They've got to know they're seeing something special.'

And he was right. My body language was wrong, I was nervously clutching the microphone close to my chest and I kept saying that I hoped they were enjoying themselves.

To make matters worse, Pontins cancelled the booking. Not because of what had happened that night, but because head office had heard I was appearing. By now they weren't happy with me at all; they'd been badgering me for months to go back and they were starting to get heavy, saying that I'd broken an agreement to return. They wrote to

Jersey and told them of a new ruling that former Bluecoats weren't allowed to work at camps as cabaret. They hadn't succeeded in making me change my mind, so this was their way of getting back at me. It was a shame, but I guess it was for the best – I'd paid my dues as a holiday camp entertainer; it was time to move on.

CHAPTER SEVEN

'Four topless birds and I can't mention 'em?'

I've always believed that you should treat people well on the way up because you're bound to run into them again on the way down. That's certainly how it's happened in my life. During the summer of 1984 there was an impresario in Jersey by the name of Dick Ray, who was the local big cheese. He ran a cabaret club called Caesar's Palace, where all the top acts appeared. They used to put on a proper floorshow with professional dancers and a real band. Dick also used to stage a show every Sunday night at the Opera House. Frank Carson was top of the bill that summer and our touring cabaret was booked to support him. I'd go on first and do ten minutes of stand-up, then I'd introduce Johnny Cosgrove, a Scottish singer who I shared a room with, he'd introduce Kate and Wendy, two female singers and the first half would end with Chris North's magic show.

The first time we appeared it went fantastically well and afterwards we all went upstairs to the Green Room to celebrate. Frank Carson and the dancers were there and we were having a great time, when Dick came in and congratulated everyone on a great show. He chatted to everyone, said how well they'd done and then he turned to me. Now at that time I did a little routine about the French and how I didn't understand them or their culture.

'I only know two words in French – fromage and vin, which means cheese and wine. On holiday I was constipated and pissed for two weeks.'

Another line would go:

'French cafés have tables and chairs outside. We have the same in Harlesden, it's called eviction.'

It was just light-hearted banter and it seemed to go down well with the audience. But in front of everyone Dick said that he thought my routine was insulting as a lot of French people came on holiday to Jersey. I pointed out that very few French people would come to see Frank Carson anyway, but I apologised and said the last thing I wanted to do was upset anyone. But Dick just wouldn't let it rest. It was obvious he wanted to try to embarrass and belittle me in front of everyone. I was into bolero jackets at that time – I was a big David Bowie fan and he wore them in the early 1980s. I'd also grown my hair long and had both my ears pierced – it was a deliberate attempt to look different from the other comics, but perhaps Dick thought I was trying to be flash. That year I'd also been named Jersey Variety Club's 'Best Young Up-and-Coming Artist with Star Quality'. They'd had an awards lunch in one of the big hotels and I'd had my picture taken with the comic Mick Miller, who'd also won an award. I felt so proud. He was one of my heroes at the time and there I was receiving an award alongside him. Whatever I was doing I was doing right, but Dick seemed resentful. Eventually he left me alone and turned to leave. Everyone was saying 'Bye, Dick,' 'Cheerio, Dick,' and of course I automatically joined in and said 'Bye, Dick' too. I was just trying to be friendly, but it was obviously a big mistake because as soon as I spoke, he stopped, turned round and glared at me. The whole room went quiet and everyone froze. 'You, young man,' he said, pausing for effect. 'You call me Mr Ray.' He made me feel the size of a mouse. I was so humiliated and I vowed there and then that if I ever got the chance to get my revenge on him one day, I would.

Despite Dick's attempts to quash my confidence I was now beginning to make a bit of a name for myself. At the end of the summer I hugged Paul Wagner and promised I'd be back to pick up where I left off the following year.

But now I had to get through the winter. I felt I'd learnt a lot in Jersey and developed plenty of new material. Now I wanted to go away and try it out in the clubs. Barry Dye, meanwhile, had set me up at Butlins in Somerset, where they wanted me to be their resident compère over the Christmas period. I was quite happy to do it as it meant I could introduce all the cabarets and do half an hour of my own material. What I hadn't anticipated was how lonely I'd be. I'd never worked at Butlins before so I didn't really know anybody there and I remember sitting in my chalet on Christmas Day, all alone. All the Redcoats knew each other and were having a great time with the holidaymakers, but I was an outsider. I remember getting myself some fish and chips and sitting there staring at the four walls while I ate them – that was my Christmas dinner. The Cratchet family were having more fun than me. I had a show to do in the evening, but during the day I literally didn't speak to a soul. I could have called my mum and dad of course, but I didn't want them to know I was lonely. I'd rather have died than admit a weakness to my dad, and as for my mum, I didn't want her to worry. She was the sort of person who would have travelled a million miles to be with me if she knew something was wrong, but I was far too proud. It was a real lesson to me that day. It made me realise how hard the business could be and that when you're a solo act travelling the country you do end up spending time on your own. I suppose at the back of my mind I'd always known it could happen, I just never thought it would be Christmas Day.

I spent New Year's Eve at Butlins and started 1985 back on the road, schlepping around the country. I was busy enough, but I was mainly appearing at hotels, compèring private functions and hen nights and not really doing my act very much. When I did get booked as top of the bill it was always at caravan parks. I mentioned this to Barry Dye and he told me not to worry as he'd just got me three weeks of stand-up gigs, seven nights a week, starting in the North-West of England, travelling through Lancashire and Yorkshire into the North-East. I borrowed my mum's Capri – even though I still hadn't passed my test. I'd already taken it once and failed, but I had to get there somehow. I was petrified the whole way there because I'd heard all the horror stories about how tough the Northern clubs could be, especially if you were a Southerner. No one had quite spelled out how tough.

And of all the places to start, please, not a Catholic Club in Preston.

I knew five minutes into my act that it was going to be an education. From nowhere this old bloke with a cloth cap and a tray of pies in his hand, limped to the front of the stage, and said to me: 'Quiet now, son.' Then at the top of his voice he shouted: 'Ladies and gentlemen, the pies have arrived.' He turned back to me. 'I think it best if you start singing now, son.' I couldn't believe it. I did as I was told and started my Elvis medley. Halfway through 'Wonder of You' I heard a shout from the wings. It was the club secretary. 'Call it a day now, son, people need to eat.'

They were actually queuing up in front of me to buy their pies. Directly behind me on the wall behind the stage was a 6ft-tall Jesus on the crucifix. Before I walked off I couldn't help myself. I had to say it. I grabbed the mike. 'Is this what you did to the comic last week then?' I knew then I'd be leaving by the back door. And fast.

Clubs in Yorkshire were just as tough, but I met some great characters along the way. One musician, who backed me in a club in Bradford, introduced himself after the gig.

'Really enjoyed your show, mate. My name's Gary, nice to meet you.'

'Nice to meet you too, pal. So is this what you do then, Gary, work the clubs?'

'No, I'm just trying to make a few quid, I'm working on some of my own songs.'

We shook hands and parted company. A few years later we were to meet up again on a Saturday morning TV show called Going Live, where he was performing as part of a new boy band, Take That. It was Gary Barlow. Good on you, Gazza.

In the North-East the heckling started before I'd even reached the punchline of my first gag.

'You posh Southern bastard.'

'Fuck off back t'London you rich twat.'

There was a lot of talk in the papers at the time about a new show that was just about to launch on BBC1. It was about working-class people living in a square in the East End of London and it was going to be called EastEnders. It went out for the first time in February while I was still in the North-East and got a fantastic reaction. Things literally changed for me overnight. It was the first TV show that had shown the lives of working-class Londoners, who, to all intents and purposes, were living like the people up North. All of a sudden that North-South divide got smaller. For the last ten days of that tour I couldn't put a foot wrong. I was coming on talking like a Cockney and they loved it.

When I got back to London, Barry told me I'd been offered £75 for a stag night, midweek at a pub in Watford. I hated stag nights. I detested the whole atmosphere and on top of that they were never the most rewarding audience for a comic because all they wanted were the strippers. However, if you can pick up £75 midweek you're doing OK, so I took it. They wanted someone who could sing a few songs, tell a few jokes and compère the whole evening. It probably wasn't the wisest decision of my life. You needed to be totally on top of your game in front of a stag crowd and I really didn't have that sort of material at the time.

The standard routine at stag nights in those days was to hire three strippers and a blue comic. Believe me, I really admire blue comics, because once you've gone down that route it's really tough to come back. The material is hard and sharp and it's never about personality, it's just about how rude the gag can be. That was never really me. I was quite happy to compère and throw the odd F-word in, but I wasn't prepared to go further than that. On this particular night I came on, told a few jokes and then introduced the first stripper. She did her stuff and got a good reception; the guys weren't too drunk so it was under control. By the time the blue comic came out they'd had a few more beers and he tore the place up. With the audience yelling for more, we disappeared to our dressing room – a tiny room with a little porthole window at the side of the makeshift stage – for the interval. During the break the strippers went out again and walked around the audience in tiny bikinis collecting money in buckets. They were already getting paid a fortune, but I'd whipped the audience into a frenzy earlier on and told them that the more money they put in the buckets the ruder the girls would get. After 15 minutes the girls came back with the best part of £200, which in the mid-1980s was a lot of money and would almost double their fee.

After the interval the comic went back out and did his second spot. This time it was a little bit tougher. The blokes were beered up and the strippers had turned them on. He'd clearly had enough and once he'd finished his act he got his money and legged it. All that was left to do in the second half was ten minutes of material from me and then the strippers in a double act. Now it doesn't get any bluer than a stag night double act. Use your imagination. Double it, then treble it and that gives you some idea of what these girls were capable of doing. I got to know a lot of strippers over the years, both male and female, and to all of them it was just an act. They never felt anything sexual, regardless of what the audience thought. They could make the men sitting out there feel like the sexiest beasts on earth, but they were doing it purely for the money. Most of them were quite hardened to it all, but this was a particularly rowdy audience and as I was about to go on again one of the girls started to get a bit upset. She felt it was getting out of hand, so I went back on the mike and asked them to calm down, reminding them that they couldn't touch the girls. I walked back into the dressing room to reassure her, only to find that she was already dressed and climbing out of the porthole. Not only that, she was taking the buckets of money with her. I pleaded with her to change her mind, but she was adamant the crowd were too drunk.

'Shane, if you've got any sense you'll pack up and go, darling,' she said.

'Well, at least leave the money so I can go and hand it back,' I said.

'You can forget that, the money's coming with me, babe.'

And that was it. I just saw her bum disappearing out of the window and then she was gone.

Meanwhile there are blokes banging on the door asking what was going on and lots of aggressive chanting from the room. 'We want tits, we want tits.' It was awful. As I was trying to work out what to do, the second girl piped up: 'Shane, I'm not staying here on my own, it's too dangerous.'

Before I had a chance to say anything she climbed out of the window too.

Left alone in the dressing room I had two options. I could go out there, tell them the girls had gone and face a public execution, or I could follow the girls through the porthole. Not the toughest decision of my life. I threw my suit carrier over my arm and started to climb out. By that point the guys at the door had grown tired of waiting. The door burst open and one of them saw me, or rather my bum wedged in the tiny window.

'You little shit,' he yelled. As far as he was concerned I was doing a runner with the money. The dancers by now were long gone in their open-top Jags; they weren't short of a few quid. I had to make my getaway in my mum's clapped-out Capri.

I jumped down to the ground, turned round and all I could see were the pub doors bursting opening and this angry mob pouring out. There was a long gravel drive between the car and me and it was like one of those terrible nightmares where you're running and not getting anywhere. I finally reached the car, praying that I could find the right key and praying that it would start. When I got inside I quickly locked the door, put my foot to the floor and screeched out of the place. The guys had caught up and were just yards away picking up handfuls of gravel, hurling them after me and calling me every name under the sun.

In the summer of 1985 I returned to Jersey. I'd learnt a lot during the winter and yet there I was touring the same hotels, so to stretch myself I'd take on different personas. One week I'd become a Scottish comedian and I'd change my whole act, from the way I spoke to the way I dressed and stood. I took it really seriously, to the extent that at the bar afterwards I'd still be Scottish. Sometimes I'd be a Brummie; other times I'd be Welsh or American. I even did an Asian comic from the Punjab called Mahatma Coat. I tanned my face, wore a turban and a white catsuit and people would come back afterwards and say to me: 'Oh, that Asian comic was so funny, where did you find him?' They didn't recognise me at all.

One guy in particular who left his mark on me that summer was Paul Wagner's brother, Jamie, who like his brother was a great singer. He was the total opposite of Paul. Whereas Paul was big, boisterous and the life and soul, Jamie was quiet and preferred to sit in the corner of the bar. He didn't suffer fools gladly and he chose his friends carefully.

He reminded me of Clint Eastwood because he didn't say a lot but still had a presence and he always wore a cowboy hat. He was a great one for sayings. 'Remember where you came from, son, because that way you know where you're going.' That was one of his favourites. If ever I moaned about a gig he'd say, 'Well if you don't like it, Shane, get out. We're lucky, we chose our jobs. Our parents didn't have any choice about what they did.' He'd also tell me that you didn't need qualifications for our job, which meant anybody could say they were in showbiz, but not everyone was successful. But the one that always stuck with me was: 'If you're going to have regrets, regret the things you've done, not the things you haven't.' I thought that was a great philosophy.

It was during that season in Jersey that my dad came to visit me for the first time. My trips home had been few and far between and when I phoned I only ever spoke to my mum. My dad and I had been poles apart when I was a child and now I'd left home and was no longer frightened of him the distance between us had grown even bigger. He was my dad and I still loved him, but we weren't in any way close and I was absolutely dreading his visit because I knew he was coming without my mum, which meant he was free to drink as much as he wanted.

I did a show at a hotel called The Metropole that week and Dad started heckling me from the audience. I always used to do a routine about mums. Halfway through the act he stood up and shouted: 'Don't ya talk about ya feckin' mother like that.' It was awful and nobody found it funny. I said: 'It's alright folks, he's my dad,' and of course everybody laughed because they thought I was joking.

Eventually he was asked to leave and I was so ashamed that afterwards I didn't tell a soul that he really was my dad. I'll never forget packing up the equipment at the end of the night. We were due to leave through the back door because our van was parked out the back, but one of the dancers ran in and said: 'There's no point going out this way, there's a drunken Paddy out there, he's collapsed on the stairs and wet himself.' I made my excuses to the rest of the cast and went outside, picked him up and walked him round to the B&B where he was staying.

That night I got a phone call from the police: my dad had been found wandering around St Helier semi-naked and drunk and didn't know where he was. Of course I went to collect him. He was my Dad. When I look back I don't think he was a bad man or that he meant any harm. He was just a drinker and that's what drink does to people. He was out of control. It drove a wedge between us for years.

It was in 1985 that I met a dancer called Dawn Rodgers. In the early 1980s there was a television programme called *The World Malibu Dance Championships*, starring the World Disco Dancing champion Grant Santino and hosted by Peter Powell. Dawn was a friend of Grant's and she was a fabulous dancer. She represented Jersey and even got to the finals. She joined our tour as part of a dance troupe and everyone liked her, except me. I found her quite aloof and apparently she didn't like me much either – she thought I was arrogant – but that ended up being part of the attraction. Eventually the barriers broke down and we got together. I remember thinking from the start that she was complex. At times it was hard to keep her jolly, but then other times we would sit for hours laughing. When the season ended in October it was time to say goodbye to Dawn. I asked her to come over to London to stay with me and my mum, but she already had some dancing work lined up so I went back to England on my own. Dawn would visit me whenever she had a few days off – we were a proper boyfriend and girlfriend – and then I returned to Jersey at Christmas to do some cabaret work at a hotel. Dawn lived with me there and we had the best time.

In January 1986 I had to leave Dawn again as I was booked to support The Nolans at a venue called The Orchard in Dartford, Kent. I know that was the month because Goz wrote in his diary: 'Shane says he's going to give one to the little chubby bird on the end.' And that was Coleen. To this day I've insisted to Coleen I never said such a thing, but Goz swears it was true.

I was a bit of a pop comic at that time and used to support all the pop bands, everyone from Paul Young to Imagination. I still had my ponytail and pierced ears and I still wore a bolero jacket. For a comic I was fairly rock and roll and my act was all about losing my virginity, drinking and pulling girls. The Nolans' audience meanwhile were diehard fans, very polite and a little bit older. I was a big fan of Paul Weller and I distinctly remember standing in the wings thinking: why can't I be supporting Paul Weller instead of The Nolans?

We did two shows – a six o'clock and a nine o'clock and I remember standing at the back of the theatre during The Nolans' final set and not being able to take my eyes off Coleen; she was beautiful. Afterwards I found their brother, Brian, who was their tour manager and asked if I could go backstage and meet them. To my delight he said they'd found me really funny and wanted to meet me too. I spoke to all the other girls and eventually plucked up the courage to talk to Coleen. We chatted and after a while she said: 'We're going to see you again this summer, aren't we?' I'd been booked to appear at a place called Tregonwell Hall, which is part of the Bournemouth International Centre. It was a room upstairs, a late-night cabaret and dining restaurant, and apparently The Nolans were appearing in Bournemouth at the same time, at a much bigger venue, supporting Cannon and Ball.

At the end of the evening I said: 'I look forward to seeing you in the summer then,' and we shook hands. I walked away and left it at that, but I knew something had happened between us. Nothing was said, but I just couldn't get Coleen out of my head. Maybe a part of it was that I was a jobbing comic and it was good for my ego to think that some-body famous like Coleen Nolan might fancy me, but deep down I know it was more than that. Something just connected.

In April I went back to Jersey and moved in with Dawn and her parents Yvonne and Denis. I was now working at a cabaret venue called the Chateau Plaisir on the Five Mile Road in St Ouen with 'The Shane Richie and Micky Zany Show'. It was our own show, which meant we could do what material we liked and we had special guests on with us. As part of the show we'd do a double act, which was great fun. It was way before the days of Vic Reeves and Bob Mortimer, but it was very much that style of humour – gags without punchlines and strange impressions such as Sylvester Stallone gardening or Mick Jagger working as a tour bus guide. It was mad stuff that made us laugh, but it didn't work in Jersey with audiences who wanted to see Frank Carson. We were banging our heads against a wall, really.

Dawn's parents were lovely people. I think they thought I was a bit of a Cockney scallywag and they liked me, too. It was a happy time and by now Dawn and I were in love, but things weren't completely right between us. I'd seen quite a change in her since we met, almost as if she had begun to feel overshadowed by my personality. She'd be the life and soul of the party and then I'd walk in and take over and she'd go quiet. I'd hear stories about how funny she'd been when I was off the island and the fun she'd got up to, but she wasn't always like that with me.

Like most couples we had our problems. She'd get quite emotional at times and say she saw me as her rock and her soul mate, but at the same time she seemed to find it difficult to open up to me about her feelings. At times it could be a fiery relationship; we were both up and very passionate, or down and not talking to each other. There was no middle ground.

In the early summer of that year we got engaged. After we'd both finished work we'd go for long walks around the island and I asked her during one of those walks, at two o'clock in the morning in a park over- looking one of the bays in St Helier. I wanted to make her feel secure and I thought that getting engaged would do that. I never really thought about marriage itself – I never really thought about the future, just the present. I had nothing against marriage; it just hadn't really entered my thoughts at that stage in my life. I'd only been going a couple of years in the business and there were lots of things I wanted to achieve. Dawn was delighted though and so were her parents, to the extent that they even put an announcement in the *Jersey Evening Post*.

The engagement was designed to bring us closer together and in many ways it did. I'd stay with her family in Jersey for a spell, she'd come back to London with me and we even scraped together enough money to go on holiday to Tenerife. We had a fantastic time, apart from the fact that I was ripped off for £5,000 by a timeshare tout. This guy showed me a beautiful timeshare apartment and I was totally taken in and ended up getting my bank to transfer £5,000 into his account. It was every penny I owned – my life savings – and as soon as he got it he disappeared. There am I, the arch blagger, getting done by another blagger. I couldn't believe it.

Even though we were now engaged, Dawn would still get into low moods. I think she found it difficult to talk to me about things. I suppose if I had problems I'd go and talk to Goz and she'd talk to her friends. Maybe if we'd spoken to each other, things would have been a lot easier between us.

In July I had to leave Jersey for my season in Bournemouth. Dawn took me to the ferry and both of us were in tears as we said goodbye. She didn't want me to leave the island, and I was heartbroken too. Now my work on Jersey was over it was going to be hard for us to see much of each other as she'd already signed for another season on the island.

While I was on Jersey I'd become good mates with a guy called Steve Christie, who was Britain's number one Cliff Richard lookalike. That was all he could do, he didn't have a proper act. He'd do 40 minutes of rubbish and then he'd come on and do Cliff and everyone would be in hysterics. His parents lived in Bournemouth so they kindly found me a tiny two-bedroom flat to rent and I turned up full of antici-pation. Bournemouth was the second biggest resort after Blackpool in those days. Cannon and Ball were in town, so was Brian Conley and the Grumbleweeds and TV's *Summertime Special* came from there. My own show was a world away from those traditional seaside variety shows, but Barry Dye said it was important just to be in the same place as acts like that.

The show I was in was called 'Les Folies de Paris' and it was a topless revue, so to get a licence and prevent the audience simply being full of dirty old men, they had to put a comic in and make it look like it was a variety show. I wasn't their first choice, but a lot of comics were a bit wary of a show like that and wouldn't do it. They knew I was up for anything on the other hand and hardly likely to turn down the chance to appear with topless dancers.

The show was produced and directed by a couple of gay guys. As soon as we started rehearsals I began to wonder what I'd got myself into. It opened with four topless dancers. One of them was a former girl-friend by the name of Sally, who I'd become close to the year before in Jersey. The others were girls in their late thirties and they weren't in the greatest shape – it was a very cheap production.

As the girls danced around I had to come out and tell a few jokes, but the producer told me that I couldn't make any reference to the fact that they were topless.

'You're having a laugh ain't ya?' I said. 'I've got to come on behind four birds who've got their tits out and I can't mention 'em?'

'No, darling,' he insisted. 'It's not that type of show, love.'

So I used to come on riding a pushbike, wearing a beret, with a string of onions around my neck singing: 'Thank heavens for little girls, for little girls get bigger every day.'

For the first couple of weeks it was empty, apart from a handful of dirty old men, but then I found that students were coming in because I was making it different every night. They still insisted I couldn't talk about the women or tell any rude jokes because it was a classy show. Now, I was never a classy comic. I still had a ponytail and a pierced ear and I'd do routines about moonwalking with Michael Jackson and then suddenly burst into a Wham song. This was a show about 'gay Paris' and I'm doing George Michael impressions and singing 'I'm Your Man'. I was a square peg in a round hole, but I started to get a bit of a following and the other acts in town would come along to see me. I'd look out and there'd be people like Bobby Davro and Cannon and Ball in the audience.

I'd been there a couple of weeks before I bumped into The Nolans again. I was with Sally in the late-night bar at the Bournemouth International Centre and The Nolans were having their opening night party in there. Their brother Brian spotted me and called me over to say hello to the girls. I chatted to them all, but I didn't dare speak to Coleen. I saw she was staring at me, but I just didn't have the bottle. Much later on I noticed she was talking to her dad, Tommy, so I made an excuse to go over and speak to him. When he eventually wandered off, Coleen and I ended up spending all night together talking at the bar. I hung on her every word and she had me in fits of giggles. No woman had ever made me laugh like that before. I was making her laugh too and she was truly interested in what I had to say. I'd only known her for hours, I had a fiancée back in Jersey and Coleen came from a different world, but at that moment none of that mattered. I was besotted.

CHAPTER EIGHT

'This is Bobby Ball, my hero, and he's threatening to break my legs'

When you're starting out as a comic you always have your heroes. People you admire and respect and who are just downright funny. For me in the mid-1980s it was Cannon and Ball. Bobby Ball was and still is one of the funniest men I've ever known. It was a thrill simply to be appearing in the same town as him. I felt like I'd made it just because I was there. Imagine how I felt then, after two weeks in Bournemouth, to find myself at a party, drinking alongside not only Cannon and Ball, but also The Grumbleweeds, Brian Conley, Bobby Davro, Russ Abbott and Keith Harris. Now, no matter what you think of these acts now, back then they were massive names with their own TV shows. And I wasn't.

I'd been invited to the party by Coleen. It was held at a huge house on the outskirts of Bournemouth that the Nolan family had rented for the summer season. Sally came with me. I drove a little white 1.6 Ford Escort at the time and as we pulled up at the house I completely lost my bottle. Seeing all the famous people inside I panicked. I said to Sally: 'I can't go in there. I'm nobody,' but she was adamant I couldn't back out.

'Come on, you *are* somebody. Just go in there and be yourself,' she insisted. So we went inside and it was celebrity excess at its finest. It was a massive house with oak-panelled rooms and a log fire, large gardens and a swimming pool. There were canapés and champagne. This was what I'd dreamed of for years: this was showbiz.

I was a bit overawed, but loving every second, as I sat quietly in a corner with Sally still feeling like I shouldn't be there. I could see all the young, good-looking male dancers chatting up Coleen. She was the youngest and, to me, by far the prettiest. Everyone wanted to be with her and I quickly resigned myself to the fact that there was no way I was even going to get near her to say hello.

To my surprise Coleen suddenly spotted me, broke away from her group and came across to ask us if we wanted a drink. Unfortunately Sally said she needed to get back and as I was driving I said I had to leave too to take her home.

Coleen looked me straight in the eye and smiled. 'Don't go, Shane, there's a bloke over there who's boring me silly. Stay and talk to me until he goes.' This bloke had his own aeroplane and I was driving a clapped-out old Escort but Coleen would rather talk to me. I could hardly believe it. Sally said she would go home on her own and drive my car and Coleen said I could get a cab home later, on the Nolans' account. I'd never even heard of cab accounts before then. I was bowled over; it was like another world.

The two of us got a drink and went through into a little alcove off the kitchen where it was a bit quieter. We sat down and chatted until the sun came up. By then it was getting cold and the party was clearing. I told Coleen I thought it was time I should be on my way, but she begged me to stay a bit longer. We came inside and went through to the sitting room and talked until nine in the morning. We talked about every subject under the sun and I hung on her every word. I was fascinated. She was a Nolan sister, after all; she was a proper pop star and had people screaming for her, but equally she seemed to like listening to my holiday camp stories, which made me feel good.

At nine o'clock I said I really had to go. Coleen walked me to the door and we went outside. It was blazing sunshine and I took her in my arms and kissed her for the first time. It wasn't a passionate kiss, I held back and just gently kissed her lips, but those few seconds felt like an eternity. From that moment on I never wanted to be away from her. It felt so real and I climbed into the cab on such a high. I waved out of the window until we turned the corner and Coleen was out of sight. It was only then that reality hit me: I was engaged to somebody else. How could I be falling for Coleen?

I didn't hold that thought for long. As soon as I arrived back at my flat, I showered and changed and then went straight back to the Nolans' house. Coleen had invited me back for brunch. Brunch? What's a bloody brunch? When I arrived Coleen's dad, Tommy, opened the door, invited me in and said that Coleen was still upstairs getting changed and that she'd be down in a few minutes.

I stood there like a little boy. I was wearing white canvas shoes, cut-off jeans like Wham used to wear, and a white T-shirt. My hair was in a ponytail and I wore a porkpie hat. I was quite trendy for those days, but at that moment I sorely wished I'd worn something a bit less conspicuous. I'd naïvely assumed that it would just be the two of us; I hadn't realised the whole family would be there along with some of the guests from the previous night.

I remember Coleen's sister Anne coming downstairs, giggling when she saw me and running back upstairs. Then Bobby Ball came over and said he wanted a word. We sat outside on our own with a cup of tea and he said:

'Reet, I've just been talking t'rest of t'sisters, don't you dare break young Coleen's 'art.'

I was confused. 'What ya talking about?'

'T'girls have told me that Coleen's really excited about seeing you again, but she's just turned 21 and I know what you comics are like; this is just going to be a summer fling for you. But I'm telling y'now, you break 'er heart and I'll break your fucking legs.'

This is Bobby Ball, my hero, and he's threatening to break my legs. I was too delighted to be scared.

We went back inside and Coleen came down the stairs. She'd

showered and was wearing a really pretty dress and looked so beautiful I just couldn't take my eyes off her. We sat down to eat and I got to meet all the family properly. I immediately loved them all; they were warm, friendly and close and I felt privileged to be a part of it. It was a world away from my own family.

That afternoon Coleen and I went out for a long walk and for the rest of that week we saw each other every night. We'd do our shows, then we'd all go back to the Nolans' for a party and the two of us would always slope off into the garden. We'd kiss and cuddle like a couple of teenagers and sit on our own chatting all night. I loved being with her. She was the first girl I'd ever met who seemed genuinely excited for me. She'd say it would be my turn one day and tell me what it would be like when I did my first press conference, my first photo shoot and my first TV appearance. I was like a sponge when I was around her because she was talking from experience. We'd stay there until six in the morning, unable to tear ourselves away from each other, at which point I'd have to go home for some sleep and a shower. I'd kiss her on the lips, never anything more, and then it would start all over again the next night.

During the day I was still speaking to Dawn. To cope with the situation I convinced myself that I was in control and that Coleen was just going to be my summer fling. She used to joke about it herself. She'd say to me: 'Oh, you're just my fella for the summer run.' I never doubted her, because that's what summer seasons were about. The comics would get off with the singers; the dancers would get off with the band. I'd seen it happen in Jersey.

It was a week later, when Coleen and I made love for the first time, that I realised I wasn't as in control as I thought. All her family had gone out to a party so after our shows Coleen and I picked up a takeaway and went back to her house on our own. We sat and talked as usual, but this was the first time we'd been in the house alone, and when it got to one in the morning Coleen asked if I'd like to stay the night. I was worried about what her family would think, but she said if we went up to her room before they got back they'd never know. We raced up the stairs giggling like little schoolkids. Afterwards Coleen fell asleep in my arms and I had the best night's sleep of my life. All the flings and one-night stands on my tours and at the holiday camps meant nothing compared to this one night with Coleen.

The next day her sisters were furious. We'd only known each other a week and they thought what we'd done was wrong, but I didn't care. From that point on I just wanted to be with Coleen, 24 hours a day if possible. Nothing else mattered – even my career – and that's when I knew how serious things were. That's when I knew I was falling in love. Real love.

By now Dawn had started to realise something was wrong. We used to speak to each other five or six times a day, but now it was just once every couple of days. My old mate Steve Christie called me from Jersey one day to tell me how upset Dawn was by this. He asked me what was happening and foolishly I confided in him. I said I had every intention of telling Dawn, but that I just had to find the right moment to break it to her. Similarly, I was still trying to find the right moment to tell Coleen about Dawn. I'd told her I'd fallen in love with her, and I just didn't know how to break it to her that I was already engaged.

In the end the decision was taken out of my hands. Coleen's brother, Brian, called me one day and asked to meet me for lunch in a local café. I was pretty friendly with the whole family by now so I didn't think too much of it, but the minute he walked through the door I knew that something had happened. His face was like thunder. 'Why the hell didn't you tell Coleen?' What had happened was that he'd been talking to a friend in Jersey and he'd told this guy that his little sister was going out with a comic called Shane Richie, who used to work in Jersey. The guy had asked if he meant the same Shane Richie who was engaged to a dancer called Dawn.

Brian held me up against the wall. 'You know my little sister is falling for you. What are you going to do about it?' I knew I had no option but to tell Coleen that day. I phoned her and suggested we meet in a little tea bar around the back of the theatre that afternoon. When Coleen walked in I stood up and put my arms around her.

'You're going to tell me something aren't you?' she asked. She knew instantly from my face that there was something wrong. We sat down.

'Yes, Coleen, I'm engaged,' I said.

Coleen was heartbroken and she began to cry. I felt like shit.

'Why didn't you tell me?'

''Cos I was scared you wouldn't want to see me no more.'

'Well guess what, Shane? I don't.'

'But I'm going to finish it.'

'Do what you've got to do, but we're finished,' she told me. 'You've lied to me.'

By my way of thinking, I hadn't lied to her; foolishly, I just hadn't told her. She was so hurt. The trouble was I'd imagined I'd see my relationship with Coleen through to the end of summer, then we'd finish it and I'd go back to Dawn. But just to make matters even worse, Steve Christie had told Dawn. He fancied the pants off her anyway and he got drunk one night and told her that I was seeing one of the Nolans.

The following day, before I'd even had a chance to decide how to sort out this mess, I received a call from Dawn. She asked if it was true and I told her it was. She flew over that weekend. We sat down and had a heart-to-heart and I told her everything that had happened. I said I was sorry and that I'd never intended it to happen. And it was true. I really hadn't planned it, but you can't help who you fall in love with. Dawn put a brave face on it and the next morning I drove her out to the airport. She gave me back her engagement ring and we said goodbye. I felt terrible that I'd hurt her. I called her a couple of times afterwards to see how she was and I met her a couple of times at various showcases and she seemed to be doing fine. Then I heard she'd met a DJ and fallen in love with him.

After Coleen found out I'd been engaged to Dawn she refused even to speak to me. Anne Nolan's daughter, Amy, who was only six at the time, used to come and watch my show night after night and sit backstage with me. I was desperate to win Coleen back but too scared to face her myself so I asked Amy to go and tell her Aunty Coleen that Dawn and I were over. She looked puzzled, but I said Coleen would know what I meant. After the show Coleen came over to see me. She said she wasn't sure about her feelings for me now and that I'd have to woo her. The following day I persuaded her to come shopping with me and as we walked down the high street I started saying to her over and over again: 'I love you and I know you love me, come on, admit it, say it, say you love me.' I used to have a trick at the time where I'd get a plastic spoon, break it up into tiny pieces and put it in my mouth. I did this and then started to spit it out as if they were my teeth. By now I was starting to get a bit of a crowd around me.

'See this woman, I love her and she won't tell me she loves me and now she's hit me in the mouth,' I shouted. The louder I got, the more embarrassed Coleen got. In the end she started laughing.

'Alright, I love you,' she said. 'Will you be quiet now?'

Not only was I now in love with a Nolan, but also I was about to get my first shot on television. The bosses at *Summertime Special* saw me in my topless revue and liked what I did. I was hired for my own six-minute slot on their show, which went out on Saturday evenings on ITV. It was a huge variety show at the time and included bands from the charts, novelty acts from around the world, top comics and a shed-load of girl dancers. Everyone watched it, including my mum and dad. My foot was finally on the ladder, albeit at the bottom.

Towards the end of the season I finally admitted to Goz and the rest of my mates that I was seeing Coleen. They all made a pilgrimage down to visit one weekend. On the Saturday night we all went to a casino together. There was Callum Rice, known as Spike, a former Bluecoat who I'd met on the camps; Stephen Murphy, better known as Spud, who worked as a roofer and who I'd met through Spike; Micky Salmon, the DJ from Bracklesham Bay; and of course Goz. We were having a great night until Spike got drunk, climbed onto a table and said loudly: 'See my mate Shane, he's only giving her one because she's one of the Nolans.' It was just drunken banter but Coleen didn't see the funny side.

'Is that right?' she asked, stony-faced.

'No,' I said. 'But it does help...'

The lads fell about laughing, but Coleen was livid and stormed out of the casino. Spike by now was in full flow. 'Well you are a Nolan, what's the big deal?' he shouted after her.

I raced after Coleen and apologised, but there was no talking her round. 'No, I don't want to see you anymore, you and all your mates are prats,' she said firmly. We split up for a couple of days over that, but in the end I managed to talk her round. Like always.

It was strange for a long time living in Coleen's shadow. Don't get me wrong, I was proud of her and I loved to show her off. Many times I'd wait for her backstage and people would push me out of the way to get to her, but it really didn't bother me. Coleen, meanwhile, would always say that one day it would be the other way round. I wasn't bothered; for the first time in my life I was truly in love.

At the end of the summer season, in October, I drove Coleen to Pontins at Camber Sands to make it up with all my old mates who'd upset her at the casino. Goz was working there as Entertainments Manager and I called him a few days before.

'Goz, I want to impress her, you've got to give us the best chalet,' I told him.

'There is no fucking best chalet, this is Pontins.'

'Well get a duvet then, the Nolans don't sleep with sheets and blankets. And make sure we get curtains that meet in the middle. And find a chalet where the door fits the frame.'

After a brilliant week at Pontins Coleen asked me to move in with her. She had a small house in Hillingdon, Middlesex – and that became our first home. She'd bought it a couple of years earlier and had lived there with her previous boyfriend, a drummer in their band called Gavin, who ended up going off with her sister Bernie. I turned up and there were still pictures of her and Gavin everywhere. I felt a bit put out, but Coleen said she'd take them down and, not only that, I was to treat the place as my own home. She was going on tour to Russia with the group for six weeks and she wanted me to stay in Hillingdon and look after the house.

I'd never been in charge of a house before and I'd no idea what to do. It was only a small house with three bedrooms and Coleen probably only meant that I should water the plants, but I got it into my head that if I was in charge I ought to try to redecorate. I was only doing a few gigs here and there, so I had plenty of time on my hands. I got the builders in and we put in a new kitchen with a little serving hatch, and at the last minute I decided to paint the bedroom. Coleen was due back the next day, so I got two mates, a comedy magician called Paul Zenon, who I'd met the year before in Jersey, and a DJ called Gary T to help me finish it in time. I found this lovely warm peach-coloured paint, bought a new carpet and curtains and put drapes over the bed. It was going to look beautiful. The only problem was that when I put the paint on the walls it looked nothing like the colour on the tin. Instead it was a horrible bright orange. Gary told me not to worry and that when I woke up the next morning the colour would have dried and calmed down. It hadn't, it was worse.

It wasn't just bright, it was bloody bright. When Coleen arrived back the next day I admitted my mistake but to my delight she loved it. It wasn't the colour she liked, but the fact that I'd made the effort.

I'd missed Coleen so much when she was away. She'd written to me every single day from Russia and I treasured those letters; in fact I still have them to this day. I've put them away so the boys can have them when they're older. We were so in love. That Christmas we spent the day alone, just the two of us. Neither of us had cooked a Christmas dinner before – Coleen had always been with her family until that year – and we ended up cooking enough for eight people because we'd no idea how much to do. The turkey was inedible because nobody had told us you were supposed to take out the giblets first, but we didn't care. This was the first real home of my own, and as far as I was concerned we were going to be together forever. Life couldn't get any better.

At the beginning of 1987 I was booked for a three-week tour of the Falklands. This was the first time I was going to be away and Coleen was devastated. She drove me to RAF Brize Norton to wave me off and couldn't stop crying. I remember being really touched; no one had ever felt like that about me going away before. I loved it out there entertaining the troops and it turned out to be the first of three visits to the place. Goz picked me up when I got home, but for once I had no tales of wild parties and bed-hopping to entertain him with; I was a changed man. At that time nothing else mattered in my life except Coleen. I lived her and I breathed her and I loved that feeling.

Things really picked up for me workwise that year and I started hosting a lot of my own shows around the country. I'd do 'The Shane Richie Show' in Great Yarmouth for one night or there'd be a comedy show in Dartford 'featuring' Shane Richie. By now Barry Dye knew how frustrated I was getting. After my TV appearance on *Summertime Special* he knew he would need help in taking my career further. Enter the Colonel: Stan Dallas.

Stan was one of the agents at International Artists, one of the biggest light entertainment agencies in the country. He'd seen me in a showcase at Leicester doing my thing and said he'd seen something in me that he'd not seen in a comic for a long time: a sense of danger. The showcase was over three days and I was the first act on the first day. The Mayor of Leicester was in the front row and I was told he didn't particularly want to be there and didn't have a great sense of humour.

'Please don't mention him, Shane,' said the compère just before I stepped on stage at 10 o'clock in the morning. It was a red rag to a bull. Not only did I mention him, within five minutes I had him up on stage doing the conga in his mayoral robes and chains. Barry put his head in his hands, but Stan loved it.

Barry and Stan did a deal, whereby Barry would look after my day-to-day stuff and Stan would look after the TV side. True to his word, Stan pulled out all the stops and within weeks he got me back on *Summertime Special*. International Artists looked after all the big stars at the time and when *Summertime Special* approached them for someone such as Hale and Pace, they'd be told they'd have to have Shane Richie as well. That was how it worked. These were the politics of the business and I was quite happy to play along with it. That was followed by an appearance on *Live From the Palladium*. It went out on Saturday nights on ITV and was a huge ratings winner. The strange thing was that while Stan had put me on a major TV show, the very next night Barry had booked me for Butlins in Bognor. That's showbiz.

In March 1988 I came home from a gig to hear a message on my answering machine from Paul Wagner, telling me the tragic news that Dawn had taken her own life. Apparently it had happened on Mother's Day. She'd gone to her room and taken some pills and wine. I was devastated. I couldn't even imagine how her family felt. I couldn't believe she was gone. I've never known how to handle death and rather than talk about it I threw myself back into work. Coleen knew me well enough not to ask too many questions; she let me handle it in my own way.

My work usually only involved a night away from home at most and if I was working in the South-East I'd always drive back afterwards. It was different for Coleen though, and when The Nolans were booked for a national tour that year I knew it meant she'd be away for months. For the first time I started to resent what she did for a living. I didn't want to share her with anyone else. There were no rows though, because I think Coleen was getting to the point where she'd had onough of touring herself. The Nolans had peaked by now. They were still selling out every show, but Coleen was finding those long periods on the road a grind and was ready to stop. It was around this time that we first talked about having a baby. I said to Coleen: 'Well, if we do you're going to have to stop touring,' and she looked at me and said: 'Well maybe that's the reason I need.'

We never spoke about it again, but every time we made love in a really romantic setting I'd wonder if that was the time we'd be lucky. I suppose it harks back to my childhood dreams about where I was conceived.

Sadly, Shane Jr's conception turned out to be as equally unglamorous as my own. In March 1988 I was invited back on another three-week tour of the Falklands and when I arrived home I was desperate to see Coleen. All the way back on the plane I fantasised about walking through the door, picking her up in my arms and laying her on a queen-size mahogany four-poster bed covered in rose petals, with Elvis gently singing in the background … whoops, that's the vision I had of my own conception!

At the doorstep I told Coleen my plan. Her face fell.

'Shane, we can't,' she whispered. 'Have you forgotten my Mum and Dad are staying with us this week?'

'So what? Your mum's slightly mutton and your dad's off drinking with my old man. Come here quick and give us a kiss,' I said with a grin. And with my bags still on the doorstep, we tumbled through into the downstairs toilet.

That spring I went on a six-week tour with Cannon and Ball as their special guest comic. Our last night was in Newcastle and after the show I called Coleen to tell her how much I was looking forward to being home.

'Shane, I've got something to tell you,' she said nervously.

'What?'

'I'm pregnant.'

'*What*?'

'You heard. We're having a baby.'

At that very moment Bobby Ball walked into the room.

It seemed right, somehow – Bobby had been there the very first night we met and had always looked out for Coleen.

'Y'alright, cocker?' he asked.

'Bobby, I'm going to have a baby,' I told him.

Bobby smiled. 'Now is the true test of a real man,' he said as he hugged me. 'So, are you going to marry her?'

Marry her? It hadn't once crossed my mind and as I drove back through the night to be with Coleen all I could think about was the fact that I was going to be a dad. When I got home Coleen was waiting up for me and we fell into each other's arms.

Unfortunately it was to be a while before we could properly share the news. Coleen and The Nolans were booked to tour Japan in June and the record company warned them that as Japan was a conservative country it would wreck the tour if it leaked out that the youngest sister was unmarried and pregnant. To hide the fact, the group had a new batch of costumes made. They were a much looser cut and hid Coleen's growing bump. If anyone still noticed they'd just say she was putting on weight.

While Coleen was away I'd get bookings around the country at various clubs. In July I took my show to Bognor Butlins and after I came off stage I stood and signed autographs at the bar. I had a bit of a crowd around me, when all of a sudden Goz tapped me on the shoulder and told me that my brother was there. He said a Redcoat had told him that Dean had turned up at the gates and they'd let him in.

'That's not like Dean,' I said. 'He'd normally phone me.' We didn't see that much of each other, but he'd occasionally ring and ask me to organise for him to come along to one of my gigs with his mates.

Then a guy from security came up to me. 'Listen, Shane, next time you want guests to come in to the camp, let us know.' I apologised and stood at the bar waiting for Dean to appear. There was a tap on my shoulder and I turned round to see a guy a few years older than me.

'Hi Shane, my name's Ricky, I'm your brother.'

I didn't know what to say or do. I initially thought somebody must have been playing a sick joke. But I looked into the guy's eyes and I could see he wasn't joking. He genuinely believed he was my brother.

'I don't know what you're talking about,' I said defensively.

'Look, can we talk somewhere private?'

He looked like me. He had the same eyes, but this guy was bigger than me and very stocky and had a broad Dublin accent.

I was pretty nervous, but I agreed and we walked back to my dressing room where he sat down and proceeded to tell me his history. Suddenly I remembered that I'd met this guy before. He'd been introduced to me years earlier when I was a youngster, as a cousin, or friend of the family, I couldn't remember which.

He explained that my dad, before he met my mum, was briefly married to a lady in Dublin and that he'd fathered a child – a boy called Ricky – but that he'd left them when he met my mum. We sat backstage for what seemed like hours and Ricky told me all about his life. He'd had it pretty tough, but he wanted nothing from me, other than to get to know me.

I got back to my hotel in the early hours of the morning and phoned Coleen. I was distraught. It felt like my world had fallen apart. Then I phoned my mum and dad and got them out of bed. My mum was in tears. My dad came on the line and I asked him why everyone seemed to know about this except me. Apparently even my brother Dean and my Aunty Mary knew, but they'd all kept it from me. My dad told me it was none of my business and that he'd only found out himself a couple of years earlier. My mum came back on and said that my career was just taking off at the time, they knew how sensitive I was and they didn't think I'd have been able to handle it.

I was furious. As far as I was concerned it was just a lie. How did they know whether I was sensitive or not? I hadn't lived at home for years. I was never angry with Ricky though and I introduced him to Coleen and gradually got to know him. I could see a lot of my family in him. He loved a drink, just like my dad and just like Dean, and I vowed there and then that I wasn't going to go down that road myself.

Coleen was great and put it all in context. 'So Shane,' she'd say, 'what's changed? Nothing's changed. So you've got another brother. But it's not as if he's come here wanting something from you.'

And she was right. Because Ricky never wanted anything from me other than the love of a real family, which sadly he never got, because that's not what the Roches are about. We didn't have a huge extended family. I was only really close to my mum, and my dad was slowly deteriorating. He was having problems with his kidneys and still drinking despite his doctor's warnings. My family now was Coleen, Goz, Stan and the baby that was on the way. I think Ricky was disappointed and we didn't see each other for a few years after that, but these days he has his own family and now we talk, just as mates I suppose.

When The Nolans returned to Britain from Japan the news of Coleen's pregnancy inevitably leaked out. What's more, her sister Maureen had become pregnant around the same time. (Nothing to do with me by the way.) With them being a Catholic family it caused a bit of a stir in the tabloid press. 'Nolans: Babies out of wedlock shock'. Jim Bowen, the bloke off *Bullseye*, gave a big interview in which he said how disgusting he thought it was and that The Nolans should know better. Everyone had an opinion.

CHAPTER NINE

A tattoo for Colin

It would have been just my luck to be on stage when my little boy was born and it could have turned out that way. Coleen went into labour on a Wednesday and that evening, when it looked like nothing was going to happen, I went off to work. I was supporting Rose Marie at the Starlight Rooms in Enfield, Middlesex. I always liked Rose Marie and believe she could have been a bigger star. She had a powerful voice and I was forever telling her that she could be the next Bette Middler. 'Ah, don'cha be worrying about dat, you just go off and be dere when your baby's born,' she'd say, in her great Irish accent. But nothing happened that night or the next day and on the Thursday night I was back on stage again. Goz was standing in the wings ready to drag me off if there was any news. By now Goz was working as my PA – he'd done the job for years anyway, ever since leaving Pontins, but he'd suggested we make it official; nothing would change except now he'd get paid!

Coleen's family had said beforehand that I shouldn't be at the birth because they knew how squeamish I was and they were convinced I'd be sick or pass out, but on the Friday when it looked like things were starting to happen, I was right by Coleen's side. I didn't know whether we were having a boy or a girl, but I didn't care, I was so excited. I had a running gag going: 'Shane Richie, at your cervix.' The nurses and midwives found it really funny to start with, but by the time I'd told the joke for the 20th time I knew I'd become a bit of a pain in the arse. Not that Coleen was any better. The doctors gave her an epidural injection in her spine to numb the pain. I asked them what it did.

'It means Coleen will feel nothing during the baby's birth,' they explained.

'A bit like when he was conceived then,' Coleen said.

Shane Christopher Roche was finally born at 11.10pm on Friday, December 2, 1988, weighing 6lbs 15oz. Shane after his dad and Christopher after Goz. When they put him in my arms I cried. I was a dad. My life seemed complete.

For the next few months I continued slogging around the clubs. In the summer of 1989 the hard work seemed to pay off when I landed a job as the warm-up man on Sky's *Jameson Tonight*. Now let me explain what a warm-up does. He comes out before the star of the show and before they start recording. It's his job to tell a few jokes, explain what the audience can expect from the show and more importantly point out where the fire exits are. It couldn't have been better. It was a five-nights-a-week chat show, I'd turn up at 6.30pm, do 20 minutes to get the crowd going (I say crowd, most nights we were lucky to have a dozen people in), I'd then leave to do a gig in the evening.

The relationship I built up with Derek Jameson was a really strong one. When his co-presenter Annabel Giles didn't come into work one day, Derek asked me if I'd like to interview one of the bands appearing on the show. I seemed to do a pretty good job and at the end of the show Derek gave me a hug and in his gruff Cockney accent said: 'Well done, young Richie.'

A few weeks later Annabel decided she'd had enough and they asked me to take over permanently. I jumped at it. As well as doing interviews in the studio they let me go out to do video links from around London – everything from catching pigeons in Trafalgar Square to learning the latest dance craze in a restaurant or sampling new food. Barbara Windsor came on the show as a guest several times and she became a great friend. She'd always say to me: 'Shane, don't worry, your chance will come.' I was flattered, but I was more than happy doing what I was doing. Bear in mind I'd only been out of the holiday camps for five years and here I was co-hosting a daily TV show, albeit one that nobody watched. Relatively few people had satellite dishes then and the only people who saw this show were a couple of posh hotels in Spain and a few nomadic herdsmen in the middle of the Soviet

Union. But Stan always used to say it was the perfect training ground. He explained that this job wasn't about gags, it was about listening to people and talking to people and knowing enough about them to ask interesting questions.

One night Derek Jameson was ill and the producer, Michael Hurl, told me I would be hosting the show. Unfortunately they had a politician booked, but Michael saved me. There's not a politician on earth who could say anything that would interest me and I think Michael knew I'd have no idea what to ask, so we pulled in some friends: Peter Stringfellow, the comic Bob Mills and David Baddiel. The mix of guests worked and Michael Hurl enjoyed it, to the extent that he even decided he could afford to give Derek Jameson some time off and let me stand in. As a result I got to interview big stars such as Phil Collins, Brigitte Nielsen and Anthony Hopkins, amongst others.

Although my career was going from strength to strength, not everything in my life was running smoothly. Once Shane Jr was a few months old, Coleen and I decided to get married. Both sets of families were excited and we set the date for September 1989. It was going to be a big church job with all the trimmings. I was marched along to see the priest, Coleen bought a big white dress and of course her sisters were going to be bridesmaids so they set about rehearsing a song.

Now this is when it went a bit pear-shaped. Of course I was head over heels in love with Coleen, I just wasn't sure I wanted a wedding right then and the closer it got the more nervous I got. OK, I'll admit it, I was getting cold feet. The problem was that Coleen comes from a big family and, as much as I loved being with them, I felt that our wedding was slipping away from me. I even rowed with Coleen's mum about the kind of food I wanted. I was used to being the one in control and this wedding seemed to be like a snowball, getting bigger and bigger and gaining momentum and rolling away from me. I began to feel that all that was required of me was to turn up on the day.

Six weeks before the big day I sat bolt upright in bed in the middle of the night in a cold sweat. I woke Coleen up and said: 'I can't do this. I can't get married. It's not about us anymore, darling; it's about our families. It's getting out of hand, we can't afford it and it's not personal anymore.' Needless to say, at three o'clock in the morning it didn't go down too well.

The next day Coleen went back to Blackpool to stay with her family for a few days to see if I'd calm down and change my mind. I didn't. Overnight I became the black sheep of the family. The flowers had to be cancelled, the priest had to be told, Coleen's dress had to go back and her sisters' song was put on hold. Not surprisingly I was about as welcome at the Nolans' house as a condom machine in the Vatican.

Thankfully, Coleen and I patched things up and after a while we decided to have another go. This time it would be done our way, with minimum guests and minimum fuss. In March 1990 we flew to Orlando, Florida and stayed at the Sheraton Hotel. Coleen's sister Maureen flew out with her fella, Richie; my best man, of course, was going to be Goz. For my stag night, Goz and a couple of British Airways stewards we'd got friendly with on the flight took me to a club called Pure Platinum. For want of a better word it was a lap-dancing club. Come on, it was my stag night!

At midnight the compère came on stage and in his best American drawl announced: 'We have a young man here from the UK, a guy by the name of Shane Richie. Shane, if you'd like to come up here for a moment.' I staggered up there as best I could after 16 Budweisers and stood there swaying, when two beautiful ladies suddenly appeared on stage, sat me in a chair, tied my hands behind my back and blindfolded me with a see-through gauze. Then from nowhere 12 of the most stunning women you've ever seen in your life came out semi-naked and – to the whoops and cheers of the audience – stripped me. Goz had set me up spectacularly, but I was too drunk to care. They kissed me all over, gave me a lovely pair of tiny pants to wear and sent me packing. I got outside and promptly heaved my guts up. The perfect stag night!

When I got back Coleen was sitting up, looking serene and doing her nails ready for the big day. Without even turning round she took one look at me in the dressing-table mirror and said: 'Don't tell me, I don't want to know.' She'd guessed straightaway what I'd been up to. The fact that my trousers were back to front and my shirt was on inside out was a bit of giveaway.

Me and the sisters: Linda, Coleen, Maureen and Bernie. Every bloke's fantasy, 'nuff said!

My Mum gave me this photo of me and my Aunty Mary.
I loved her so much.

I know I started the holiday camps at an early age, but Coleen drew the line at Shane Jnr, not even a year old, packing his nappies and dummy and leaving for a life of bingo and glamorous grans…

After a day at Disney with Coleen and the boys I couldn't resist doing gigs in the evening.

My happiest times. A family holiday in Orlando with Coleen and the boys.

Robin Williams – Genius. It was during this meeting he was giving me advice on playing Peter Pan and how to rearrange my nuts!

Me, flying as Peter Pan in Lewisham. If you look closely you can just see my nuts in my throat.

The closest I got to being a model. (Trust me, I didn't need two hands to cover em!)

I can't believe I had a quiff way before I started in *Grease* – and I think I've just burped!!

SHANE RICHIE

BARRY DYE
BARRY DYE ENTS.
9, OLD FOUNDRY RD,
IPSWICH, SUFFOLK.
TEL: 0473 216677

STANLEY DALLAS
INTERNATIONAL ARTISTES,
235-241 REGENT STREET,
LONDON.
TEL: 071-439-8401

Guess what I was promoting here?

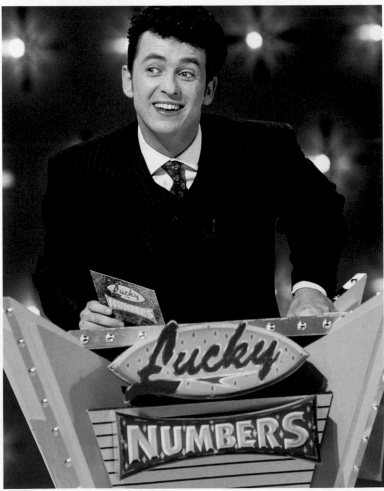

Lucky Numbers, ITV
I had a ball doing this show, calling bingo for a living!

Me and Robbie Williams in bed on *The Big Breakfast*. And yes, we are naked from the waist down!

Me and Peter Simon, BBC Children's TV. Some of our gags would go way above the kids heads – and Peter's!

On *The Shane Richie Experience* I finally got to sing with the Osmond's. Donny couldn't make it – so guess what?

On *The Shane Richie Experience*, doing 'Don't Rain on My Parade'. Bit of an ugly bird, aint I?!

We married on 8 March in a small gazebo by a lake. It was one of the best days of my life – it was so personal and at that moment I felt I would love her forever. She was now Mrs Roche. I was so proud. That night we went to a restaurant where they sang opera, which was a fabulous experience as neither of us had been anywhere like that before. It was a present from friends and we had the best seats and ended up drinking one bottle of wine too many. As you do.

The other thing you do on your wedding night is, of course, the obvious. That bit we didn't manage. We'd knocked back so much wine that we spent our wedding night crashed out in separate beds in our hotel room, snoring loudly (and that was just Coleen). But you know what? We were so much in love and so comfortable with each other that it just didn't matter. We had a blissful honeymoon and flew back a fortnight later.

It was the flight from hell. We took off on a Sunday evening and 45 minutes into the journey the plane suddenly dropped and levelled out again. I assumed it was turbulence until I saw a stewardess running up the aisle screaming her head off. At this point the pilot announced that we were diverting to JFK airport in New York because of engine failure. We sat on the tarmac for two hours and then took off again. Half an hour into the flight the same thing happened again, but this time there was a loud bang from one side of the aircraft. No one screamed but everyone went quiet and Coleen grabbed my hand. It was one of those terrible moments where everything runs through your mind, but you sit there in silence afraid to voice your fears in case it makes them come true. The pilot announced that we would have to go back to JFK a second time. It was now 1am and we were all taken off the plane and put in motels for the night.

The next morning all the passengers met up again at the airport. It was only as we were about to board that Coleen and I realised it was exactly the same plane. At that point I decided I'd had enough. I'd row a boat back, anything, rather than go through that again. To get away with it once is fine, twice you're pushing it. I wasn't going to put us through it a third time. We caused a bit of a stink and eventually they agreed to get our luggage off the plane. Coleen went straight over to the Air Lingus desk and of course because of the Irish connection they couldn't do enough for us and put us on their next plane back, with VIP treatment the whole way. It was only after we'd landed that we heard that our original plane had encountered problems for a third time and had been forced back to JFK yet again. That changed my feelings about flying forever. I still go on holiday abroad, but I'm not the greatest flyer.

Coleen and I returned from our honeymoon on such a high, but I came back down to earth with a bump very quickly. I returned to the news that the powers that be didn't feel *Jameson Tonight* was pulling in enough viewers and was to be axed. Thanks to Stan I wasn't allowed to sit at home and twiddle my thumbs for very long. He booked me guest slots on every TV show going, from *321*, to *The Les Dennis Laughter Show*, to *Des O'Connor Tonight*. Noel Edmonds was great to me and would invite me on his *Noel Edmonds Saturday Roadshow* whenever he could. Another of my big supporters at that time was a great presenter by the name of Judith Spiers, who hosted *Pebble Mill* from Birmingham every afternoon. She'd have me on the show from time to time and we'd always have great banter.

With each appearance I felt I was getting stronger and stronger. On top of that, each time I appeared on television my money went up. I'd started out as a £150-a-night-comic and now Stan was getting me £500 a time. He was also getting me bookings in theatres, supporting acts such as Johnny Mathis and Dionne Warwick. For the first time in my life I actually had a bit of money and Coleen and I could enjoy a better quality of life. We loved Orlando and we bought a lovely house out there – 10531 Satinwood Circle, Cypress Springs, Orlando.

That summer the BBC approached me to see if I'd be interested in taking part in a new comedy sketch show called *Up To Something*, which would go out on a Tuesday night. It would be myself, Mike Hayley, Dave Schneider, Lewis MacLeod, Frances Dodge and Suzy Aitchison. I was in awe of these guys. We were from different backgrounds and our views of comedy were quite different. I wanted to go for the big laughs and they were quite happy with subtle humour; and the two seemed to work well together.

The show aired in August 1990, which is never a good time because most people go away in the summer, so it didn't set the world alight. But those who watched it seemed to like it and people within the business noticed I had something to offer. What's more the national press were now taking an interest in me. Until now I'd been lucky to get my name in the *Willesden & Brent Chronicle*, but suddenly both *The Sun* and the *News of the World* wanted to interview me. Did I think I'd hit the big time! When the papers came out I bought up a dozen copies in my local newsagent, I was so proud. The *News of the World* even described the show as 'the sensation of the summer' and called us the new Young Ones. Sadly, good reviews don't pay the bills and when the series ended in the autumn I was back working the clubs and pubs as well as entertaining the forces in Northern Ireland, Germany and South America.

There was also another tour of the Falkland Islands, this time with Micky Zany. We decided to recreate what we'd done in Jersey and put on a double act. We performed at three bases up in the mountains – Mount Byron, Mount Alice and Mount Kent – and we got a great reception. They were just so pleased to see some fresh faces. We had a great blag going where we'd get six squaddies up on stage and sit them in a circle. We'd go round the circle and each one would have to tell us a gag. If we couldn't get the joke before they finished, we'd give them a fiver, but if we got to the punchline first they had to give us a fiver. Of course Micky and I knew every joke going – we'd been telling them for so long – and we raked it in.

One massive TV event that I was thrilled to be a part of that year was a show called *Night of 100 Stars*, which took place at the London Palladium and was a tribute to David Bell, who had been the producer and director of *Summertime Special* for many years. He'd discovered a lot of people during his career and anyone who was anyone was on the show. I'd thought I'd be appearing on stage as part of a group tribute, but I actually had my own six-minute slot between Michael Barrymore and Joe Longthorne. I was now becoming part of the comedy establishment and boy, did that feel good.

After the curtain came down there was a huge do, backstage. All the dignitaries from the Palladium were there, alongside the press, producers, directors and of course all the entertainers from the night. It was like a Who's Who of showbusiness. I spotted a group of mates over at the bar and as I approached they started to applaud me and told me how well I'd done. All of sudden I noticed that standing there in the group was Dick Ray, the guy who'd done his best to humiliate me in Jersey all those years ago. He'd clearly forgotten that we'd met before. I hadn't.

'Right can I get anyone a drink?' I went round the group, taking their orders, all but Dick's, and then turned to walk away. He clearly thought I'd forgotten him.

'Oh Shane, mine's a glass of champagne,' he piped up.

I turned slowly and looked him straight in the eye.

'You call me Mr Richie.'

Everyone else thought I was joking and Dick clearly had no idea what I was talking about, but I did. It's not normally my style but I couldn't let it pass.

I started 1991 with more gigs and it was around this time that I had my first and last taste of Ecstasy, albeit accidental. I'd been doing stand-up comedy in a club in London and finished at 1am. Afterwards Goz suggested we make a night of it, so we ended up at the Middlesex and Herts Country Club, in Stanmore. It was nicknamed 'The Middlesex and Tarts' – it was full of flash blokes with the latest Porsche and Page 3 girls. The clientele seemed to have more money than sense. I used to go every couple of weeks with a gang of mates just to let off steam. All the boys would meet up there. There was Micky Salmon, who I'd first met at Pontins in 1980 when I was 16 he was everything I wanted to be. He was a few years older than me and striking-looking with a great personality and now he was making a name for himself on the stand-up circuit. Then there was Jeff Stevenson, Spike, who was now working as a DJ and Spud who was still a roofer.

On this particular night we got to the club at close to 2.30am. We had a couple of drinks and then hit the dance floor when all of a sudden I started to feel a bit strange. Something wasn't right. Now bear in mind I was suited and booted and I was on the dance floor surrounded by beautiful girls. Suddenly I felt a tremendous rush and all the girls' faces started distorting and melting. The music was getting louder and my stomach started to turn. I realised straightaway that I needed to get off the dance floor, but my legs wouldn't go anywhere. I grabbed a bottle of water from Goz and drank it down in one, but it didn't help. From nowhere I suddenly started to projectile vomit into my hands and all down my suit. I tried to make my way outside as inconspicuously as possible, but of course everyone could see what had happened and all I could hear around me were shouts of: 'Oh look, Shane's been sick!' I was mortified. That night when I got home I threw up for hours and I found out the next day that Goz had been the same. I later found out that some smartarse had spiked our drinks with ecstasy.

Around that time I got two more bookings for BBC shows. The first, called *Paramount City*, was hosted by two black comedians called Curtis and Ishmael, and was shown in America. The second was a light entertainment show called *You Gotta Be Joking*. This was another sketch show, but it was going to be different from *Up to Something*. It would be much frothier, aimed at a younger audience and the comedy would be much more pie in the face.

The show opened with myself, Billy Pearce, George Marshall, Maddie Cryer and Annette Law sliding down a fireman's pole and doing one-liners to the camera. It gave me the opportunity to create charac-ters and there was one in particular that seemed to go down well with viewers. He was a guy called Snakebite who was a West Country heavy metaller who never quite got it right. Instead of Iron Maiden he was a big fan of the Barron Nights and had a catchphrase: 'Snakebite 'ere and I'm 'ard'.

It was while I was recording the show that I realised what a worka-holic I'd become. I'd go home, sit up half the night trying to write material and end up chucking dozens of screwed-up pieces of paper around the room. By the time I did get to bed I was so wound up I'd have nightmares. I'd start going through my lines in my sleep and even started sleep-walking, practising my routines pacing around the room. On one occasion Coleen woke up to find me rehearsing an American football routine naked at the end of the bed.

'Shane, bed, now!'

'What? What? What?'

It wasn't a pretty sight.

That summer my desire for perfection led me to take a huge gamble. I'd met a guy called Paul Berg who was a schoolteacher from Portland, Oregon and was headmaster at the American Community School that Shane went to. We'd put Shane there because we hoped and believed that one day I'd end up working in America and it would make it easier if he was used to the American education system. I became friendly with Paul and he knew what I did for a living and when he got back home to Oregon for the summer he gave me a call. He knew someone who ran the local comedy club and he'd told them all about me. Apparently they wanted me to go out for a couple of weeks and do a few slots.

Coleen was going to spend the summer in Blackpool singing with her sisters and I'd been offered a season there myself, but I really didn't want to do it. I was bored doing the same jokes for the same audiences in summer seasons and wanted to try something different. This was my chance. Coleen packed me 14 pairs of socks and undies and headed off to Blackpool saying she'd see me in a fortnight.

I flew to Oregon and when I turned up at the Silver Dollar Comedy Club I couldn't believe my eyes. This wasn't a smoky room above a pub, it wasn't the scruffy back room of a restaurant – it was a proper comedy club. At that time stand-up comedy in Britain was very much a working-class thing, whereas in the States it was viewed more as an art form. People would dress up and go to a comedy club for the night like people go to the theatre here. As a result they had huge venues dedicated solely to comedy.

They promised me two slots a week and when the night came I was billed on the board outside: 'Direct from the UK, England's Number 1 Stand-Up comic'. I was far from that, but I wasn't going to put them right. I was curious as to how I'd be received, but I needn't have worried; I tore the place up and ended up appearing six nights on the bounce. The great thing was that in Britain I'd been used to doing an hour. Here they only wanted 15 to 20 minutes max, so I could condense it down to my best material.

One night a comedy booker was in the audience and afterwards he came backstage to tell me that if I was interested he had some dates for me along the West Coast. Coleen gave me her blessing and said I should go off and enjoy myself for a couple more weeks. I laundered my 14-days worth of clothes and with my tiny suitcase in one hand and the phone number of a friend of Paul Berg's in LA in the other, I headed off to the airport.

I rented a car and for the next ten days I cruised down the West Coast, stopping off at different towns along the way. Some places were comedy clubs, some were hotels, but I didn't really care because it was a new experience and I was learning. But as the tour progressed I noticed something strange happening along the way: the closer I was getting to Los Angeles the harder the gigs were getting. An English comic in Oregon was a novelty act, but closer to Los Angeles they weren't taken in by the London charm or accent.

When I arrived in LA I called Paul's friend as arranged. He turned out to be a great guy by the name of George Lyle, who was high up in banking and owned a beautiful apartment overlooking Manhattan Beach. He said any friend of Paul's was a friend of his and that I was to use his home as a base for the rest of my stay. Not only that, on the nights I wasn't working he'd show me around town.

That night I was booked to appear at a club called The Improv in Santa Monica. It was on the beach, right amongst the beautiful people, as they like to call themselves, and was the place to be seen. Stars such as Robin Williams, Eddie Murphy and Billy Crystal had all appeared there and their pictures were plastered all over the walls. These guys were my heroes. The way it worked at the club was that the bigger the name, the earlier you appeared on the bill. So you'd get someone who was a TV star on first, and the guys who were just starting out in the business coming on at the end. I was fifth, which meant I was on at about quarter past ten.

'Please welcome all the way from London, England, the guy who's been wowing 'em up the West Coast for the past coupla weeks, Mr Shane Richie.'

I walked on to a rapturous round of applause. It was to be the last applause I would hear for the next 12 minutes. I'd built up such confidence performing in these clubs in tiny towns that I ended up playing it all wrong. Even to this day I don't know what it was, maybe I was too cocky, but I just wasn't funny. I suppose, like anyone, comics have bad days, and that was certainly one of mine.

The crowd sat there stony-faced and then the heckles began: 'Ged off, ya limey bastard!'

'You're trash, go back to England!'

To make matters worse, George had brought along a group of his friends and told them how funny I was and they were all witnessing this. Because I'd done so badly I was moved down the rankings for the next night and went on at 1.15am. And for some reason, I stormed it. It was the same material and the same club, just a different audience. That can happen sometimes.

There was an agent in that night who hired acts for a place called The Laugh Factory on Sunset Boulevard. I got talking to him after the show and he'd obviously no idea who I was, other than what he'd just seen on stage, so I told him all about my sketch shows back in Britain for the BBC. I knew Americans were suckers for the BBC, and before I knew it I'd blagged myself two nights supporting Jerry Seinfeld and Rosie O'Donnell at his club. Both were big stars in America at the time, although I didn't really know them because *Seinfeld* hadn't made the same impact in the UK back then.

There was a Mexican bar across from The Laugh Factory, which was known for loud music, tequila and the fact that Billy Idol drank there. After my second night one of the other comics asked if I'd like to go across and meet him. Now of course I knew all about Billy and we even shared some mutual friends in Essex, but we'd never been introduced so I jumped at the chance. We walked into the bar and he stood out like a sore thumb, dressed from head to toe in leather with this dirty big mop of white hair. He had no idea who I was, but after a few drinks together we were swapping stories like old mates. After a while the conversation switched to his tattoos. He's got so many the topic is hard to avoid. He was proudly showing them off and explaining what they meant and why he'd had them done, when he suddenly turned to me and said: 'Man, you gotta get a tattoo done. If you wanna prove your love to somebody, you gotta get a tattoo.' Every week I seemed to have been ringing Coleen to extend my stay and she was getting a bit fed up. What better way to get back in her good books? Or so it seemed after my 15th tequila slammer...

George was with me and in the early hours of the morning we piled into a load of cars and followed Billy and his entourage down to a place on Venice Beach, about 20 minutes outside LA. It must have been about four in the morning but the streets were still full of people and we strolled along in the warm night air clutching our bottles of Jack Daniels, laughing and joking. Billy eventually led us to a little alleyway and pitched up outside a tiny backstreet tattoo parlour. A lovely Vietnamese lady welcomed us in and asked me where I'd like my tattoo.

'I'd like a little love heart on my bum and in the love heart I'd like you to put Coleen,' I explained, between gulps of JD. Now she didn't speak good English and bear in mind it's four in the morning and I'm off my face, so I wasn't speaking good English either.

'Colin?'

'No, it's Coleen.'

'Colin?'

'No, Coleen, C-O-L-E-E-N.'

'Ah, understand, Colin.'

By now I was lying face down on a makeshift bed with a light bulb hanging over it, with my trousers round my ankles. She pulled out a drill.

'Coleen, you know how to spell it, yeah?' I said.

'Yes, OK, now we start.'

As anyone unfortunate enough to have seen my bum will know, I still have her handiwork to this day. A wonky heart with Colin in the middle of it. And to any Colins out there that I've met over the years – no, it wasn't for you. Some years later I had it changed to 'Co', but it still looks like a dirty great birthmark and I hate looking at it. So if you're reading this, thanks Billy. A bunch of flowers for Coleen would have been a whole lot easier.

While I was in LA a comic introduced me to a teacher called MK Lewis who was running comedy classes in Santa Monica. Apparently he'd worked as a comedy scriptwriter on movies in the 1970s and was very well respected in the business. I was introduced to one of his assistants and gave them a show reel of my stand-up and the sketch shows I'd done. MK watched them and loved what I did. He adored British humour – Morecambe and Wise and *Fawlty Towers* – and he agreed to enrol me for the eight-week course.

Eight weeks? Bear in mind I'm father to a three-year-old boy and I haven't seen him or my wife for a month. Another week would have been all right, but eight was pushing it. Coleen just laughed. 'What de feck are you up to now?' She knew I had to do it, if only to get it out of my system. Coleen's mum always used to say, 'God loves a trier'. And that was me. Always trying.

The course concentrated on comedy in film and was fairly intensive – 9 to 5 every day, and on top of that we'd be given homework at the weekends, where we'd have to watch a pile of comedy films. I was in my element and loved every minute of it, although to this day I'm not sure how much I learnt because I've never had the chance to put it into practice. I'd like to think that one day somebody will give me a shot and all that hard work will pay off.

There's something about LA though that gives you an attitude – I don't think it's necessarily the healthiest of places. It really is dog eat dog out there and if you stay for any length of time you end up acting like that yourself. That had never been my style before. Yeah, sure I'd always been ambitious, but all of a sudden I wanted to be the best. I called Stan back in Britain and asked him to make some calls and get me some meetings with some casting directors. But it was always the same: 'OK, let's look at your profile, turn right, turn left, look at me straight on, my you're a good-looking guy. I like what you do, who knows? Maybe we can do something with you in the future. We have your name on file, young man, you have a nice day now.'

And that was the last I'd hear from them.

One day I went along to a restaurant to meet a casting agent from 20th Century Fox. She'd seen my show reel and CV and liked them, so I felt I was in with a chance. We chatted away for a while, went through the routine of looking at my profile, and everything seemed to be going well. Then suddenly she caught me on the hop. Was there a demand for me in my own country, she asked? Now it would have been so easy to do a blag at this point. I could have convinced her I had the BBC and ITV fighting over me, but there was no point, because she could so easily check up. No, I admitted. I was just a jobbing actor/comic, trying to get work.

'Well, I'm sorry, but until you're a big star in your own country, you'll find it difficult to find a TV or film company in Los Angeles prepared to plough money into you. They need to know you're in demand.'

For once I'd found someone honest enough to tell me how the system worked. It hurt. But it fired me up as well. I phoned Stan and told him what had happened. 'Don't worry, Shane, success is where preparation meets opportunity,' he told me. He was right as always. It was time to come home.

CHAPTER TEN

'Mummy, I've got glitter in my eyes'

By now I was on a roll and had high hopes for 1992. When I returned from America at the back end of 1991, the BBC approached me to host a new Friday night show called *Caught in the Act*, which was very similar to ITV's *You've Been Framed*. They didn't want gags, they just wanted a cheeky chappie to present it. We recorded 12 episodes and it was a smash. It pulled in 10–12 million viewers and during its three-month run I was on the cover of every magazine. Photographers followed me wherever I went and I got a real kick out of it. I believed this was the beginning of something fantastic. I thought I'd finally made my name and all the hard work had paid off. Here I was, 28 years old, with my own show in the top ten and talk at the BBC of developing me as Mr Saturday Night Television, Mr Light Entertainment.

Not only that, but I was earning bundles – £5,000 to £7,000 a week – doing stand-up. The fact that I had my own TV show had bumped up the money massively. We'd just bought a lovely new house in Hillingdon, a few miles from where we were before. It was our dream home, a five-bedroom detached house on the corner of a cul-de-sac overlooking some fields. Coleen and I were blissfully happy together and we'd just discovered that she was pregnant again with our second child. Things couldn't possibly get any better.

And they didn't. They got worse. I was sitting at home watching *Points of View* with Anne Robinson one night when she started to read out letters criticising *Caught in the Act*. Some of the viewers felt I was too working-class – a Cockney oik who didn't pronounce his words properly. They interviewed Jim Moir, then Controller of BBC1, who reassured viewers that *Caught in the Act* wasn't very BBC. He said it was a show that they'd tried, but that they'd made a mistake.

A mistake? I thought I was the future of the BBC, now I was being written off as a mistake! And what a way to find out. Sitting at home watching *Points of View*. I was gutted; I'd done everything they'd asked of me. I'd dressed the way they wanted, said the things they wanted me to say. I was quite happy to be their puppet. If they felt the show was cheap and tacky was it my fault?

Although the bosses at the BBC felt I wasn't suitable for prime-time television, they came back to me and rather sheepishly said they had found a role for me – kids' TV. It was a brand new show called *Run the Risk*, which was a Saturday morning children's television version of *It's a Knockout*. It appeared on BBC1 as a segment in *Going Live* and involved teams of children competing against each other in various challenges involving lots of gunge. Every time I asked the teams questions I'd ask them to 'Turn and face the legend', which became my catchphrase for a while. At the end of each programme I'd push my co-presenter, Peter Simon, into the gunge. It was what it was, which didn't worry me – I thought if I could get the kids to like me then hopefully they'd grow up with me and follow my career. It worked for Lenny Henry.

Every now and then I'd be asked to stand in for Philip Schofield on *Going Live*. Usually they gave me notice, but not always. On one particular occasion I'd been out doing a stand-up show. I'd gone out for a few drinks afterwards celebrating a friend's birthday and eventually strolled in at 4am. There on the answering machine was a message from BBC saying that a car would be picking me up at 5am to start rehearsals at 6am to stand in for Philip.

At 8.29am the countdown started for us to go live. Five, four, three, two, one … and as we went live I gave out the biggest belch anyone has ever heard. I was still drunk! How I got through that show I have no idea. There were times I didn't know who I was. I had the director talking through my earpiece telling me what to say and which camera to look at and on top of that I had Gordon the Gopher, the show's glove puppet squeaking in my other ear. I needed another drink when I came off to recover! I never was going to be the new Philip Schofield …

After I finished recording *Run the Risk* I went back out on the road trying out new material. It didn't always work. I went back to Jersey, six years after my previous visit and this time I was top of the bill at the biggest venue on the island, Inn on the Park. At the time I was going through a phase of making my comedy angrier. My opening comment when I walked on stage was: 'I can't believe this island. You can't dance on a Sunday, but you can sleep with your gran.' Jersey had a reputation for being an incestuous place and it had archaic laws about dancing, but the locals didn't find me funny. In the interval Paul Wagner put his head in his hands. 'Shane, I know where you're going with this, son, but it's not going to work on the island.'

Did I listen? Not a bit. I followed it up with a routine about the Germans occupying the island. I said they'd made a mistake, thought it was the Isle of Wight and were disappointed. It went down a storm with the young people, but the pensioners were furious. It was my own fault. They were expecting this nice young man they'd seen on television and I'd come on stage with a cigarette, leather trousers and attitude.

When I came off stage there were two policemen waiting for me. They said I'd broken the obscenity laws on the island. They'd been planning to charge me, but Paul Wagner apologised to them and said I hadn't intended any offence. Even so, they took me back to my hotel. They even stayed there all night to make sure I didn't leave my room. The next morning they escorted me to the airport and told me never to come back: I was officially banned from Jersey!

Although the clubs were generally going well, it wasn't enough anymore. I still wanted more from TV than a kids' show and I began to let myself go, ballooning up to 15 and a half stone, mainly through boredom and dissatisfaction. I could see the careers of others around me really taking off, but nothing seemed to be happening for me. I still co-presented on children's television with Philip Schofield and Sarah Greene but it didn't seem to be going anywhere. Philip meanwhile seemed to be the new kid on the block. He'd done *Going Live*, *Live and*

Kicking and he was now being groomed for grown-up television. I'd complain to Stan and he'd joke:

'Yes Shane, but he talks proper.'

'Alright Stan, 'nuff said.'

I was still perceived as the cheeky Cockney wideboy. For a time I tried speaking posh, brushing up on my vocabulary and pronouncing my words a bit better, but I didn't stick with it for long. It didn't feel right and I knew people would see through it.

I needed a new challenge, so when Jon Conway approached me and said he was planning to stage *The New Adventures of Peter Pan* at a theatre in south London in the summer, I told him I was interested. Although I wasn't a big fan of panto I loved the idea of playing the boy who never grew up. It sounded familiar. I sat down with Jon, who is a director of Qdos, the biggest pantomime producers in the world, and he said it would be a very different production. The Steven Spielberg film *Hook*, starring Robin Williams, was just out and it had raised people's interest in the story, so we sat down and came up with a new concept. The original story was about the little boy who never grew up and the film was about the boy who did grow up. We decided we should do the story of what happened in between – of how Peter grew up.

Jon told me that I would be playing Peter Pan and that he wanted to make it a very acrobatic role, with even more flying around the stage than normal. I vowed to get myself in shape and enrolled at the Hillingdon School of Gymnastics, where Michael Crawford trained for his *Barnum* role. I even took a course in fencing, but I was still doing late-night club shows – travelling back at night, stopping at 24-hour garages and eating the usual diet of Pringles, a Ginsters Cornish pasty and a Fab lolly, all washed down with a Diet Coke. I was struggling. I had no real incentive other than the panto, which wasn't enough. Although I knew it was going to be good fun I was literally doing it for the money.

I had some photos taken in my Peter Pan outfit, which were blown up and put outside the theatre. I looked awful. My head was the size of a mini and at the time I had bad acne, so I ended up with this huge spot on my chin that on the posters looked like the size of a rugby ball. Had no one on the production heard of Cover Stick?

During rehearsals I got a chance to meet one of my all-time heroes, Robin Williams, who was over in the UK at the time promoting *Hook*. When I heard that Jonathan Ross was interviewing him on his TV show *The Last Resort* he kindly arranged for me to meet him. Harry Enfield was due to meet him at the same time, but Harry being a shy bloke bottled it at the last minute, so I was left on my own with Robin. I told him that I was appearing in panto as Peter Pan and he asked me if I would be flying.

'Yeah, of course,' I said. I'd been a fan of Robin's since I was a child when he appeared in *Mork and Mindy*. I'd followed his career ever since, adored his comedy and thought he might be about to give me a few tips on how to make the part really work. He looked at me and raised his eyebrows. 'Well, with all respect to you, Shane, you're going to need several guys to pull you. How much do you weigh?' I told him I was 15 and a half stone and when he converted it into pounds he was flabbergasted. I had my picture taken with him and invited him to the show, but unfortunately he was going to be back in America at the time, so he gave me his address and asked me to write and let him know how it went.

When the opening night came I was fired up. Jon's idea was that I would be on a wire and strapped into a harness and the show would open with me leaping off the dress circle, flying through the air and landing on the stage. There was a huge build-up with dramatic music and then suddenly the searchlights shot around the theatre in a figure of eight while 1,200 excited paying punters shouted: 'Where's Peter Pan?' When the lights hit me on the edge of the dress circle I shouted, 'Here I am, everyone!' and that was my cue to go. Unfortunately with all the excitement my adrenalin was pumping, so instead of stepping off, as I'd been instructed, I took a running jump. This totally threw the guys with the ropes and they couldn't hold me, so instead of flying gracefully across to the stage I plummeted six feet. All of a sudden there are kids and parents screaming as this 15 and a half stone bloke with bad skin dressed in tights comes hurtling towards them. I dangled there, for what seemed like hours, in absolute agony. At that point, with my nuts squashed up around my throat, I suddenly knew exactly why a girl always played Peter Pan.

When they finally got me airborne again the next idea was for me to hover across the stalls and throw handfuls of glitter out as I flew past. It was a lovely idea and looked really magical when we practised it in rehearsals. The only difference was that on the opening night I had 400 kids staring up at me. This glitter fell like sand, so in what was supposed to be a really dramatic moment, all I could hear was 400 kids crying: 'Mummy, I've got glitter in my eyes, I can't see anything and it hurts.'

Things went from bad to worse. Because of the momentum I crash-landed headfirst into the MDF forest at the back of the stage. I hit it so hard I thought I'd broken my nose. As if that wasn't enough, the guys on the ropes lifted me up again slightly with my wire. So not only are my nuts around my throat, my nose is the size of a grapefruit and the colour of a beetroot, but I'm now swaying from side to side on tiptoe as I try to deliver my dialogue. Meanwhile Goz has appeared on stage dressed as an Indian squaw and wearing dirty big white Reebok trainers. Goz thankfully realised what was happening to me and managed to wave backstage, but they misunderstood so instead of lowering me they started to lift me even higher. At this stage the rest of the cast had no option but to start ad-libbing.

'Peter, you're not leaving already are you?'

Leaving? I was still struggling to get there. When the show eventually ended I sent Robin Williams some pictures of me dressed as Peter Pan and I got a lovely note back saying, 'I hope your nuts held up.' If only he knew…

We always planned to have a second child and on 16 September, 1992, Jake Peter Roche was born weighing 8lbs 4oz. We chose Jake because he'd wriggled around so much inside Coleen while she was pregnant that she'd nicknamed him Jake the Snake. Peter was after Pete Suddaby, who was Coleen's sister Maureen's ex and a good mate of mine.

I was feeling fairly cocky when I arrived at Hillingdon Hospital with Coleen. Having been present through Shane's birth I had a sense of been there, done that. I set up the video camera in the corner and sat and waited. When we look back and watch it today, it's all there on film

– apart from the vital moment. At the first sight of Jake's head I slithered down the wall and passed out. I looked so ill, apparently, that the doctors had to leave Coleen for a while and attend to me. Typical. I was never one to be upstaged.

That year we had a fantastic family Christmas, but I couldn't help but feel my career was in the doldrums. Help came when I was least expecting it. At the start of 1993 a guy called David Ian became close to my sister in law Bernie Nolan. David was an act I'd met previously, he was part of a cabaret called 'Boys Will Be Boys', and we became drinking buddies again. He told me that he was now a producer and was on the verge of working on a stage musical – *Grease*.

'What? *Grease* the John Travolta movie?' I said.

'Yes, it used to be a stage musical before that.'

I hadn't known, but I told him I'd love to do something like that.

'What would you do?' he asked.

'Well I'd play Danny Zuko, you muppet,' I told him.

'You play Danny Zuko? No, we need a big star,' he said. Boy did that hurt.

David told me they were planning to get Craig McLachlan, who'd had a couple of chart hits and was a big cheese from the Aussie soap *Neighbours*. Undeterred I asked him if I could audition for one of the smaller parts. I'd already been up for one musical earlier that year – *Me and My Girl*. It was down to me and Brian Conley and they said they'd loved what I'd done, but that Brian had his own TV series and was a bigger star. I'd seen him in it and he was perfect for it. Perhaps *Grease* was my chance.

'Well, can you dance well enough, Shane? You'll be alongside professional dancers. This is a multi-million pound show. Robert Stigwood, who produced the original film, is producing the stage show too.'

Robert Stigwood? A light went on inside me and I pleaded with him.

'Well OK, but I can't get you a private audition, you'll have to come along to the open auditions and you'll be there with loads of others. What's more, I'd better warn you now, the pay's no good. All the money's going to the stars of the show, Craig McLachlan and Debbie Gibson.'

147

I really wasn't bothered. I wanted to be in a musical. International Artists at the time managed both myself and Brian Conley and some of their agents mocked us as the funny men without acts. I suppose to a certain extent they were right. We were funny, but we didn't have the strongest of acts. We were personality comics, but the plus side of this was that we could adapt. Put us in a holiday camp, put us in a university, put us in an empty swimming pool and we would make it work. Could I do the same in a musical?

They were holding auditions at the Cambridge Theatre in the West End. I went along not looking my best. I'd managed to drop a stone for the panto, but I was still heavy. I sat down in the hall next to the other hopefuls and ended up chatting to a few of them while we waited. They were amazed I was there. They couldn't believe that someone they saw on television would queue up for an audition. It didn't bother me. If I had to audition for a part, then so be it. I wasn't proud. I've never believed that a star should automatically get a job just because they're on television and I detest big names who do that, especially when they're not up to it.

When my time came I went up on stage and sang 'Sandy'. I thought I did OK. Afterwards I walked back to Stan's office, which wasn't that far away. When I got there Stan said they'd already called and wanted me to go back in a couple of hours to try some dancing.

'Dancing? You're 'aving a larf ain't ya, Stan? I'm wearing tight jeans. Dance in 'em, I can just about walk in 'em,' I told him.

To make matters worse I knew that I was now up against trained guys in their late teens. I could move a bit and hold a tune, but I was neither a trained dancer nor a trained singer and I was 28. When I arrived back these guys were limbering up, pulling their legs over their heads and I couldn't even touch my toes.

David Ian was there and I called him over.

'Listen, mate, you know I had an injury in panto?'

'No.'

'Didn't I tell you I've got shin splints?'

There was the first blag. So far so good, until Arlene Phillips came across. Now Arlene is one of the most respected choreographers in the business. She was the name behind Hot Gossip and went on to choreograph some of the biggest pop videos in the 1980s and shows such as *Starlight Express*.

'Why is this young man not dancing?' she asked.

David stepped in. 'Oh hello, Arlene, this is Shane Richie.'

She had no idea who I was.

'But why isn't he dancing?'

'Oh, he's got a problem with his knee. He injured it doing a big stage show at Christmas.'

'Oh really, what was that?'

'Er, Peter Pan.'

'What, you do panto?'

For some reason people in musical theatre really look down on panto. Arlene turned her nose up and walked away.

I realised there and then that if Arlene had a say in who was in the show, I'd had it. There was only one thing for it – I needed to schmooze Robert Stigwood. Robert is a big Australian, who managed The Bee Gees and Olivia Newton-John and had produced the film versions of *Grease* and *Saturday Night Fever*. When he spoke, everyone listened, and he was never surrounded by less than half a dozen hangers-on, but I persuaded David to engineer an introduction and then proceeded to turn on the charm. I knew if I could make him laugh I was in with a chance. I told him all about my days in the holiday camps and he loved hearing the panto story about me dangling by my nuts above 400 screaming kids.

The following week I phoned Stan every hour asking him to call them, but he was adamant we should play 'wait and see'.

'Listen, Shane, if they want you, they'll phone. If I chase them then they'll know you are desperate and they'll tell us what the rules are.' Stan stuck to that philosophy until the day he retired and he was probably right. If I learnt one thing from Stan it was how to be patient, although it didn't feel like it at the time.

Two weeks passed and I was pulling my hair out. At the end of February, Coleen and the boys and I flew to Orlando for a holiday. While I was there I did a few gigs in Tampa and Orlando, managed to lose a bit of weight and returned in a much better frame of mind. We got back on a Sunday and that evening Stan phoned to say they wanted me to read for the part of Kenickie, the chain-smoking tough guy who gets his girl pregnant. The audition was that week and they wanted me to take along a favourite passage from a story or a play. A bit of Shakespeare, something like that.

I called David the next day. I said I was really pleased they'd asked me back, but that I'd be no good at reading a serious play.

'I thought I'd write my own thing, do a bit of stand-up,' I told him.

'Shane, you can't, you're auditioning for bloody *Grease*,' he said. But once I'd made my mind up …

I set off for the audition determined to win them over. I'd dug out a leather jacket from the back of the cupboard and had somehow managed to style my hair into a quiff. I must have looked a right prat sitting on the underground all the way from Hillingdon to Tottenham Court Road. There I was, a slightly overweight 28-year-old in a leather jacket, tight jeans, boots and a white T-shirt, with a ridiculous quiff. I could see kids whispering:

'Mummy, is that the man who does the gunge show on television?'

I got there an hour before my audition and drank coffee and chain-smoked fags until I was called. On stage I knew I had my work cut out. Robert Stigwood was watching with about eight people around him: his driver, his secretary, his PA, his PA's PA, you name it. Arlene was there too and I could tell she still wasn't impressed. Even though she now knew who I was, she didn't like the idea of a children's presenter in a multi-million pound musical.

I took a deep breath, turned my back on them, lit up a cigarette, pulled out my comb and turned round to face them.

'Are you looking at me?' I was Robert De Niro.

As soon as I said it, the laughs started. I'd got them. I had an audience.

For the next seven minutes I did a routine about chicks, fast cars, smoking, drinking, under-age sex. Everything American you could think of, I threw at them.

'Well, if you like me, my name's Kenickie. If you don't, screw you.'

There was silence, then suddenly a loud round of applause and they said they'd be in touch.

It was weeks later before I heard. The good news was that they wanted me. The bad news was the pay. David had been right – it was terrible. Even after Stan's tough negotiations they could only up it from £625 a week to £750, and that was only when the show started. In the ten weeks before that I'd get £200 a week for rehearsals.

How was I going to tell Coleen? I know for a lot of people £750 was a lot of money – it would have been to my mum and dad, but we'd got a new baby and a huge new mortgage that I'd taken out when I was earning up to £7,000 a week. I went home that night and broke the news. Coleen was elated. She couldn't care less about the money; she was just so proud that I was following my dreams. She was even prepared to go back to work. There was a summer season coming up in Weymouth and she offered to go back on stage and join her sisters. She was prepared to do anything for the boys and me. That is the kind of woman she is.

The rehearsals took place in a warehouse in the East End on the banks of the River Thames. At that time I had a black Jaguar with a V12 Le Mans engine that I'd paid 12 grand for. It was my pride and joy. The first morning it took me three hours to get across London and I was half an hour late. I couldn't find anywhere to park, so I ended up leaving the car on a council estate. I ran in and everyone was there except me. David immediately piped up:

'Oh, sorry Robert, I meant to tell you that Shane was going to be late because he had to do an interview today.' David was forever covering my back.

When I came out that night to collect my car the tyres had been slashed, the car had been broken into and everything had been nicked. I sold it the next day for a couple of grand and bought myself a second-hand red Fiat Uno for £400, with windows that wouldn't close properly.

The previous year when I was on television I'd had courtesy cars pick me up and drive me to the studios, or if I were doing a gig Goz would drive me there in the Jag. Now I was travelling around in my beat-up Fiat or on the bus or tube. As all the money I earned was going towards the mortgage, Coleen and I ended up living in one room of the house because we couldn't afford carpets, curtains and furniture for the rest of it. Worst of all I had to let Goz go. Goz had been my driver and PA for years, but I couldn't afford to keep him on anymore. He got a job as an airline steward, or as I called him, a Trolley Dolly, so he was fine, but we were both sad about it.

Craig McLachlan, meanwhile, as the star of the show, was living the life of Riley. A Daimler would pick him up from his luxury flat in the West End every morning and the producers would take him out for lunch most days. At times it felt like some of the cast were embarrassed for me, but if that was the way it was going to be, then so be it. I remembered what Jamie Wagner had said to me in Jersey some years before – I made my own choices. It was time to put my ego to one side and swallow my pride. How things had changed in a matter of weeks. I'd go home deflated sometimes, but Coleen would always pick me up: 'Eh, c'mon Shane, your time will come again.' And she was right. I knew I'd been given a great opportunity to re-invent myself and that was more important.

At ten o'clock every morning we started with an hour-long physical warm-up – stretching, bending, bending, stretching – followed by a vocal warm-up for half an hour with the musical director Mike Dixon. The warehouse was split into three sections – the Dance Room, the Singing Room and the Acting Room, where we'd go through the script with the director, David Gilmore. So if you weren't singing you were dancing, if you weren't dancing you were acting, and on and on and on. You get the picture. That was a typical day.

As we rehearsed I found that I was fine with the singing and the acting, but the dancing was proving to be a problem; I was struggling with the choreographed moves. I was playing opposite Sally Anne Triplett, who played Rizzo. She could do everything and do it really well and would help me out when Arlene shouted out obscure dance terms in Latin.

'Right everyone, *grande jeté*!'

'What?'

'Now, *entrechat quatre*!'

'Eh?'

'*Sauté*!'

'Sally, what the hell does that mean?' I'd whisper as everyone else sprang into position.

'That's a triple somersault into the splits,' she'd say, as Arlene shouted out yet another load of old nonsense, before quickly pulling me into the right place. In one rehearsal we practised a move called the pencil lift where I had to throw Sally's legs in the air, with her arms resting on my shoulders. I timed it badly and she came down so hard that she fractured her foot and was out of rehearsals for three weeks. Arlene saw all this and wasn't pleased.

Stan had it written into my contract that throughout rehearsals I could still do comedy gigs, so at the end of the day I'd jump into my car and drive to Newcastle, Manchester, Great Yarmouth, anywhere that would take me, just to try to get some money together to cover the mortgage. Many was the time I'd have to call Stan at lunchtime and ask him to cancel my gig for that evening because Arlene was keeping me behind for an extra two hours practice. On the plus side though I was finally getting fit. Craig and I had become great mates. He was a fitness fanatic and every lunchtime he'd drag me to the gym. I got down to 13 and a half stone and was now even getting a bit of a six-pack.

During rehearsals I took a day out to appear on a children's BBC TV show called *Hanger 17*. Goz drove me to the BBC studios at Elstree in Hertfordshire and we met up with Anthea Turner. I'd known Anthea for years and she was always up for a laugh. We cottoned on to the fact that this was where they filmed *EastEnders* and we found a little back way through to their studios. We were like kids in a sweetshop – here we were running around the actual *EastEnders* set. We found the Fowlers' house and ended up jumping up and down on Pauline and Arthur's bed giggling like mad. Security guards heard us and we scuttled off to hide behind Ian Beale's house. Eventually they disappeared, but just before we left I decided I had to leave my mark. I pulled a marker pen out of my back pocket and quickly drew a knob on Pauline Fowler's fridge. Childish I know, but it had to be done. Blame Anthea!

Grease opened in July 1993 at the Dominion Theatre in Tottenham Court Road in front of the world's press and a star-studded audience, including Mick Jagger, Sting and The Bee Gees. Sadly Coleen couldn't come because she was working in Weymouth, but I managed to blag all my mates in – Spud, Goz, Spike and Micky Salmon. The show couldn't have gone better, though typically I was sick just before I went on stage. I'd always had a problem with my nerves before a show and before any gig or live TV show I would inevitably throw up. It's probably why I've struggled with my weight, because I can never eat before a gig, so I end up gorging myself afterwards, eating in China Town or Tom's Burger Cabin on the A40 at two in the morning.

The next day I rushed out to grab the newspapers to read the reviews. Now I'd expected Craig and Debbie Gibson to dominate the stories, but no one mentioned me whatsoever. I'd kind of expected it, but I was disappointed.

One night Sting came to see the show. Both Craig and I were big fans and we were excited when he came backstage after the show with his kids. He asked us if we'd mind autographing some pictures and albums for his children so we sat there for several minutes signing away – 'With lots of love', 'Best Wishes', 'Lots of kisses', 'Hope you enjoyed the show', 'With love and kisses', more kisses. We were almost writing stories on our photos to make Sting's kids feel special. Then I quickly ran down to my dressing room and found my copy of Sting's album *Ten Summoner's Tale*s.

'Sting, before you go, mate, could you sign this for me?' And he wrote on it: 'Sting'. Nothing else. And it didn't even look like Sting, it looked like Snigliiiiii.

One of my great mates at this time was Tamzin Outhwaite, who was in *Grease* alongside me as Patty Simcox. We were like a couple of kids who viewed the Dominion Theatre as our playground. In between shows we'd do stupid things like play Knock Down Ginger on the dressing room doors and then run off before anyone answered. Why? Because we could! That was our afternoon entertainment.

As the weeks passed *Grease* became like a regular nine to five job. I was enjoying it, but now that I couldn't do the comedy gigs any more money was even tighter. It was time for another blag. Ticket touts were a particular problem with *Grease*. One of the producers knew I moved in those circles and knew a lot of the lads, so he asked me if there was anything I could do to sort it out.

'No worries, I'll have a word with a friend of mine,' I promised him.

What he didn't know was that I'd got my mate to put the touts there in the first place. Mark Sutton, who had his own security company, was known as Big Mark because of his size, and somebody I'd become mates with a few years previously. We were part of the same crowd and had always got on well. I went back to him and he asked the lads to go missing for a few weeks to get me a few brownie points. The producer was so delighted that he started giving me free tickets as a thank you – the best seats in the house at £40 a time. I gave them to Big Mark and we sold them on for £60. Over six nights that was an extra £200–£300, which Coleen and I sorely needed. To this day some of those touts from *Grease* are still my mates and they'll still help me out when I'm stuck and get me tickets for a show.

Although the ticket money helped, I was still relieved when Stan called me to say that Scottish Television wanted me to screen test to host *Win, Lose or Draw*. This was a game show that was on ITV every weekday morning at 9.25am. Danny Baker had made it his own, but he was leaving and they wanted someone to take over. It was between me, Nick Hancock and Bob Mills. Stan went along for a meeting with Sandy Ross, one of the bosses at STV and immediately played hardball. 'Are you looking for Danny Baker Number Two or are you looking for Shane Richie Number One? Because if you want a new Danny Baker then don't bother,' he told him. Stan always used to say things like that. It must have worked because they chose me. I was given two weeks off to record 50 shows – five shows a day, five days a week – and for that I'd be paid £10,000, a king's ransom – which by now we owed to the bank.

When the show came out at the beginning of 1994 it was an immediate hit. I was trim, I had a quiff and was full of confidence. By now I knew exactly how to work shows such as this. I had celebrity guests on and they were all friends of mine – people such as Cannon and Ball and the cast of *Grease*. I even managed to get a slot for The Nolans. We got the highest daytime viewing figures on ITV, 2–3 million, which was half a million more than Danny Baker. Sorry, Danny mate, it must have been my hair. Pretty soon the papers were describing it as a cult show. ITV were now jumping over themselves thinking they'd found some new guy, which made me laugh as I'd been schlepping around for years.

The upshot was that people were now booking tickets for *Grease* after watching me on *Win, Lose or Draw*. What's more, the show meant we had a bit of extra cash coming in. It meant we could finally afford carpets and curtains for the downstairs. Not that we got them. The day the first cheque came in I went out shopping with strict instructions from Coleen to come home with two sets of curtains.

I returned home that afternoon not with the curtains, but as the proud owner of a stunning 1964 Rockola juke box. I couldn't resist. It was worth £800, but I'd managed to blag it for £500. What a bargain. Coleen wasn't best pleased, but I got round her. How? By filling the juke box with Nolans' hits of course!

CHAPTER ELEVEN

'That's for you, Danny Zuko'

A year in a show like *Grease* is a long time and quite rightly Craig McLachlan and Debbie Gibson decided they wanted to move on. Stan called me and said the producers wanted me to do a private audition for the part of the male lead, Danny Zuko. I couldn't believe my luck, but Stan said he'd turned them down.

'The only way Shane is going to audition is in front of a live audience,' he told them.

In March 1994, just after my 30th birthday, I got my chance. It was a Friday night and Craig had taken an evening off. He was due to return on the Saturday and then work through until the end of his contract a couple of months later. I got tickets for my mum and dad, Coleen and my boys and some of my family even flew over from Ireland. Word got out in the press beforehand that I was to be Danny for the night: and every ticket was sold. They put a sign outside the theatre that night 'Appearing tonight as Danny Zuko for one night only: Shane Richie. Sold Out.' When I walked into the theatre and saw that it was a great feeling.

Stan came backstage to wish me luck.

'Go out there and make 'em have it,' he used to say to me before every big show.

'OK, Colonel.'

I called him the Colonel after Colonel Tom Parker who looked after

Elvis. I've no idea why, but it caught on and even today people still call him that.

Once Stan had gone the realisation hit me: now I was on my own. I sat in my dressing room petrified. I'd been sick so many times there was nothing left in my stomach and all I could hear were chants of 'We want Shane, we want Shane!' I got my call and shakily took my place on the balcony. The *Grease* theme opened up and the lights hit my face. Before I could even sing a note the place erupted. Over 2,000 people were shouting my name and stamping their feet. It was the first time I'd heard girls screaming for me. For a moment there I could have happily given up the business. I couldn't see how it could ever possibly get better than that. I wanted so much to put my hands in the air and shout 'Yes! I've made it!' But I couldn't acknowledge the audience because that would have been Shane Richie and right now I was Danny Zuko. I launched into 'Sandy', even though I couldn't hear a note and the theatre finally went quiet.

When the show finished I knew I'd held my own. Everything I'd worked hard at had finally come together. At the end of the show Danny and Sandy took their final bow as usual to the cheers of the crowd. Craig and Debbie always walked off arm in arm at this point and that signalled the end of the show. But as I walked off with Debbie I had other ideas. We got to the wings and I turned round and walked straight back on stage alone. I could see Debbie looking at me as if to say, 'What the hell's he doing?' With the audience still cheering, I took the comb out of my back pocket, twiddled the front of my quiff with two fingers, looked up into the box where Robert Stigwood was sitting with the other producers, blew them a kiss and then threw the comb at them. It landed on Robert Stigwood's lap. I made the Number One sign, pointed to myself and then walked off.

That night there was a huge party in my dressing room. All my family and friends were there, crowded around me, when Robert Stigwood walked in. He worked his way through the crowd until he was right next to me and then tried to speak. Unfortunately, my mum had no idea who he was.

'Feck off, Shane's busy,' she said crossly.

'Mum, that's Robert Stigwood.'

'I don't give a damn who it is, I'm talking.'

When Craig came back on the Saturday he told me he'd heard I'd done well, but the relationship between us changed. All of a sudden the part was no longer just his. He was still a great Danny Zuko, but somebody else had played him now. And I'd done it differently. Craig was never a fan of the movie and made that very clear, whereas I'd grown up with the film, and Jake watched it constantly, so I played Danny more like John Travolta. I dyed my hair black and adopted the walk; I'm a great believer in giving people what they want, as opposed to what you think they should have.

As if playing Danny Zuko wasn't enough, ITV came back and offered me a second series of *Win, Lose or Draw*, but Stan turned it down. He said I'd re-invented myself now and it was time to move to prime-time programmes. Meanwhile we'd had a call from Granada Television. They'd come up with a bingo show called *Lucky Numbers*, which would go out on a Friday evening and they were interested in me as the presenter. I liked the idea. I'd called bingo for years at the holiday camps and knew I could do it with my eyes closed. We had meetings upon meetings with Kenton Allen, who had produced Jonathan Ross on radio and television. We became really close and we'd sit for hours talking excitedly about the show and how good we could make it. Granada was prepared to sign me up exclusively with a £1m two-year golden handshake deal.

Granada was confident that *Lucky Numbers* would be huge because it tied the show in with *The Sun* newspaper. Readers would get their game cards with their Friday *Sun* and then play along, so on the show I'd be talking to the viewers at home as well as the people in the studio. This was the sort of prime-time show that went to established stars – the likes of Cilla, Bruce or Barrymore – and here I was, just turned 30. Not only that but there would be the possibility of other shows and more importantly for me they said they wanted to develop me as an actor as well. That was the sucker punch; that was what brought me in. Was I on a roll now!

With a deal like that I could easily have said goodbye to Kenickie,

Danny Zuko and musical theatre and concentrate on my television. But then word got around that the producers were still planning to audition for a new Danny Zuko to take over when Craig left. I felt really hurt by this. If they hadn't thought I was good enough on the night when I played Danny then they should have told me. At the same time Craig was planning to take a two-week holiday and they'd asked me to stand in. It was all a bit unfair as they'd not offered me the role permanently and by rights it was the job of the understudy anyway. He was a guy called Glenn Carter, who could sing and dance me off the stage, and not surprisingly for a short while it caused a bit of friction backstage. I took the part though and treated every night like an opening night. By the end of the second week I had Danny Zuko down to a T.

This time surely they couldn't ignore me. They didn't, and shortly after my two-week run came the phone call I'd been waiting for – they were offering me the role of Danny Zuko for a year. I'd wanted it so badly – my name in lights in the West End. At that time the West End was using a lot of TV stars to put bums on seats. They'd already had Jason Donovan and then Philip Schofield in *Joseph and the Amazing Technicolor Dreamcoat*, and also Brian Conley was starting in *Jolson*.

To be honest I was so delighted I'd have done it for an extra £50 a week. I'd already proved it wasn't about the money by playing Kenickie for peanuts. But Stan was having none of it. He pushed it and pushed it. Every time the producers came back with a better offer he'd go away and think about it and then go back to them and say it still wasn't good enough.

What swung it was when the producers realised I'd signed a deal with ITV to host a prime-time Friday night show in association with *The Sun*. Now Stan had them. 'He's going to be on television on Friday night, with a quiff. Now what's he going to talk about? He's going to talk about *Grease*. He's going to be promoting the show,' Stan constantly reminded them. And they bought it. Not only did they agree to pay me £10,000 a week, not only would they let me have time off from the show to record *Lucky Numbers*, but they would also continue to pay me while I was out recording. Stan pinned them down to every deal possible – a share of the merchandise, paid holiday and, as daft as it sounds, I even got a car park space. It was unbelievable. In July Stan walked into my dressing room after one of my final performances as Kenickie and plonked a magnum of champagne down on the table in front of me.

'That's for you, Danny Zuko,' he said proudly, as he hugged me.

What was lovely about landing the job was that Goz was able to come back and work for me. We'd missed each other when he was off on the airlines and it was good to be together again. When Craig left we moved into his dressing room and totally changed it. We asked for new carpets, curtains and lampshades and a new leather suite. We even had new lights around the mirror and a new shower and toilet.

As well as Craig, Debbie Gibson was also going on to pastures new and the powers that be needed to find a new Sandy. Apparently they auditioned everyone from Denise Van Outen and Danniella Westbrook to Dannii Minogue. David Ian eventually broke the news to me.

''Ere Shane, we've found you a new Sandy.'

'Who've we got then, Dave?'

'Sonia.'

My heart sank. By all accounts Robert Stigwood had taken a shine to the little redhead, who'd had a few chart hits a few years previously. Now don't get me wrong, I had nothing against her personally and I still don't, I just thought that she was miscast. I know I'm not the greatest dancer in the world, by any stretch of the imagination, but I'd worked my nuts off in the routines to be as good as the people who'd trained for years to do that job. I didn't want people ever saying 'Oh, he's only up there because he's Shane Richie.' But that's exactly what they did with Sonia. Routines we'd spent a year doing night after night now had to be changed. Not only that, I'm 6ft and in Danny Zuko's heels I'm close to 6ft 2. Sonia? I don't know, 4ft 6? Maybe even less. She was tiny. So tiny that I was told I now had to wear flat boots and we had to change the choreography drastically to suit her. In 'You're the One That I Want' Sandy is supposed to skip across the stage, but because Sonia had such small legs she could never do it. I hated that. I hated the fact that the show had to be compromised in that way. I've never seen Sonia since. We never fell out particularly, but we had nothing in common. She didn't like my sense of humour and I didn't particularly like hers.

As I was now the lead I decided to brush up on my singing. I asked around and a singing teacher called Mary Hammond was recommended. She was well respected in the business and had helped big stars such as George Michael and Michael Crawford. Mary looked like a very strict schoolmistress and I sat down for my first lesson feeling very nervous. We chatted for a while and I noticed how tactile she was, to the extent that I wondered if she was flirting with me. When the lesson began I became convinced of it. Instead of asking me to sing a song, Mary asked me to lie on the floor. What's more, she then came and lay next to me.

'Sing aah,' she told me and at the same time lifted up my shirt and put her hand on my stomach. I couldn't believe it. Wey hey, what's going on here then? I've come here for a singing lesson, I thought to myself. We stayed like that for the next half hour, at which point Mary jumped up and said: 'Right Shane, see you at the same time next week.' I immediately realised what an idiot I'd been. Of course Mary wouldn't have looked twice at someone young and daft like me and I now know that's exactly what happens in a singing lesson. But in those days I was just a boy from Harlesden with a very vivid imagination.

Many celebrities came along to see *Grease*. I had the pleasure of meeting Dustin Hoffman one night. He was a strange one. He'd come to see the show with his family and they were put in the Royal box. What was odd was that he didn't sit down for the entire show; he just stood behind the curtain and watched from there. I don't know if he was trying to go unnoticed, but if he was it didn't work and every so often I'd throw in a bit of dialogue from his movie *Rain Man* just to let him know I'd clocked him.

That year I was invited to perform at the *Children's Royal Variety Show*. I'd sung at the *Royal Variety Show* the previous year as part of the cast of *Grease*, but this year I was out there on my own, singing 'Jailhouse Rock' and backed by 30 dancers. It was a proud moment.

By now *Grease* was huge and at the end of the show the stage door at the Dominion was always heaving with hundreds of people. By the time I'd finished signing autographs and having my picture taken with fans it could take me the best part of two hours to get out. I was more than happy to do it most nights, but occasionally when I was meeting up with friends in a restaurant I needed to make a quick getaway. It was Goz who came up with a great plan – I'd take the final bow, run into the wings and take off my microphone, where Goz was waiting for me with a big coat. I'd put it on, squash my quiff under a hat, nip through a side door into the stalls and then literally follow the audience out, listening to their comments about the show as I shuffled along. And no one ever cottoned on.

At the start of 1995 I could do no wrong in the eyes of *The Sun*. The journalists there loved me. They printed stories about me every week and there was never a bad word said against me. Of course there wasn't – they were sponsoring *Lucky Numbers*. Meanwhile the *Daily Mirror* was trashing me. I'd be photographed walking out of a club and the caption in *The Sun* would say 'Shane Richie, enjoying a well deserved night out with friends'. In the *Mirror* it would be 'Shane Richie in drunken nightclub frenzy'. It was the first time I saw how it worked with the press and how they could take one single fact and give it so much topspin that the final story ended up a mix of fact and fiction. The funniest thing was that a year later, when *The Sun* stopped sponsoring the show and the *Daily Mirror* took over, it all changed round. I'd come out of a restaurant with Coleen and it would be 'Shane Richie enjoys quiet evening out with his lovely wife' in the *Mirror* while in *The Sun* it would be 'Shane Richie in restaurant bust-up with missus'.

I started *Lucky Numbers* on 9 January, 1995. Granada had high hopes for it, but I don't think any of us had anticipated just how big it would be. It was Britain's first interactive game show, with a prize of £20,000, which at the time was telly's biggest cash prize. Contestants had to answer questions to cover up numbers on their board. Of course, every game show host has to have a catchphrase and the producers told me I'd need one myself. The show started with the audience sitting with large bingo balls in their hands and I'd pick out three of them, so I said, almost without thinking: 'Put your balls in the air'. That soon progressed to 'Show us your balls'. You name any balls jokes going and I'd find 'em!

Within weeks the show was pulling in ten million viewers and I couldn't walk down the street without kids shouting out to me. I loved it. I was only 30, I wore sharp suits and had my hair in a quiff. Unfortunately sections of the press accused me of acting like some big time Charlie. I never meant to, it's just that I was confident about the show because I'd called bingo so many times at Pontins. Had I known that was going to be people's reaction – that I'd come across as arrogant – I'd have toned it down a bit, but I really didn't see it coming.

In the meantime I was appearing six nights a week at The Dominion. On Saturday 11 February, 1995, I came off stage as usual, dripping with sweat and full of adrenalin. I went back to my dressing room expecting to find the usual mixture of mates and cast knocking back champagne, but there was no one around. Goz was always there, so I knew instantly there was something wrong. I sat there on my own and after a few minutes Goz came in, looking pale.

'I've got some bad news, Shane.'

'What?'

'Micky's dead.'

I couldn't take it in.

'What you talking about?'

'Micky Salmon died today.'

Micky was a big football fan and supported Watford. That afternoon he'd run to the game. When he got through the turnstile his heart had just packed up and he'd collapsed and died. At that moment nothing else in the world mattered. Micky had been one of my best mates for the past 15 years and now he had gone.

His family asked me if I'd say a few words at his funeral in Ruislip. I remember standing at the front of the church. It was packed to the rafters and all I could see as I looked out over the congregation was blonde hair. Micky loved a blonde. It made me giggle inside – even after his death Micky could still pull a blonde.

I made a speech. How I got through it, to this day, I'll never know, but at the end of it I did something that I knew he would have appreciated.

'Ladies and Gentlemen, the one and only Micky Salmon.' And everyone stood up and gave him a standing ovation.

To this day I still think about him. He'd been the lynchpin of our group; it was always me, Goz, Micky, Spud, Spike and Jeff. He'd held us all together and from the day he died our group never saw each other as much. Now every time the sun shines I think of him. He touched my heart. Things ain't the same without you, pal.

CHAPTER TWELVE

'Tell me the fucking numbers'

Nothing raises your profile like a TV advert and in the spring of 1995 I was approached by Procter and Gamble and asked if I'd like to take over from Danny Baker in the Daz adverts. It seemed like I was constantly picking up his cast-offs. Little did I know that it was going to be one of the toughest gigs of my career.

Now everyone always assumes that the women who featured in the Daz adverts were actresses. Let me tell you, they most definitely weren't. This is how it worked. We'd head off to a town or city and a team of market researchers were sent off to a local supermarket, incognito. They'd make a note of all the women who bought Daz and then catch them on their way out.

'Excuse me, we're doing a survey on washing powder, do you use Daz?' They'd obviously say yes and the market researchers would take their address and then ask if it was alright to give them a call in a couple of hours time to ask about the results of their wash. In return they'd get a shopping voucher.

It was that simple. We knew there'd be a lady at home. We knew she used Daz and we knew she'd just done a wash. The woman knew that someone would be in touch, but what she didn't know was that I was suited and booted and quiffed up, waiting around the corner. I'd ring her doorbell, the lady would open it and look suitably shocked and I'd say:

'Good morning, this is the Daz Doorstep Challenge. Do your whites wash whiter than white?'

She'd giggle and I'd say: 'Can I have a look at your laundry?' We'd go in, film it, I'd do a piece to camera. We're out. 30-second ad.

It sounds easy, but what a nightmare they were to film. Had we actually used real actresses it would have been a whole lot simpler. Sometimes I'd ring the bell and rather than open it the lady would shout:

'Who is it?'

Obviously I couldn't say.

'Can you come to the door, please?'

'No, not unless you tell me who it is.'

And all this conversation would go on through the letter box.

Other times the ladies didn't seem that pleased to see me and the producer would cut it and make us do it again. If they'd been actresses, fair enough, but you try getting a punter to act surprised a second time. It stuck out like a sore thumb.

The producers were very pedantic, even down to how I rang the bell or knocked on the door. I had to hold the microphone in my right hand, the Daz box in my left and somehow knock on the door with the Daz logo at all times facing the camera.

'Shane, are your fingers clean? We've got a close-up on the box.'

'Shane, your thumb is slightly over the D, can you move it?'

'Shane, can you hold the box closer to your chest, with your index finger and your thumb under the box?'

'Shane, can you tilt the microphone 45 degrees, please.'

'Hold on, he's got a mark on his jacket.'

This went on for hours and it drove me mental. We hadn't even opened the bloody door yet and we had ten doorsteps to film in a day.

Then there was the ring. Often they didn't like the sound of the real doorbell so they dubbed it over later. Once we got inside it was no better. Up to 15 people would traipse into a tiny terraced house. Along with me there were cameramen, sound, lights, producers, make-up artists and a representative from Procter & Gamble. For 20 minutes we'd take over the woman's entire kitchen, setting up lights and moving everything around. We'd then film her putting in her washing, with perhaps a close-up of a child's T-shirt covered in blackcurrant juice stains, and then we'd come back an hour later and film it when the washing came out.

Now I may be wrong, but all soap powder seems the same to me. The only thing that changes is the smell. Sometimes I couldn't see the difference and nor could the lady, but I'd whisper to her:

'Ooh, doesn't it look great?'

'Do you think so?'

'Ooh, definitely.'

And I'd end up convincing her. Of course it was clean, but I don't know that it was any whiter than before it went in. This was the blag. It was about fooling the general public. And if you do it with enough confidence and a big smile on your face, you can fool anybody.

It went according to plan so rarely that if we got one in ten that were usable we were lucky. The main problem was getting the ladies to be enthusiastic enough at the end. I could stand there and rave about how great Daz was until I was blue in the face, but what they needed was a testimony from the women.

One day in Preston the challenge seemed to be going like a dream. The woman was well spoken and attractive and when I opened the door her face lit up.

'Wow, isn't this exciting! Please come in, Shane.'

Brilliant, we were on a roll here. We could be out of here in an hour with one in the bag. We started to load her machine.

'Daz really is a miracle wash, isn't it?'

She was using all the right words. We got down to the testimony at the end and she let rip.

'Nothing washes whiter than Daz. It brings out the white in my children's clothes. My husband's never been happier since we changed to Daz.'

This was it. Hallelujah! We'd got the ad of all ads. I'd got the box in shot, I'd held the microphone right and this glamorous woman was saying all the right things.

'Well, there's one lady who's happy with her wash.' Cut. We started to pack up and the producer went over to hand her the shopping voucher.

'No, I don't think so,' she said. 'I want paying for this.'

'Sorry?'

It turned out that this woman was an out-of-work actress and she'd known exactly what she was doing. The producers were furious, but I thought it was hilarious. Somebody who knew how to play the game.

The ads went out in May and sales went up an extra 16 per cent. Unfortunately, despite its success, the Daz Doorstep Challenge was deemed a bit naff. I kept trying to change them, but they were having none of it. They wanted to stick with the original and for every Daz door I opened, another door closed on my career. I could do musical theatre and game shows, but there was no way I was going to be taken seriously as an actor after that. Too many people thought it was too cheesy.

What it did give me was financial security. Thanks to Stan I was earning a fortune. The Daz deal was close to £500,000 over two years and all I had to do was work 21 days in a year. I'd spent years going around clubs, theatres, appearing on dodgy TV shows and panto and schlepping around America and here I was getting half a million pounds. And for what? Knocking on women's doors and asking to see their underwear. Coleen always used to say she couldn't believe I was getting paid for something I'd spent all my life doing for nothing. On top of that I got extra money for doing radio interviews and more for letting them put my face on the Daz box.

In addition Stan had driven such a hard bargain with *Grease* that even when I was let out to film the Daz ads and *Lucky Numbers*, *Grease* would still pay me my £10,000 a week. He convinced the producers that as long as I had my quiff on television I was still plugging the show. Even though I wasn't mentioning *Grease* it would remind people. They agreed, but Granada weren't too keen on the idea, so we compromised and I had a half-quiff – but Grease still paid me the money.

On top of that I'd already signed a million pound two year deal with Granada. Every day Stan would open the post and there'd be cheques from *Grease*, or the merchandise, or the Daz ads or back payments from *Lucky Numbers*. So many cheques were coming in that at one point I didn't know where they were coming from. Coleen said to me one day: 'Shane, there's a cheque here for £30,000, what's it for?' And you know what, neither of us could work it out.

Did the money go to my head? What do you think!

I've always been a car nut, so I went out and bought a Rolls Royce for £12,000 in cash. Don't ask me why, I never needed a reason. I already had a new BMW sports and a white Porsche, which I'd bought off a mate, and Coleen had the latest people mover. I had the Rolls Royce for three months and I only drove it twice. It was a 1964 Silver Shadow, from the year I was born. Goz used to drive me to the Dominion in it and we'd cruise down Marylebone Road, with the windows down in the lovely summer of '95, wearing shorts and baseball caps, eating McDonalds and singing 'Town Called Malice' at the top of our voices. 'Better stop dreaming of the quiet life, cos it's the one we'll never know.' I'd always loved The Jam and that song seemed to sum up my life. People would recognise me and shout and wave and I played up to it. I'd make a point of going through Harlesden, past the streets where I grew up. It made me feel good, for all the wrong reasons. But I just wanted to say 'Look, I've made it now.' And that's what I believed. I thought I was the Number One and was set up for life.

I knew the Rolls had to go though. We used to park it outside the stage door and one night I came out to find that someone had scraped 'fuck you' into the side of it with a key. I stood there and laughed, because I remembered when I was 11 someone had parked a Rolls Royce outside my dad's club and I'd keyed the same words into the side of it. It was karma and I got rid of it the very next day.

Because I didn't have a TV set as a child until I was ten, I put a television in every room. I made sure Coleen and the boys had the best of everything and of course I blew thousands on some of the strangest things, in particular *Planet of the Apes* memorabilia. It was my favourite TV show when I was a boy and I couldn't resist. I bought original costumes and the original wagon, which was used to transport Charlton Heston in the movie. I bought posters, masks and the original movies on film and DVD and a 6ft gorilla that I stood in my hall. And of course I bought the original toys. I built up one of the biggest collections in the country. It all harks back to my Christmases as a boy when my mum and dad couldn't afford to get me much. I remember my mum putting her arm around me and saying: 'One day, son, you'll be able to have what you want.' And she was right. It had finally happened.

Despite all the money coming in, I didn't put a single penny to one side. I had no savings accounts and no pension. Rightly or wrongly my philosophy was, 'Treat every day as if it's your last, because one day you'll be right.' Everyone was on at me to save – Coleen, her family, Stan, even my mates. Goz would say: 'Put some money away for a rainy day.' And I'd say, 'It ain't ever gonna rain, I'm alright.' Little did I know that pretty soon the clouds were going to open.

Coleen used to despair sometimes. I'd pull up in the drive in a brand new Jag and she'd come out.

'Oh, no, what have you bought now?'

'It's alright, babe, it was a bargain.'

And it was, because I'd always get them to knock something off. I could afford £20,000, but I'd barter and get it for £16,000. It was what my mum had taught me as a child when she took me shopping round the market – try to get a bargain, always do a deal.

But for me money was for spreading around. When I fancied treating my boys to some new toys, Hamleys opened up at night for me to go shopping. I'd go to restaurants with my mates and pick up the bill at the end of the night. I even put a down payment on a house for Goz. I wanted to treat my mum and dad to a new house, but they refused to budge from their terraced council house in Wembley. All their friends were there and they said they were happier staying there, too.

I couldn't refuse begging letters. (I can now, so don't even think about it!) It would be £500 here, £1,000 there. Coleen and my office begged me to stop, but I'd paid my dues and worked hard to get to where I was and I believed now I'd made it, the money was never going to stop coming in.

That year, like millions of other people, Coleen and I sat down one night and watched a television documentary called *The Dying Rooms*. We were heartbroken by what we saw – in orphanages across China, tiny babies were shown tied to their cots and starving toddlers were left to die alone in darkened rooms. It was one of the most horrific things I've ever witnessed. There and then we vowed to do something about it. We had a fantastic life and two wonderful healthy boys. The little girls in the orphanage had nothing and nobody. We could talk about nothing else for days and found out everything we could about the situation. Then we contacted Hillingdon Council and said that we would like to apply to adopt one of the abandoned children in China. We had meetings with social worker after social worker and had review after review. It went on for months. Meanwhile the abandoned children were still stuck in the orphanages. Eventually they came back with their verdict. In their opinion Coleen was two stone over their limit – unless she lost weight we couldn't adopt. We were devastated. It seemed a crazy decision. These kids were desperate for someone to care for them and we had everything to offer, but someone sitting in an office somewhere had come up with some arbitrary weight limit. We were determined not to give up though. If the council wouldn't help us we'd just have to think of another way.

During the time I was doing *Lucky Numbers* I received a phone call from Big Mark saying that Reggie Kray wanted to meet me – apparently he was a big fan of the show. I drove down to Maidstone prison with Mark and Goz and I was excited the whole way there. I couldn't really understand why Reggie would want to meet me, but if Reggie Kray says he wants to see you, you don't turn him down, do you? And besides, I was curious. Let's be honest, who wouldn't be? He's part of folklore.

Mark said there was nothing to worry about, but all the way there he kept telling me not to mention *The Krays* movie. Apparently Reg was a bit sensitive about it. We'd sit there in silence for a while and then Mark would start up again.

'Right, winkle,' that was his nickname for me, for some reason, 'remember – don't mention the film.'

'Alright, I'm not going to mention it.'

'He won't like it.'

'Shut up, I ain't gonna mention it, alright?'

We were suited and booted and looking pretty good. When we arrived we waited in the pub opposite the prison as instructed. Two of Reggie's mates came across to collect us.

'Are you here to see Reggie?'

'Yes.'

'Mark, have you told Shane not to mention the film?'

'I know not to mention the film, alright?'

We got to the jail, were frisked by security and shown through a maze of corridors. I was signing autographs as I went. Eventually we were shown into the meeting room, which was like an eerie version of a school canteen, with prison guards at either side. We sat down at our allotted table and the place fell quiet. They all knew who we were waiting for. It was like a meeting with the Pope. When Reggie walked in everyone's eyes dropped to the floor reverentially.

Reg walked slowly across to the table, sat down and put his arm around me. 'Alright, Shane, how's it going?'

'Reggie, nice to meet you, mate.'

'Alright son. Now, down to business. You know we all play *Lucky Numbers* in here. We get banged up at 8 o'clock, but it's on at 7.30. So, what are the numbers?'

'Sorry?'

He put his arm around me.

'Come on, son, you can tell me.'

'Tell you what, Reg?'

'The numbers.'

'What numbers?'

He leaned in close and with a big grin on his face said: 'The fucking bingo numbers.'

'Reggie, I don't know the numbers and even if I did you've gotta 'ave a bingo card.'

'Tell me the fucking numbers.'

'Reg, I swear…'

'Tell me the fucking numbers. We'll make a few quid.'

By now I was slightly panicking inside, but still doing my best to stay cool.

'Reg, it ain't like that. I've recorded all the shows. And anyway I don't know the bleedin' numbers and even if you knew 'em, you've gotta 'ave the bingo card.'

Here I was with Reggie Kray, Britain's most notorious gangster, talking about *Lucky Numbers*. I couldn't believe it. But Reg wasn't going to give up.

'Now the thing is, Shane, I can get the bingo card, all I need are the numbers.'

I looked across at the prison guards hoping they might pick up on my panic, but I couldn't even catch their eye. Reggie Kray in the flesh looks like your grandad would look if he'd worked out for 20 years. He had piercing eyes and when he spoke everyone listened. I had only one option. I'd have to blag it.

'Right Reg, here's what I'm gonna do for ya. I'm gonna phone my mate at Granada and I'm gonna get him to give me the numbers. Ring me tomorrow and I'll give 'em to you.'

You'd think he'd won the Lottery the way he hugged me.

'Sweet, thanks very much.'

And at that he relaxed. He asked about my work, my boys and my mum and dad; he seemed to know a lot about me and particularly about my dad, who had worked as a doorman in the mid-1960s. We chatted about every subject under the sun and I began to feel really comfortable in his presence. Maybe a bit too comfortable. Here came the million dollar question…

''Ere, Reg…'

'What son?'

'What did you think of the movie *The Krays*?'

Big Mark became little Mark all of a sudden. He shrank in his seat and I saw him lean across to Goz. 'He's only gone and mentioned the fucking movie,' he muttered.

It seemed like the whole room had gone quiet. Reg pulled his chair out and faced me.

'Have you seen it?' he asked.

'Yeah, course I 'ave.'

'I'll tell you what I thought, son…' and for the next 20 minutes he proceeded to tell me all about it. What he liked about the film and what he didn't like. Which bits were true and which weren't. No one had ever had the bottle to ask him before, but far from being upset he was actually excited to talk about it for the first time.

After an hour the warders told us our time was up. I got up to leave.

'Now before you go, Shane, is there anything you need from me?'

'Funnily enough, now you ask, Reg, there is…'

In the late eighties I'd done some gigs at Butlins for an agent who never paid me. He owed me £8,000, which was a lot of money back then. When I asked him for it he told me to stick my request up my arse because I didn't have a contract. I'd trusted him and he'd tricked me. I told Reg that this guy lived in Canvey Island and that I was trying to take him to court to get my money back.

'Who is he?' Reg growled.

I told him the guy's name and thought no more of it.

I don't know to this day exactly what happened, but word has it Reggie made a call, the agent told him where to go and, lo and behold, soon after, his office was burnt down. A week later I had a cheque sent to me for the whole amount, flowers for Coleen, toys for my boys and an apology.

Coincidence? I don't think so.

The day after the visit I called one of my mates at Granada and asked for the winning bingo numbers for the following week. He obviously wanted to know why.

'Don't ask, you wouldn't believe me if I told you.'

I got hold of the numbers and managed to get them to Reg. Now I don't know if this is true or not, but rumour has it that Reg somehow managed to get some bingo cards made up, which he sold to all the inmates. And guess what? Reg got the winning card.

After that Reg and I struck up a friendship that would last until the day he died. I'd visit him as much as I could and he'd ring me at least two or three times a week. There was never any fear after that first visit: it felt more like I was talking to my grandad. He'd call my mobile just before I went on stage in Grease and Goz would hold it up to the speakers. Reg would get a group of prisoners round and they'd listen to the first half of the show before lock-up, so he got to hear me sing 'Summer Nights' and probably half of 'Greased Lightning'. To this day I still have two fabulous pictures he drew for the boys. I remember him telling me that the last show he'd seen before he was banged up was Half A Sixpence. He wanted to raise the money to stage it again with me in the lead role. We even got as far as having meetings about it and

Tommy Steele, who starred in the original, was up for me doing it, but sadly Reggie died and the whole idea went with him.

I think Reggie knew my background and he liked where I'd come from. I was part of the petition to get him out of there. He'd put two fingers up to the Establishment and they wanted to make an example of him. Other people could commit the most terrible crimes and not get half the sentence he did. In return, any time I needed him he was there for me. If someone screwed me over I'd think, 'Right, do I get a lawyer or do I tell Reggie?' And Reggie would make a call and it would be sorted.

Reggie wasn't the only one looking out for me. I was invited to a big do one night in the East End of London with Craig McLachlan. I was standing chatting to the TV presenter John Leslie and Big Mark, and over Mark's shoulder I could see three shaven-haired blokes giving me the finger. I told Mark that I thought it might be better if I went home. One of the blokes' girlfriends had been talking to me, he'd got the wrong impression and now it looked as if it was all going to kick off.

Mark simply said: 'Go to the toilet, winkle.' I did what he said and as I was standing there these three guys came in. One stood either side of me and one behind me.

'Who do you fucking think you are?' one of them began to sneer. I thought I was finished. But before I had time to speak Mark had burst through the door and asked me to leave. I have no idea what happened next, but a couple of minutes later Mark walked out on his own, picked up his hamburger from the bar where he'd left it and casually carried on the conversation we'd been having before.

''Ere Mark, what happened?'

'Oi, winkle, sorted.'

That was Big Mark.

When the summer came, my *Grease* contract came up for renewal and the producers made me an offer I couldn't afford to refuse. Not only that but the show was going to take a turn for the better with a sexy new Sandy played by Samantha Janus, who was taking over from Sonia. There was an immediate rapport. We fancied the pants off each other as Sandy and Danny and when we were on stage it was electric. Sam was great fun and very confident on stage, but even she was petrified when she heard that Olivia Newton-John was coming to see the show. Olivia was in Britain briefly on a promotional tour and Robert Stigwood persuaded her to come along. This was the woman who'd played Sandy in the film and here she was coming to watch Sam and I in the West End.

There was pandemonium outside and things weren't much better backstage. Luckily the show went without a hitch and 2,000 people went crazy. At the end of every performance I'd made it my trademark to throw my comb into the audience. Now Olivia Newton-John was sitting in the stalls about 12 rows back. For a second it crossed my mind to throw the comb to her. Then I stopped myself – I could do better than that. Instead I jumped off the stage, fought my way through the crowd, handed her the comb and gave her a kiss and a hug. It was an emotional moment. This was the real Sandy, after all. On a high, I turned round. Now all I had to do was run back down the aisle and jump back on stage. Easier said than done. As I jumped I tripped and gashed my leg. Of course I couldn't let on that I'd hurt myself, but instead of the usual Danny swagger I limped off stage that night like an old man. That'll teach me to show off! That night Olivia came out to dinner with us. She told us stories about when she made the movie and happily posed for pictures with her daughter. I went home that night thinking I'd met someone really special.

Another special night was when Princess Diana brought her boys to see the show. I'd always liked the Royal Family and Diana was my favourite. The producers took me to one side before the performance and warned me that at all costs I must stick to the script word for word. There must be no references to the fact that Diana was in the audience. Then her aides came backstage – on no account must I make eye contact with her during the show.

Of course, all this was like a red rag to a bull. One of the most beautiful and famous women was sitting in the audience watching my show and I couldn't mention it or even look at her. They were having a laugh, weren't they?

The show started and I immediately spotted Diana sitting at the front of the circle. My opening song was 'Sandy' and I was supposed to look dreamy as I sang it and gaze into space. Well, as soon as the opening notes struck up I turned my whole body round, looked up at Diana and sang the whole song to her. There was a bit in the middle where I had to speak the lyrics: 'Sandy my darlin', you hurt me real bad, you know it's true. But baby you gotta believe me when I say I'm helpless without you.' The crowd loved it and I saw Di tilt her head and give that little shy look that I'd seen in pictures a million times.

In the interval the company manager pulled me over furiously. 'Shane, what are you playing at? You sang directly to Diana, we told you not to.' I chuckled to myself when he'd gone. 'You ain't seen nothing yet.'

In the finale we did a mega-mix of the show's big songs. When it came to my turn to sing 'Greased Lightning' I gyrated my tiny waist – 30in at the time – for all I was worth, grabbing my crotch and pointing at her. She tilted her head again, but I could see she was giggling. Her boys both had big grins on their faces; they were lapping it up too. Afterwards she came backstage and we met very briefly. She said how much she'd enjoyed the show, but then she had to go. It was a shame. She was a beautiful lady and seemed so down-to-earth; I could have talked to her all night.

We also had a visit from Sarah Ferguson. It was a charity night and she brought her daughters along and of course we were all told to line up at the end of the night to meet her. Sweat was dripping off me, I was tired and basically all I wanted to do was get out, have a drink and a fag and a shower. As Fergie came along the line, all the girls in the show curtseyed and all the guys bowed and eventually she reached me at the end. The stage manager introduced me:

'This is Shane Richie, who plays Danny.'

'Hi, how ya doin'?' I said, in my best American accent.

'Oh, I didn't know you were American,' Fergie said.

'No, I was acting, love.'

All the cast laughed at this, but Fergie clearly thought I was taking the Mick, dropped my hand like a hot potato and quickly walked on, giving me a look over her shoulder as if to say 'you prat'. No Royal garden parties for me then.

Another visitor to the show that summer was Robbie Williams. He'd just split from Take That and we got really close. He'd come and sit in my dressing room after the show and then we'd go out and party. We really hit it off and ended up presenting Channel 4's *The Big Breakfast* together. I was really flattered because he'd told them he didn't want to do it without me. He'd often tell me that he didn't quite know what to do with his life. He was thinking about trying to make it as a solo artist, but was nervous because so many singers disappear into oblivion when their bands break up. Even just chatting in the dressing room I could see he'd got star quality. He could so easily have done a game show or musical theatre. Thankfully he chose a different route; it meant there was one less talented person I'd have to compete with!

After yet another a drunken night out with Robbie I was making my way past the Dominion Theatre when I noticed that the illuminated names outside the theatre had been tampered with. It normally said, in huge neon letters: 'GREASE STARRING SHANE RICHIE AND SAM JANUS', but someone had smashed the S H A N E R and the S A M J. it now read 'GREASE STARRING ICHIE ANUS'. The Dominion staff weren't too impressed but it had me in stitches. Good on you, whoever did that.

By July *Lucky Numbers* was on its second series and a great success, when Granada Television contacted me to say they'd come up with a new idea that hadn't been done before. The idea was that they would get three couples who were already engaged to compete to win a wedding on television. They hadn't decided on a name at this stage but there were various contenders: The Wedding Show, The Wedding Game, Let's Get Married, Always and Forever, The Love Game.

The show was something new. It was colourful, it was loud, it was brash, it was variety. I'd ask a series of cheeky questions: 'What part of your body does your boyfriend consider your best feature?' 'What's the most unusual place that you and your partner have engaged in making whoopee?' Then there'd be games. In one the women dressed as jockeys sitting astride a giant mechanical hen, which fired out eggs that their partners, dressed as stags, had to catch in their antlers. I dressed up as Elvis and sang with a choir of Elvis lookalikes and the finale featured a game called 'Down The Aisle', in which the would-be bride took a step down a staircase every time her other half got an answer right. It was like *TGI Friday* meets *House Party* meets *Lucky Numbers* meets *An Audience With…* and I was really excited about doing it.

The only thing now was to come up with a title. And yes, I'll hold my hands up, it was my idea to put my name in there. When they said it was meant to be a bit of an experience and not just a game show it came to me straightaway – *The Shane Richie Experience*. Why not? I was now a big star in *Grease*, I was Mr Daz man and I was the host of *Lucky Numbers*. Polygram Records had even given me more than £100,000 to make my own album, which we called *Shane Richie: The Album*. There's imagination run wild. It was basically an album of cover songs from the 1970s and 1980s, with a few originals thrown in. My career was on the up. I couldn't put a foot wrong, or so I thought…

The pilot show was screened on 26 August and more than eight million tuned in. The figures were great, but we were ripped to pieces in the press. *The Sun* called the show 'awesomely tacky, tasteless and smutty', while the *Daily Mail* described it as 'an insult to the institution of marriage.' The opening paragraph of a two-page diatribe began: 'Deep within the recesses of Granada, once one of Britain's proudest ITV companies, a highly-paid team of executives is working on a £1m series which marks a depressing nadir, even by the often-lamentable standards of light entertainment.' Newspaper letters pages were filled with complaints and even the Church of England joined in. Everyone seemed to hate it.

I was shocked, but not too worried, because everything else seemed to be going so well. So well that I'd just been nominated for Most Popular Entertainment Presenter in the National Television Awards alongside Michael Barrymore, Noel Edmonds and Chris Evans. These were the biggest names in showbusiness and my name was up there with them.

What's more, ITV still believed in me and in the show. The BBC approached me, but ITV were so keen to hang on to me that in September they offered me a new two-year contract. It would involve a third series of *Lucky Numbers*, my own sitcom and would kick off with an eight-episode series of *The Shane Richie Experience* to be screened the following year.

I sat down with Mike Dixon, the show's musical director, who I'd also worked with on *Grease*, and we drew up a wish list of people we'd like to appear as guest stars. We quickly signed up pop bands such as Eternal and Boyzone, but we also managed to pull in big names such as The Beach Boys, Lulu and Status Quo, who I got to sing with. The highlight for me, though, was persuading The Osmonds to re-group. For the first time in 15 years the Osmonds would appear on British television and it was going to be on my show. It was a childhood dream come true. Alan, Merrill, Wayne and Jay flew over – sadly Donny and Jimmy couldn't make it. The guys already knew I was a fan because whenever I got the chance in interviews I'd talk about them. People would laugh at me, because The Osmonds weren't very credible in the 1990s. What a load of old tosh – I could never understand the credibility thing; I just liked them. They appeared on the show in dinner suits and Granada made me a Donny outfit – a white jumpsuit and a flat cap. The guys thought it was hilarious. I came on and sang 'Puppy Love' and then I got to sing 'One Bad Apple' with them.

At the same time as filming *The Shane Richie Experience* I began to look at scripts for potential drama and comedy series. I read for a sitcom called *Thicker Than Water* and there was even talk of a new comedy drama series called *Cold Feet*. Everything seemed to be ticking along nicely.

In October word went round that *This is Your Life* was about to do a hit on a TV personality currently appearing in the West End. Well, of course that was me. Once I found out I noticed strange things starting to happen. All of a sudden I discovered that my old friend Paul Wagner was coming over from Jersey for the weekend. I hadn't seen Micky Zany for a while – he'd been on tour – and he was going to be around too. Goz seemed to be acting very suspiciously and as if to confirm it, when I phoned to speak to Coleen just before I went on stage, there was nobody home. This was it. Michael Aspel was going to get me with the big red book. I was made up. After all, it's one of the two big accolades isn't it? If you're on *Parkinson* or *This is Your Life*, you've made it.

The show ended, I took the last bow, threw my comb into the audience and started to look round into the wings. This was it; Michael

Aspel was coming to get me. I stood there just a little bit longer than normal. Right, here we go. Mike Dixon caught my eye and stared as if to say, 'Come on, Shane, get off stage, we're going to be here all night.' Eventually I walked off. Perhaps he'd been held up. To give him another chance I walked back out again. More bows, more applause, but still no Michael.

OK, he wasn't going to get me on stage, perhaps he was going to surprise me later when I got out of the lift and headed to my dressing room. I got in the lift barely able to contain my excitement. The doors opened…deadly quiet. Right, Michael Aspel is going to be behind the door of my dressing room. I composed myself. Here it comes, here it comes…I tiptoed in. The room was empty. I sat down, puzzled. Where was everybody? Perhaps Michael was going to get me when I left the theatre. Perhaps that was it. At that point Goz came running in. 'Shane, quick, we've been invited to a party. *This is Your Life* have just done Brian Conley, on stage in *Jolson* down the road.' Did I feel a prat, or what?

It was around this time that I got a rude awakening as to the effect fame and money can have on those around you. In October of 1995 I got a shock opening the *Daily Mirror* one day and seeing a big double-page spread interview with my brother Dean. He'd talked about our tough childhood and posed for pictures next to my poster outside the Dominion Theatre. I was hurt because he'd never warned me and it caused a few problems between us at the time. Today we get on fine – I'll always be his big brother, that will never change. Our lives just took different paths. I'd left home when I was 15 and Dean was 11. Whenever I rang home from Pontins I'd always ask my mum how he was and he was usually in trouble with school or the police. At one time he was even threatened with borstal. Dean always had a great singing voice, but you can't treat showbusiness as a hobby. You have to give it 100 per cent. It takes discipline to handle rejection and then hold your head up high and try again; maybe that's something Deano just couldn't handle. But he had nobody to guide him and to tell him right from wrong. I should have been there for him and the fact that I let him down is something I have to live with.

1996 kicked off with the launch of *The Shane Richie Experience*. The first show went out in March and pulled in ratings of 7.5 million, but within a month it was down to 5.7 million. If you get those figures now you've got a hit on your hands, but in the mid-1990s it was death. I'd read the papers every week and I'd be ripped to sheds. Everyone seemed to hate it and my name was in the title – boy, did I make a mistake there.

There's been a lot of debate about what went wrong. Looking back I guess some of the games were too tacky. We had one in which the grooms had to stick their bums through a hole and the brides had to walk along the line feeling the bums and guess which was their partner. The show was probably too busy as well. There were too many fancy camera shots; it was like watching MTV. That's fine for a certain audience but not for prime-time Saturday night TV. Perhaps it would have worked better as a straightforward variety show without the marriage element. Who knows?

I was gutted by the reaction, but at the same time I simply assumed I'd survive it. After all, I'd had a phenomenal couple of years. *Lucky Numbers* had been commissioned for a third series and *Grease* was still going strong. I was Shane Richie, singer, actor, and TV presenter. Why would I imagine that the next two years would be any different? How naïve was I?

CHAPTER 13

'Would you like some Pringles, Mr Richie?'

Sometimes in your life you make a decision that on the surface seems so obvious that you hardly give it a second thought. It's only afterwards that you realise that seemingly straightforward decision has ended up wrecking your life.

My simple decision was this: after three years in *Grease*, I was finally going to call it a day. I'd proved to the country and to myself I could sing and dance and by now I was hosting Friday and Saturday night television shows, so it seemed a good time to hang up my leather jacket when *Grease* decided to open another production in Manchester in January 1996. If only I'd stuck to my guns.

Instead the producers came back in the April and made me an offer I couldn't refuse. My salary would be increased from £10,000 to £20,000, plus I would be guaranteed a split of the box office profits and the merchandise deals. I sat down with Coleen and it was a decision we made together – she agreed that with that sort of money on offer I should go to Manchester with the show. We didn't want to disrupt the boys' lives and education, so we decided that Coleen would stay at home in Hillingdon and I would rent a place with Goz in Manchester for the summer of 1996. It would only be for five months and then we'd be back together again, a great deal richer.

I headed up North with Goz a couple of weeks before the show opened to look for somewhere to live, as I didn't fancy being in a hotel for all that time, and we ended up finding a remote olde worlde farm-house out in Cheshire. As soon as I saw the place I knew we had to have it. It was stunning, with six bedrooms, all mod cons and a heated indoor swimming pool, done out with Roman pillars. But what really won me over was walking into the master bedroom. There was a big heart-shaped bed and when you pressed a button a television came out of the ceiling. It had party written all over it.

The problem was that by now I was beginning to believe my own publicity. I thought I was invincible. *The Shane Richie Experience* had been panned, but that just seemed like a hiccup. *Lucky Numbers* was still successful, I was still on TV most nights with the Daz ads and with *Grease* I could do no wrong.

The show had been big in the West End, but in London there were lots of other big shows and big names. In Manchester it was just *Grease*, Manchester United and *Coronation Street*. Corrie had a cast of 40, Manchester United had a team of 11, oh sorry, 12 – of course there's the guvnor, Sir Alex. With *Grease* there was just me. Of course now I realise how fickle and shallow fame can be, but at the time I lapped it up and was soon wrapped up in the whole rock star lifestyle.

Within weeks of arriving in town I went along to a car showroom in the centre of Manchester wearing sunglasses and a bandana – the whole celebrity bit – to test drive a Ferrari. I decided I didn't like it and went along to another showroom to see the new M3 Evolution. I walked in and the guy didn't recognise me.

'Hi, I'm interested in buying the M3 Evolution.' The guy took one look at me dressed in dirty trainers, tracksuit bottoms and a scruffy t-shirt and didn't even bother to get up.

'Yes sir, of course you are.'

'Well, how much is it?'

'£43,000.'

'How much for cash?'

I remember him yawning at me as if I was wasting his time.

'£40,000.'

'Right,' I said and walked out.

I went back the next day and walked in and put down £40,000 in cash on his desk in front of him. Well, you can imagine the difference. The champagne glasses came out. 'Would you like some Pringles, Mr Richie?' They couldn't do enough for me.

Within weeks *Grease* was so big that you couldn't get tickets and people that I considered to be big stars were desperate to meet me. I'd been a big Manchester United fan since I was a boy, yet I'd get a message that Sir Alex Ferguson wanted to have a chat after the show and I'd say casually, 'Yes, in a minute, I've just got to get changed.' David Beckham was such a big fan that he would come to see the show at least once every ten days and he'd bring somebody different with him every time. It might be a member of his family, or Nicky Butt and Paul Scholes or Giggsy and Giggsy's mum. He'd come to see me backstage and get autographs for his friends. He was a huge star in Manchester, but I don't think the England career had quite kicked in then and he was dead shy.

I remember once asking him to call Shane Jr at home to wish him Happy Birthday. He pulled out his mobile and dialled the number.

'Hello Shane, it's David Beckham here.'

'Dad, stop winding me up, is that you?'

I grabbed the phone from Becks.

'No Shane, it really is David Beckham, he's ringing to wish you Happy Birthday.'

I gave the phone back to David and he proceeded to sing 'Happy Birthday' down the phone to Shane, with me and half the *Grease* cast joining in in the background. Years later I was at a movie premiere with my boys and David saw us and went straight up to Shane and asked him if he remembered it. He was great with my boys and I'll always be grateful to him for that.

But it wasn't just Manchester United that followed the show. All the teams in the North seemed to – Liverpool, Manchester City, Newcastle United and the rest. Stars from *Emmerdale* were always in the audience and half the *Coronation Street* cast were regulars. I remember Tracy Shaw had only just started on the Street; she didn't know many people and she latched onto the show big time. I'd come off stage sometimes and she'd be sitting in my dressing room. She was a shy little girl who seemed to have lost her way and she'd sit and pour her heart out. I think she liked my flippant, carefree attitude to the whole business. She found it difficult handling the attention, whereas I took it head on.

By now I was living the rock and roll lifestyle to the limit and if I ever announced we were going out to a nightclub we'd get a police escort. There was one particular Wednesday in the school holidays after a matinee where the police had to redirect traffic around Manchester city centre because 2,000 screaming 14-year-olds were going mad outside. Police cars with sirens turned up and officers had to come into the theatre and take me out.

Meanwhile there were parties almost every night. I was constantly surrounded by beautiful women who all wanted a piece of Danny Zuko. *Grease* was about rock and roll sex and when the curtain came down the show carried on. There's not a bloke alive who wouldn't be affected by that. I defy anyone not to let it go to their head.

It was only a matter of time before I was out of control. Claire was a dancer in *Grease*. Her name at that time was Louise St Claire, which on my advice she later changed to Claire Tyler. She was 22 at the time and I was 32. She was a small, petite, pretty girl, but what made her different from all the other girls in the show was that she wasn't sycophantic. The whole Shane Richie thing didn't blow her away and that was a great attraction. She'd been away working on cruise ships for quite a while and she maintains to this day that she didn't know who I was, or that I was married. It was probably just her way of trying to justify an affair with a married man to herself, but I believed her.

Once I'd decided I wanted her I went out of my way to impress her. Claire had never been in a limo before; she'd never been in a top class restaurant before. Shops in Manchester would stay open until 11 o'clock at night so I could shop after the show and restaurants would close so I could take a party from *Grease* there. Claire loved all that and I loved doing it for her.

We finally got together at a big party I threw for the cast. I'd invited all my mates from London, but I spent the whole night talking to Claire. After downing several bottles of champagne we ended up in bed together, but nothing happened. She was adamant that she wasn't going to be another notch on the bedpost. As the weeks passed I found myself spending more and more time with her – we were soon an open secret amongst the cast. Claire would end up staying at the farmhouse two or three nights a week. I'd ask her to stay other nights, but she'd say she had something else on. I think it was all to keep me interested and it worked, because the nights she didn't stay I'd miss her. Friends, and in particular Goz, started to warn me that I was getting in too deep, but I never agreed. I convinced myself I wasn't emotionally involved. Who was I kidding?

I'd have told Claire anything to keep her happy. I've spoken to other blokes who've had affairs and they've done the same thing. I think blokes can lie quite easily. Everyone says it's just because I'm an actor, but no, it's because I'm a bloke. The strange thing was that although it went on for months it never felt like an affair. There were loads of other mates doing it and it was as if it was part of the job; this was what came with showbusiness. It was arrogant, I know, but it almost felt like it was my God-given right: you're Shane Richie, you can walk on water. What a prat I was.

There were times when Coleen would call me at the farmhouse for a chat while I was in bed with Claire. I'd get up, walk out of the room to talk to Coleen and tell her that I loved her; and I did. Sometimes though I would concoct a row just to ease my guilt. I was drinking quite a bit by now, which gave me that extra bit of bravado.

Coleen would say: 'What are you up to?'

'Nothing,' I'd reply.

'What? Nothing at all?'

'Are you calling me a liar?' I'd shout and then slam the phone down. It was a horrible thing to do but it made me feel better about the terrible way I was behaving.

In August Coleen and I had our marriage blessed in Blackpool. It was something we'd agreed to do for the sake of her dad, who wasn't well at the time. None of our parents had been at our wedding in Florida and this was our way of making it up to them all. For her dad it was the opportunity to give her away in a white dress. Family and friends travelled from all over the country to share the special day with us. Everyone thought we were the perfect happy couple – and before Manchester we were – but Coleen sensed there was something wrong. She couldn't put her finger on it, but of course I knew exactly what it was. I was in too deep with Claire and my life was starting to spiral out of control.

Grease was due to finish in September, but the box office was doing so well that they extended our contracts until January 1997. I discussed it with Coleen and she asked me to turn it down, which wasn't like her. When I insisted on going back she was immediately suspicious and kept asking if there was something wrong. Of course there wasn't, I lied. I headed back to Manchester and during the following months my visits to London grew less and less frequent. Goz by now had realised how serious things were becoming with Claire and he tried to make me go home, but I'd always make an excuse. That's when it started to get dangerous. The lying really started and I'd get mates to cover up for me.

Once I told Coleen I couldn't come home on my day off because I was doing a charity go-karting event – I spent the day with Claire. Another time I made an excuse to Coleen and went to meet Claire's family.

I think by now Claire was in love. I wasn't sure how I felt but I started to fall into that trap that blokes do when they feel cornered and I began to lie even more. I'd tell Claire that things weren't going well at home, that Coleen didn't understand me, she'd put on weight, sex wasn't great between us, she didn't love me the way she used to. Of course these were all lies. I had no intention of leaving Coleen, but I still wanted Claire and I'd say whatever it took.

When Christmas came I went home for a few days and acted as if everything was normal. I'd only been home a couple of days when Coleen opened a letter as we sat at the breakfast table. I could see instantly from the shock on her face that something was seriously wrong. Without speaking she handed it over to me. It was anonymous and said that I had been having an affair with one of the dancers from *Grease* and that the affair was still continuing. There was a photograph of Claire enclosed and the letter finished, 'Enjoy Christmas – it will be the last one you have as a family.' Without hesitation I ripped it up and threw it straight in the bin. 'Surely to God you're not going to believe that? It's just some spiteful hate mail,' I snorted. I strode out of the kitchen with as much confidence as I could muster and acted as if nothing had happened for the rest of the day.

Coleen seemed to believe me, and the rest of the Christmas holiday passed without incident, but we weren't together for long because by New Year's Eve I was back in Manchester throwing yet another party at the Victoria and Albert Hotel. I turned up with the *Grease* crowd and when we got there we discovered *Coronation Street* were having a party there too. *Grease* always had the best parties – of course we did, we had the best singers and the best dancers – and the Corrie crowd were leaving their party to come and drink with us. Footballers were popping in and out – it was one of those nights, a bit of a free-for-all.

Anyone who was anyone was there and I had a great night, chatting to everyone, talking about showbusiness and getting more and more drunk. I ended up getting so smashed that I was put to bed in one of the suites at the hotel. Now as anyone who has stayed at the Victoria and Albert will know, all the rooms there are named after various television programmes. Of course I was too drunk to read the name on the door of my room and simply collapsed into my bed fully clothed. When I woke up the next day on the first morning of 1997 I was convinced I'd died and gone to hell. Staring down from every wall were dozens of pictures of me grinning madly. They'd only gone and put me in the bloody *Shane Richie Experience* suite.

By now *Grease* was developing a cult following and fans would come from all over Europe to see the show. Not only that, but many of them would go to extreme lengths to meet me. It happened once after I'd been forced to go on stage when I was feeling really ill. It was a day when I'd been out for lunch with Tracy Shaw. We'd come back and were sitting in my dressing room and she kept going off to be sick, so it was pretty obvious something she'd eaten had upset her stomach. Soon after I started to feel ill myself.

'Mr Richie, Act One, beginner's call.'

It was too late to tell anyone. I took my position on the balcony 15ft feet up and the music struck up. Screams filled the theatre and the lights were on me, when all of a sudden the room started to spin. I started to make my way down the ladder and then my legs went. The next thing I knew I was being picked up and carried across the stage to the dressing room. All around me were frantic shouts to close the curtains and an urgent announcement was put out across the Tannoy: 'Ladies and gentlemen, unfortunately there has been a slight hitch in the proceedings, is there a doctor or nurse in the house?'

I came round in my dressing room with a pretty girl standing by my side. She'd come backstage after the announcement and she sent somebody out to get me a glass of water. She said I was very hot and told me to take off my jacket and shirt and undo my trousers. She then proceeded to mop my brow.

'Who's she?' I said to Goz weakly.

'Oh, they called out for a nurse, she's a nurse,' he explained. The girl looked puzzled.

'No I'm not, I was in t'audience. Me name's Susan, but you can call me Sue. I've come all the way from Barnsley to see you. Can you sign me programme?'

When I finished in *Grease* at the end of January 1997 Ian Kelsey picked up the T-Bird jacket and took over. I found it difficult to say goodbye to Claire. Goz had been right, I was now in too deep – I was in love with her. *Grease* went from Manchester to Birmingham and Claire went with it, while I went back home to Coleen. I assumed that once I got home I'd get Claire out of my system and things would gradually get back to normal, but of course because I'd been away for so long, Coleen had found a whole new set of friends. Meanwhile I'd made a new bunch of mates in Manchester and I missed them and the lifestyle I'd had with the show.

Perhaps to distract ourselves from the growing gulf between us, we threw ourselves into a new project – buying a new house. For months we'd been getting all sorts sitting outside the house from morning until night. They'd scrawl graffiti on the wall and shout to my boys that they knew who their dad was – we began to get a bit worried for their safety. People would follow me home and the paparazzi would hang around in the street. We decided to look for somewhere more private.

We very quickly found the perfect spot. It was a large six-bedroom mock Tudor house, built from two barns that had been knocked

Craig and me tearing it up in *Grease*.

Samantha Janus was the perfect Sandy.
No two shows were ever the same. Bloody
beautiful!!! She ain't bad, either (joke!).

Me and Debbie Gibson trying out
costumes for *Grease* months
before we opened.

Me, Jake and the T-Birds in my dressing
room, Dominion Theatre. Jake knew the words
to 'Summer Nights' long before he could
say "Daddy".

After three years
of *Boogie Nights*,
I was finally having
enough…

Lisa Maxwell and me
at the launch of *Boogie
Nights* in the West End.
In Trafalgar 'Bloody'
Square, with bird shit
everywhere.

Me and Jake on stage in *Boogie Nights*. He knew every word,
every song and every move. In fact, he knew them better than me!

Goz, Spud and me on a balcony in Cannes on our way to the Monaco Grand Prix. (Spud could never resist my charms!) Oh, and check out the tattoo…

Claire deserved better than someone like me. I was unhappy and angry. She was beautiful.

For a while I refused to wear a smart suit whilst appearing at Butlins…

Me and my Dad. We now finally understand each other.

Me and Coleen on a rare night out without the boys.

Me and my Mum. She would occasionally turn up and surprise me while I was on tour!

The only photo of us all together; Mum, Ricky, me, Dean and Dad. Things could've been so different.

In *Jack and the Beanstalk*. This is what Christie saw on our second meeting. C'mon who could refuse that?

Finally making it to Santa Monica – not sure about going home though!

Me and Goz share a moment on the road from San Francisco to LA.

With my new family in Albert Square. Alfie, Nana Moon and Spencer.

With Phil Dale, my mate and manager.

Me and my girl Christie. My rock, my love. I adore and love her.
I love being in love!

39, slightly overweight,
divorced with two kids:
'Soap's Sexiest Male' –
lovely jubbly!
My boys now have this
award in their bedroom
back home in Blackpool.

Me and Joely Richardson in the movie, *Shoreditch*.
I poured my heart and soul into this project. Oh yeah,
and the best part of £700,000 and for what?
I don't know yet.

When I'm with my boys nothing else matters. I have these pictures and many more on my wall in my dressing room at *EastEnders*, coz wherever my life takes me they will be there, always and forever. I love them so much.

together. Nobody had lived in it before; the builder was planning to live in it himself and then decided to sell it. It was on ten acres of land in a quiet spot in Buckinghamshire. The asking price was just under £1million. The money I had from the Daz ad would be a down payment, we sold the house in Orlando to raise more funds and we could get a mortgage for the rest of it. Coleen loved it, I wasn't so sure, but I thought It would be a good investment and we went ahead. It was probably the one and only sensible investment I ever made.

The house was called Hedgerows Farm, but I wanted to call it something different. Something that people would remember. How about this? Fir Kew Hall. Geddit? Fir Kew Hall – say it faster. Genius! Shame the council didn't feel the same way, or the teachers at the boys' school. The local council sent me a letter within weeks. 'We appreciate your sense of humour, Mr Richie, and it's given our staff some amusement here at the offices, but we would appreciate it if you could re-name your property.'

But I wasn't just spending on the house. I was still regularly going out shopping and coming back with a new car, and once I came home with a horse and two ponies for Coleen and the boys. The plan was that we'd put them in the fields next to the house. Of course none of us had time to look after them, so we moved them to a stable three miles down the road. I don't think we ever saw them again. We ended up giving them to a disabled riding school.

Sometimes you make decisions for the wrong reasons. I'd become friends with Tony Lambrianou, an associate of the Krays, and he invited me to go to see a play in Hornchurch, Essex. It was called *Inside the Firm* and it was all about his time in prison. I really enjoyed it and at the end he told me they were looking for someone to take over the lead. I really wanted to develop my acting and with hindsight I should have done it. Instead I turned it down, did some more Daz ads and went back into *Grease* – all purely for the money.

Grease re-opened on 7 April at the Cambridge Theatre in the West End and finished in July but after that I found I had nothing to do. I was in heaven being with my boys again, but when they were at school I found myself sitting in front of the television, having endless boring meetings or pushing a trolley round the supermarket. It was all a bit of an anti-climax after the buzz of Manchester. I felt like Joe Nobody.

To make myself feel better I'd disappear for two or three days to spend time with Claire, telling Coleen that I'd got a gig. When Claire had finished in Birmingham she'd moved to London and I'd started seeing her every week. I was still in love with Coleen, but at the same time I'd lie to Claire and tell her my wife and I were in separate bedrooms. I wanted my home life with Coleen and my boys, but I was addicted to this other lifestyle I'd had. Although I couldn't see it at the time my life was slowly starting to descend into chaos.

CHAPTER FOURTEEN

'Shane, she knows'

If my private life was in turmoil at that point, professionally I was dead in the water. Granada had followed up *The Shane Richie Experience* with a spin-off called *Love Me Do*. They changed the title, changed the format, and got rid of the dancing and the game show element. It went out in June 1997. I don't suppose anyone remembers it much today. More people were watching *Countdown*. I never felt very comfortable with it. I was on television, promoting monogamy and there I was slap-bang in the middle of an affair. I had to do it – I was still under contract to Granada, but it was never my sort of show and was more suited to somebody like Cilla or Dale.

When it ended Granada didn't know what to do with me. No one wanted to take the blame for *The Shane Richie Experience* and I ended up carrying the can. I can look back and laugh about it now and in many ways I'm still proud of what it achieved. I like to think we pushed back parameters, but people just weren't ready for it in the mid-1990s. Granada told me they were having a major shake-up and my contract was finished. I'd been hung out to dry. Stan was always positive and was forever telling me not to worry, that we'd find something, but I believed my television career was over. I knew that you were only as good as your last TV show and that all the work I'd done in the past meant nothing.

All of a sudden nobody wanted to know me. Just a year earlier I'd been a huge star, always surrounded by a crowd of friends and hangers-on, and now I'd go to awards ceremonies and friends I'd known for years who were also in the business would dig each other in the ribs and look embarrassed when they saw me. I was only 32 and I'd spent the last 15 years slogging my guts out and it seemed like it was all for nothing. Nobody would even have me on their chat shows. I was a has-been. I'd even started to appear in newspaper 'Where Are They Now?' columns.

At the same time I parted company with International Artists. Stan was moving to a new company called AMG, who later changed their name to Qdos. I always said that if Stan worked out of a potting-shed in the middle of a turnip field I'd have gone with him. Stan said it was a fresh start and I realised he was right. I needed to re-invent myself.

It was then that *Boogie Nights* was born. Jon Conway was one of the guys in charge at my new agency and together we came up with the idea of a play called *Tank Tops and Tarts*, loosely based on my childhood. It would be about adolescence and growing up on a council estate in the 1970s and would examine father/son relationships, mixed-race relationships and teenage pregnancy. The two main characters were Roddy O'Neil and Debs. Debs was based on Lisa Cross, my first teenage love, while Roddy's dad Eamon was based on my dad; he was a big Elvis fan and he liked a drink. I remembered what I was told by Barry Williams back in the Pontins days – always talk about what you know.

We wrote it in the basement of my house along with a good friend of mine, a writer called Terry Morrison. Terry had worked with me on *Run the Risk*, *Lucky Numbers* and *The Shane Richie Experience*. He bore the brunt of the fall-out from Granada with me and when I was dropped, he was dropped too.

We workshopped it in the house for weeks on end, with myself, the actress Lisa Maxwell and the actor Steve Serlin, both of whom I knew from *Grease*, and a comic called Peter Piper, who was an old friend of mine. Then we realised that if we put in a few 1970s songs we could actually make something of it. We'd decided by now that *Tank Tops and Tarts* was too much of a mouthful so we played around with other titles – Boogie Wonderland, Nights on the Boogie and Saturday Night Fever, but apparently that had already been done. I actually argued against *Boogie Nights* because I knew there was a film about the porn industry about to be released with the same name and I didn't want there to be any confusion, but I was out-voted, so *Boogie Nights* it was.

Boogie Nights premiered at the Churchill Theatre in Bromley in November 1997. We'd planned to have a two-week run there before a national tour. The show was my baby. I'd sweated over it. I'd co-written it, I was starring in it and I was co-producing it, with Jon and Qdos. The last person who'd done that was Noel Coward. I was kind of proud, but no one ever picked up on it, they just thought, 'Oh, it's only that Shane Richie bloke.'

On the opening night I laid on a car to pick up Coleen, my boys, my folks and my Aunty Mary. It meant a lot to have them there. My mum was one of the few people who'd stuck by me during the wedding show. She'd always say, 'Jayzus Shane, don't you be worrying about it, der'll be something else.' My Aunty Mary had been having treatment for breast cancer so I was glad she could come. Unfortunately my dad wasn't well either, so it was a rare outing for him. He was still having problems with his liver and kidneys. He'd been put on dialysis three times a week and it was knocking the stuffing out of him. All of a sudden I saw this big, strong man turn frail and old, with very little to say because he couldn't drink anymore.

After the show my mum and Aunty Mary were due to come down to my dressing room for a drink, but my mum appeared on her own and told me that my Aunty Mary wasn't feeling well. She was at the top of the stairs outside my dressing room and she couldn't breathe. I went out and as I got to the top of the stairs my aunty started crying. She started to panic, but told us not to make a fuss. We could tell this was something serious and my mum called an ambulance. I organised a car to take us all to the hospital and we had two anxious hours until a doctor finally came out and told us that she was alright and was resting. Goz drove my mum and dad home and I stayed at the hospital so that she would have someone there when she woke up. At four in the morning a nurse came out and found me asleep in the waiting room. She gently shook me awake.

'Mr Richie, I'm really sad to tell you that your aunty has passed away.'

I was broken-hearted. One of my own family had gone. I stood up in a daze trying to hold back the tears and set off to find a phone to break the terrible news to my mum. As I walked out I just happened to glance through the double doors to my right and saw my aunty lying there. She had a peaceful look on her face, which I'll never forget to this day. *Boogie Nights* was never the same for me after that. In my mind every show was dedicated to her and every time I sang 'Sorry Seems To Be The Hardest Word' I thought of her.

When I was a child it was my aunty who held my hand when I was scared, it was my aunty who made excuses to my dad when I wanted to wear make-up and it was my aunty who defended me when I went off to work on a holiday camp. To this day I miss her with all my heart and I still keep her ashes in the house. My friends are bemused by it but my theory is that by keeping her ashes there we're encouraged to talk about her and that way her memory lives on.

That Christmas Coleen and I organised a trip to Lapland. It was probably the most magical family holiday we ever had. We called it 'The Search for Santa' and for five days me, Coleen and the boys hunted for him – on sledges, on skis, on skidoos, by reindeer and snowmobile. On the final day we found him. For those five days I believed in something I'd never been able to believe in as a kid. I believed in Santa Claus. I believed in the magic.

By the end of 1997, Stan was getting very uneasy about my affair with Claire and was urging me to end it. In Manchester it had seemed so easy to hide, but now it was happening in London he was terrified the papers would get wind of it. And it wasn't just the papers. Coleen was more suspicious than ever after finding a receipt for a Gucci watch. She accused me of buying it for a girlfriend, which wasn't true. The receipt was for a watch that Goz had bought his girlfriend, but Coleen wasn't that far away from discovering the truth, because on the same day in the same shop I had a bought a watch for Claire. I'd got out of it by the skin of my teeth, but I should have guessed that a showdown wasn't that far away.

It came at the end of January 1998 after I was booked to appear in a variety show for a big corporation in Crete. I fell sick with food poisoning while I was there and was rushed to hospital. I asked Goz to call Coleen and let her know what had happened. When he came back to my bedside he was ashen.

'Shane, she knows,' he said. I knew instantly what he meant.

That Christmas I'd bought Coleen a computer and what neither of us knew, because we weren't very computer-minded, was that it had an answering machine built in, so as a result it was picking up and taping every call. While I was away, Coleen eventually worked this out and went through all the calls to see if she'd missed any messages. One of the calls it had taped was me talking to Claire.

'Hello darlin', what time do you get off stage? OK, I'll call you back. I love you. Bye.'

The other was me talking to my mate Paul Spong, better known as Spongo. He was a musician who I'd met back in 1982 at Little Canada and we'd been mates ever since. I'd confided in him about my affair with Claire and in the taped call I could be heard telling him that I really wanted to see Claire, but that she was going out with friends and that I was planning to call her later because I was really missing her.

I didn't dare phone home. The next morning I was due to be discharged from hospital and was flying back anyway. However hard it would be, this was something I had to deal with face to face. When I walked in the door the boys were still up and Coleen was calm as if nothing had happened. That evening, after they went to bed, I poured us both a glass of wine and we sat down.

'What do you want to do?' I asked nervously.

'I don't know yet,' Coleen answered.

I'd been afraid that Coleen would throw me out without a chance to explain, but suddenly I saw that I still had a chance to talk my way out of it.

'Let's sort this out, it's not an affair, Coleen, it's just one of the dancers and it doesn't mean a thing,' I begged. Coleen believed me and I think I believed it myself. When she suggested that we go for marriage counselling I happily agreed.

We had an initial honeymoon period when I was at home, but once I went back on tour with *Boogie Nights* in March the problems started. Coleen couldn't trust me and she'd constantly check up on me, asking where I was and when I was next going to ring. On top of that I became convinced that it wouldn't now take much for Coleen to have an affair herself. Why shouldn't she? I'd done it. I couldn't understand how she could be so forgiving.

To make matters worse I wasn't over Claire. Although I'd planned to end it with her I'd never actually gone through with it. In desperation I'd get friends to cover for me as I sneaked off to see her again and again. I'd go to extraordinary lengths to cover my tracks. I remember Coleen once asked me what I was doing at the weekend and I told her I was going go-karting in Belgium. What made me say that? To this day I've no idea. The next day I went to a travel agent and picked up a brochure of Belgian hotels and left it in my bag. That way if Coleen ever checked she'd see it and think I really had been.

As hard as I was trying to cover my tracks I was also making plenty of careless mistakes. I'd buy gifts for Claire on a joint credit card – I bought her a ring, a Lladro porcelain figure and I was forever sending her flowers. Of course Coleen was reading these statements every month and she sussed exactly what I was up to. Did I want to be caught? I'm not sure. I think the problem was that I was lying so much that I couldn't remember which story I'd told to each of them. And I'd lie to cover up the lies.

It just wasn't working and in early June 1998 I moved out to a rented flat in Pimlico, central London. I'd told Coleen it was a vile bedsit with a mattress on the floor and that I needed time on my own to clear my head so we could sort things out. It wasn't the truth. It was actually a nice flat and Claire spent a lot of time there, but I couldn't let Coleen know that. I suppose a part of me wanted to see if it would work with Claire if I got out of Coleen's life, but equally I needed space to sort myself out.

One sad consequence of our break-up was that we had to abandon our plans to adopt a child from abroad. After our first failed attempt two years previously we'd contacted a charity, The Children's Society. They'd sent us all the forms and we were at the stage of filling them out when Coleen found out what I'd been up to.

It didn't take the press long to discover what had happened. On 16

June the story broke. Under the headline 'Shane and Wife Split After 8 Years' the story blamed the pressures of work. The hardest part was breaking the news to the boys. They were so used to me being away touring that we hadn't needed to explain that I'd moved out, but if the story was in the papers then friends at school would end up telling them, so we had no choice. Coleen took them up to the bedroom and gently explained that we'd grown apart and had decided to separate for a while. Shane Jr, who was nine at the time, went hysterical, screamed the room down and then curled up into a foetal position sobbing uncontrollably for 20 minutes. Jake, who was four, was too young to realise what it meant, but he knew something was wrong because his brother was upset and he started to cry, too.

The following week on 21 June the *News of the World* splash was 'TV Shane Caught Cheating By Wife'. It had taken them just seven days to find out the truth about our split. They had the full story and ran it alongside a picture of Claire. I was devastated. Not so much for me, or even Coleen, but for my boys. Shane was at that age where he was reading the papers and so were his friends. I felt I'd let so many people down. That Sunday I sat down to talk to Coleen. As far as I was concerned this really marked an end to my relationship with Claire. I couldn't go backwards. I wanted to make things work with Coleen. I know I didn't deserve it, but she agreed to give me another chance and I moved back into the house. The following week she even came on tour with me. We were determined to save our marriage.

For the next couple of months I continued to tour with *Boogie Nights*. Whoever put the tour together must have needed their head testing. I'd be in Hull one week and then straight down to Southampton, from there I'd go to Liverpool, from there to Plymouth, from there to Bristol and then up to Glasgow. We were all over the place. My job was to keep it afloat and keep the publicity going, so I was away for weeks on end living in digs and for a time I didn't get to see Coleen and the boys at all. I put all my time and energy into the show to forget what had happened to me personally, and I ended up so wrapped up in the business and my own self-importance that I didn't see what I was doing to my own family. I ended up too busy to sort out my problems with Coleen; too busy to take the kids to school or even look at their homework.

At the same time I started to see Claire again. It wasn't that I didn't love Coleen, it was just that I missed the excitement of being with someone new. Coleen knew I was still talking to Claire, but she believed me when I said that we weren't seeing each other. Word was going round in the press though that I was out of control, drinking a lot and still with Claire. It was only a matter of time before I'd get caught out. In August a girl came forward and told a tabloid that I'd slept with her after appearing in *Boogie Nights* on tour. Under the headline 'Shane's Sex Shame' she claimed I'd charmed her into bed and then dumped her. 'He wants to use some of that Daz washing powder he's been advertising on himself. It's a long time since he's been whiter than white,' she complained. I don't know if it was true or not. I thought I might actually have been with Claire that night, but I couldn't be sure.

Coleen and I were sleeping in separate bedrooms at this point and that Sunday morning Coleen walked into my room and threw the paper at me. 'Not only have you cheated on me with Claire, but you're doing this now,' she shouted. She was furious, but I had to admit to sleeping with this girl. If I hadn't been with her then I'd have been with Claire and I couldn't tell Coleen that. That was how big a mess my life had become.

CHAPTER FIFTEEN

'You've let down the general public'

Although *Boogie Nights* was going from strength to strength, my personal life was crumbling around me. Coleen suspected I was still seeing Claire and Claire knew I was still sleeping with Coleen. I was lying to both of them, trying to cover my tracks. The whole thing was a mess and I was all over the place. Slowly I was turning into my dad. I was drinking heavily, I was putting on weight, I was verbally abusing people and I had no time for anyone. I started to hate myself and everything I stood for, to the extent that I couldn't even look at myself in the mirror. Drink was my only escape. I'd end up having another Jack Daniels and another late night and find myself in bed with some strange girl whose name I didn't know and couldn't be bothered to find out. Goz told me to take a look at what I was doing to myself, but I was too wrapped up in my own pain to listen. I've always hated self-indulgence in other people and yet here I was wallowing in self-pity.

Things came to a head in August 1998 when we took *Boogie Nights* to Southend. It was the last town on the tour before the show went to the West End and we'd organised a big aftershow party as a way of wishing ourselves luck. Coleen had brought my boys along to see the show and after the final curtain call they headed off to the bar for the party and I set off for my dressing room to get changed before joining them.

Before I reached it my leading lady, Lisa Maxwell, who was playing Debs at the time, ran up to warn me that Claire was in my dressing room crying. She'd turned up at the theatre during the final act and had talked her way in.

'Oh God, you're joking. Coleen's here. What am I gonna do?' I was in total panic. The only thing I could think of was to get rid of her as quickly as possible. I walked into the dressing room and, sure enough, there was Claire, sobbing her heart out.

'What's the matter?' I asked, taking a deep breath.

'You know what's the matter,' she screamed. 'You've been seeing someone else.'

I couldn't deny it. I'd had several drunken, meaningless one-night stands during my tour with *Boogie Nights*. One night in Liverpool I'd even woken up to find two rucksacks at the side of the bed. Next to me were two naked girls. Apparently they were backpackers who'd been to see the show the night before and decided to pull me. Typically I couldn't remember anything about it.

Now Claire had found out about one of these nights. When I admitted it, she completely lost control. She jumped to her feet screaming and crying and took a swing at me, which caught me full in the mouth. I couldn't blame her. Then she threatened to go and find Coleen and tell her what had happened. I knew I had to calm her down and persuade her to go home. Her mum had driven her down to Southend and was waiting in the car. Wouldn't it be better if she just went straight outside and went home again? After 15 minutes of pleading with her, she eventually agreed.

I slumped into the chair in my dressing room and breathed a huge sigh of relief. But it wasn't over. As I started to change out of my stage clothes, Coleen appeared at the door.

'Is there anything you want to tell me?' she asked.

'What? No,' I lied.

'Have I just seen Claire?'

'No.'

'Don't lie to me. Please don't lie to me, Shane,' Coleen begged. The strange thing was that she'd never met Claire, but when she saw this girl dashing past her in the corridor she just knew who it was; it must have been sixth sense.

'OK, you're right,' I admitted. 'But it's not what you think.'

I told her that Claire had been in, but that we'd had a huge row and I'd ended it for good between us. *Boogie Nights* was transferring to the West End in October, which meant an end to touring. I'd be home every night and this was going to be a brand new start for us. We went to the party together, both feeling very shaken and Stan came over and sat with us. We'd always been close and I told him what had just happened.

'I need to change,' I told them both. 'I'm sorry for what I've done and it's time to move on.' And at the time I really meant it. I could see the hurt I'd caused both Coleen and Claire and it was starting to affect my relationship with my boys. I couldn't do that to any of them anymore.

Claire refused to talk to me after that night and had gone on holiday to Barbados with some friends to sort her head out. At the same time Coleen and I went away to Majorca to talk about our future. At the end of it we decided that we would have a separation. I promised I wouldn't see Claire during that time and that I would go back to Pimlico and spend some time on my own.

The trouble was, I was confused. I couldn't get Claire out of my mind. At the same time, when I saw Coleen things didn't feel right between us anymore. We'd never taken up her suggestion of marriage counselling and as a result we'd just swept our problems under the carpet and tried to carry on as if nothing had happened. But it wasn't working; things weren't the same. I felt that we were just clinging on by our fingertips for the sake of the kids and that maybe our marriage was over after all.

I knew Claire was still away but in despair I went round to see her mum and told her that I thought I still loved her daughter. I think I needed to know if Claire still felt the same way about me. When she came back her mum passed on the message that I'd been round and Claire got back in touch. She was understandably cautious after what had happened in Southend, but soon we were meeting up again a couple of times a week. Coleen, meanwhile, knew I was screwed up. She knew I still had feelings for Claire and that I was doing too much booze. I'd go to clubs and bars and drink until the early hours and then stagger back to the flat in Pimlico with a gang of new mates I'd only met a few hours earlier. I'd wake up the next morning and there'd be five or six strangers sleeping in the spare room and on the floor. I had no idea what was going on.

Coleen would tell me she could cope with my affair, but not my indecision, but I kept sitting on the fence. I'd tell Coleen that I was going to finish it with Claire and I'd tell Claire I was going to finish it with Coleen. I was all over the place. I remember Claire asking if she could come to the opening night of *Boogie Nights* in the West End in October, but I made up some lame excuse about why it wasn't possible because I wanted Coleen to come with me instead. We had the aftershow party at the Hippodrome off Leicester Square and it was as if nothing had happened. We were the way we used to be. We laughed, danced and drank the night away and typically the evening ended with us sloping off and getting fruity in an abandoned office.

Detailed stories about our marriage problems were now regularly appearing in the papers. It was always 'a close friend said this' and 'a close friend said that'. For example, one night Jake sat up until midnight with Coleen drawing a picture for Claire. Of course Coleen was upset by this and told me that night over the phone. Twenty-four hours later the story appeared in a national newspaper. I couldn't understand it. How did they know? Who was telling them? And why?

Coleen was convinced it must be one of my mates and of course I was convinced it was one of hers. For a while we both went round in this constant state of suspicion. I didn't know who to trust. I wondered if it was Stan, the Colonel, who I'd been with for years and who normally I'd trust with my life. I blamed Claire. I'd shout at her and ask her to stop telling people what was going on, which was ridiculous because there was stuff in the papers even she couldn't possibly know. Was Big Mark telling people? Was he making money? I even suspected Goz, which was awful as he'd been my closest friend for years.

I pulled in favours from some journalist friends and begged them to tell me who was leaking these stories. They gave me the name on the condition I never told anybody. When I heard who it was I couldn't believe it. Surely it wasn't true. When I told Coleen she was devastated. Not only had her husband let her down, now one of her own family had too. We'd shared meals with this person, sat drinking with them and discussed our problems with them, even our most intimate secrets. We thought about confronting them and I so badly wanted to do it, but Coleen thought nobody would believe me. Why would they? I'd been lying for years about having an affair. And she was right.

I had to do something. How crazy is this – I even considered having their pet dog killed. Big Mark knew a bloke who apparently used to do it for a living. He was the gentlest of blokes, but if you paid him a couple of hundred quid he'd kill someone's pet. I had it all planned. I wanted to hurt them so much – as much as they'd hurt Coleen and the boys. I had it all set up, to the extent that I'd even given him an address and told him when they would be out and the dog would be left at home. Thankfully I came to my senses. What the bloody hell was I thinking of? That wasn't me. Of course I couldn't have done it, I love animals far too much.

Once we knew, the hardest part was having to talk to this person as though nothing had happened. They were still a part of the family and we still saw them at all the usual family get-togethers. To this day I loathe and detest them, but I've caused enough hurt to Coleen's family and I know I just have to let it go. They know who they are. And I hope they sleep easy in their bed at night.

Other than planning to assassinate a pooch, the only other time in my life I've fantasised about doing something like that was several years earlier when a musician took a fancy to Coleen. He was persistent to the point that she got frightened. I warned him to stay away a hundred times, but he just laughed in my face.

'You're Shane Richie, what are you gonna do?'

That was the last straw. This guy was, and still is, a professional pianist and through a friend of a friend I made inquiries about hiring someone to go round and cut off his little finger. It was all set up and I sat there sweating about it until the day came round. It got to just a couple of hours from when it was to happen and I called the whole thing off. But I made sure he heard what I'd had planned and I never heard from him again. Believe me, I'm not proud of any of this. It's just that I wasn't clever enough to think of any other way.

I felt under such huge pressure with the mess my life was in, and one of my favourite ways of letting off steam was go-kart racing. I'd always loved it and now I was back in the West End I was going out to Daytona most Wednesdays or Thursdays and racing from midnight until four in the morning with my mates. One particular night I received a call from Charlie, the owner, to say that a big star had asked if he could take over the place that night instead. I was a bit put out until he told me it was Tom Cruise. Not just that but Tom had invited Goz and I along to race with him and his friends. The second I came off stage I rushed straight round – my eyeliner still intact.

'Hi Shane, I'm Tom and this is my wife Nicole.'

'Hi mate, I'm Shane and this is my wife Goz.'

What a top bloke he turned out to be. We talked for hours about everything from my kids to how he threw up when he was filming *Top Gun*. And you know what I loved about him? He had no idea how big a star he really was. He really didn't. He'd say things like:

'Hey, did you guys ever see a film over here called *Days of Thunder*?'

'Did we see it? You're kidding ain't cha Tom?'

I felt so relaxed in his company that I even opened up to him about Coleen and what was happening in my life. We raced and talked until the early hours of the morning. Between races we'd sit at the side of the track, sharing a Coke and singing songs from *Boogie Nights*. I might have been the better singer, but he whupped my arse on the track.

At the end of the night we swapped numbers and Tom wished me luck with my personal life. I walked outside and the paparazzi were waiting for me. They took their pictures and went home happy. Little did they know that one of the world's biggest movie stars was just the other side of the doors.

I'm a sucker for a charity and find it hard to say no, even when I'm at death's door, so when I was asked to appear at an Oxfam charity gala at the Prince Edward Theatre to raise funds for the victims of Hurricane Mitch in December I promised I'd be there. I was on antibiotics for a chest infection, but what was waiting for me backstage? A bottle of Jack Daniels, of course. I was appearing with the cast of *Boogie Nights* and I was told that we were going to close Act One. The cast of *Miss Saigon* were also performing, along with Brian Blessed, Frankie

Vaughan and the harmonica player Larry Adler. I was really disappointed at the turn-out and when I went on stage I made a crack that people had paid £50 for a ticket and I was the only person there they'd heard of. It was only a joke.

When I came off I was told that the schedule had changed and that now I'd be closing the end of the show. By now I'd teamed up with Sam Janus and Lisa Maxwell and we decided to go for a drink. When we returned two hours later I was slightly tho worse for wear. I stood in the wings watching two great singers from *Miss Saigon* performing the big number 'Last Night of the World'. It was a beautiful love song and contained the lyric 'a song played on a solo saxophone'. Ah-ha! Idea! Being the prat I am, I persuaded one of the band to lend me his saxophone and I walked on behind these two girls playing the *Pink Panther* theme. Nobody laughed, except for Lisa and Sam standing in the wings. As if that wasn't bad enough I then walked back across again the other way, to the absolute horror of these two singers.

I was pulled off and given a dressing-down, but it was water off a duck's back. It seemed like a bit of a stuck-up do and I was like a fish out of water. This wasn't my audience. These weren't the sort of people who watched *Lucky Numbers* or *The Shane Richie Experience* or used Daz. They certainly wouldn't have come to see *Boogie Nights*. They had no idea who I was.

A bottle of Jack Daniels later, I went on to close the show as arranged, but just before we started singing someone shouted from the wings, 'Shane, can you stretch it out a bit?' Could I stretch it out a bit? You give me three minutes and I'll turn it into three hours. For some reason I started to do jokes about Brian Blessed climbing Everest. To me it was hilarious, but it wasn't the funniest of routines and after a while they turned off my microphone and spotlight. I stood there in the dark and heard someone in the wings whispering, 'Get off now, you're embarrassing yourself.'

Did I listen? What do you think? Quick as a flash I pulled out a lighter, held it under my face and started singing 'One voice, singing in the darkness...' At that point the whole audience started to slow clap me. To be honest it wasn't my best night, but the charity made around

£23,000. The following day when the press reported what I'd done and gave the charity a mention, that amount doubled. The organiser even rang and asked me if I'd do my own show the following year. They didn't put that bit in the papers though, did they?

The final straw for my marriage came in April 1999 when I told Coleen that I needed some time away on my own to clear my head and that I'd booked a ten-day go-karting holiday in France with some mates. What I actually did was fly to Tunisia with Claire. Before we left I told Claire's mum that Coleen knew all about the holiday; of course I was lying and she knew it and the day before we were due back she called Coleen to tell her. She didn't feel I was being fair on either of them and that Coleen had a right to know the truth.

I called Coleen from the airport and she said: 'How is Claire?' I asked her what she was talking about and she said she knew. I came off the phone and started shouting at Claire. 'Why's your mother called Coleen? What's she playing at?' I immediately blamed her mother for the mess. When I landed at the airport I went to stay with Goz and when I went round to see Coleen the following day we agreed it would be for the best if I moved out permanently. I moved into a flat in Chiswick with Claire, but before long I was spending every weekend back with Coleen again. I didn't want to hurt her or Claire, but I cared for them both and just didn't know how to resolve things.

In June 1999 the decision was taken out of my hands when Coleen decided to call Claire and sort things out once and for all. When they finally spoke Claire did all the talking. She told Coleen everything I'd promised her and all the lies I'd told her about the state of my marriage. The next day Coleen went to Blackpool with the boys to stay with her family for a couple of weeks and told me our marriage was finally over. She had waited around long enough hoping and praying that I would sort myself out. She couldn't wait any more. How could I blame her?

Now I had to make it work with Claire. So I decided to take her and the boys on holiday together to Florida the following month. I needed Coleen's blessing obviously and she agreed, but she said that if Claire was going to be a part of her sons' lives then she wanted to meet her.

I so badly wanted her to change her mind, but she was adamant. I told Claire and to my surprise she was OK about it. The week before we left I drove Claire round to my place. I walked into the kitchen and the two of them came face to face for the first time. Exactly what they said to each other that day I'll never know. I just couldn't handle it – I made some lame excuse and walked out. Cowardly, I know. Claire told me later that Coleen had made her a cup of tea, which I thought was really good of her. If I'd been Coleen I'd have poured it over her head. But that's Coleen all over; she's dignified and she's always known how to handle things. Jake was too young to understand what was going on and of course took a liking to Claire instantly. She was a singer and dancer and Jake loved all that. Shane was different. He just wanted his mum and dad to be together, so it was always going to be hard for anyone who came between them.

When Claire and I returned from Florida, Coleen announced that now I wasn't there she wanted to leave the house. She'd never liked it that much, she found it too big and creepy and remote and she said I'd be better off living there. I re-mortgaged my house and bought a place two minutes up the road for Coleen and the boys, and moved back into the family home myself with Claire.

To mark the start of her new life, Coleen did her story with *The Sun*. Over three days in August I woke up to terrible headlines about how I'd betrayed her, how I'd lied to her, how I'd cheated on her. I was angry that she'd done it, but what I couldn't stand was that almost every word of it was true. By now, every time I featured in a newspaper story I was described as a love-rat. Unfortunately the bad publicity was about to take its toll.

Out of the blue Stan called me to say that one of the top executives at Granada Television wanted to take us both to lunch at The Ivy. With him choosing such a smart London restaurant I'd assumed that we'd be discussing them re-commissioning *Lucky Numbers* and *Love Me Do* and I chatted away quite happily without suspecting a thing. It was only over the second bottle of Chablis that the conversation suddenly became serious.

'Shane,' he said, 'I'm afraid we feel you've really let down the general public.'

I was staggered. 'Why? People break up all the time. I'm sorry, but it happens. Why should it affect my TV career?'

'But Shane, you've had an affair. You'll need to lay low for a few years and maybe then we'll see where we stand.' A few days later I found out that he'd left his wife and kids for another woman. But it made no difference to me. I was still out of favour as far as television was concerned.

With little enthusiasm I went back on tour with *Boogie Nights*. I had to do it, the money was drying up and there was nothing coming in. TV didn't want to know anymore, my contract with Granada was over, and the Daz ads were finished. One of my first ports of call was Glasgow. While we were there one of the cast knocked on my hotel room door one day and said that Billy Connolly was filming round the corner. I'd never met him, but he was one of my heroes and I couldn't pass up this opportunity. I went out into the street, found him in his caravan and introduced myself and sat for a whole hour with him. He was a complete stranger, but for some reason I felt able to confide in him. I thought I'd achieved everything – I'd earned lots of money, I was touring with my own show, I had a wife and two lovely kids – but it was all unravelling. I'd been having an affair and TV companies didn't seem to want to use me. I told Billy all this and he listened in silence. When I'd finished he looked me straight in the eyes.

'Shane,' he said. 'The true strength of a man is how he rises after he falls.' They were powerful words, words that were to stay with me for a very long time.

The cast for *Boogie Nights* by now included Claire. But the problem was that now Claire and I were official the thrill had gone. Meanwhile, perversely, now Coleen and I were apart we were getting along better than ever. And now she no longer wanted me, I wanted her again. She was looking fantastic and when I was home from tour she'd go out with her mates while I'd look after the boys. She was still my best friend so whenever I was having problems with Claire it felt natural to pour them out to Coleen. The difference was that Coleen knew me before all the money and the fame and I felt comfortable around her, but with Claire I felt I had to keep up the pretence. It seemed to me that she wanted to go to every premiere, every opening of a restaurant, every new club – she wanted to be seen out with Shane Richie. It was only Coleen who knew the real me. One day I was round at her house and we were joking around when Coleen started giggling and saying: 'You know Shane, I could have you any time I wanted.' I was joking back, 'No you couldn't, get out of here.' But you know what? She was right. Out of nowhere we started kissing. Before I knew it the inevitable happened. Afterwards we were like two giggling school kids sharing this little secret. But funnily I always felt it was all right because she was still my wife – I never saw a problem with it.

Pretty soon it was a regular thing and I was sneaking round in the afternoons, while the boys were at school and Claire was busy else-where, for a bit of how's your father. Coleen would cover my back and if Claire ever phoned she'd say I wasn't there. How bizarre was this: Coleen had ended up becoming the mistress, Claire was now living in the marital home and I was cheating on her. Other times I'd tell Claire that I had to go round to see Coleen to discuss our separation and then we'd go out for dinner or to the pictures. I think Coleen quite liked the idea that she was getting one back on Claire. Now she'd met Claire she was also a lot less fazed by the whole thing. Claire meanwhile was worried. Now she'd met Coleen she couldn't understand why I'd left her. Coleen and I shared the same sense of humour and the same personalities – in many ways we were very alike. Understandably it made Claire feel very insecure.

Unfortunately I wasn't going to get away with seeing both of them for long. After a few weeks of this, Coleen lost her temper one day and went round and told Claire that we were still sleeping together. She'd had enough of me lying to them both again and decided that she'd drop me in it. I can't blame her. Claire was putting all Coleen's possessions in bin-bags and asking her to come and collect them and at the same time I was telling Coleen to leave her stuff at my house because it would all blow over with Claire eventually and she'd move back in. At the same time Claire had been boasting to Coleen that I would never ever do the dirty on her, which Coleen not surprisingly took as a bit of an insult.

The two of them ended up spending three hours together and

Coleen told Claire every last cough and spit about me. They were even planning to set up a trap and then confront me jointly and throw all my lies back at me. When I got back that night Claire went ballistic. It was my fault, of course, but I didn't see it that way and went mental. Coleen had me by the nuts. Now she was the one with the power and boy, was she using it.

What finally brought it home to me that our relationship was over was when Coleen told me that she'd met a guy called Dave and that he'd invited her away to the Lakes for the weekend. I begged her not to go and said I thought we might be able to make things work. She asked if I could promise that and I said I couldn't, so she went. The damage had been done and Coleen finally couldn't take any more.

CHAPTER SIXTEEN

Cracking up

I was so excited when *Boogie Nights* went to Blackpool because it meant I would get to spend some time with my boys, who were on holiday there with Coleen's family. We were booked to do six weeks at the Opera House in the late summer of 1999 and I naïvely imagined I'd have a ball – spending time with Shane and Jake in the day, performing on stage at night and then parties afterwards. Unfortunately it wasn't to work out like that.

The problem was, in Blackpool I had to face up to the mess I'd made of things. When I was at home I could forget about the separation and the fact that my boys weren't with me anymore, but here it was staring me in the face. Of course it was great seeing them, it was just painful because I realised that they now had lives of their own. If they weren't with Coleen and her family in Blackpool then they were at their new home in London with their own bedrooms, their own friends and their own interests. Of course we had a great time when we were together, but the truth was I was a part-time dad now. I was someone who would come and go and not be there for them day to day.

At the same time Coleen seemed to be happy with Dave, who was the exact opposite of me – calm, steady and fairly quiet. Everyone seemed to be getting on with their lives, except me. The only way I could handle it was by drinking. I'd always enjoyed a few jars when I was out with mates, but that was simply social drinking.

At times I'd lie to Claire and tell her I was going to meet some friends, then I'd go to a bar wearing a hat and glasses so no one would recognise me and get absolutely trashed. Other times I'd sit on my own in my dressing room until I got drunk. It was only then I felt confident enough to go out and be Shane Richie. A lot of it was anger. I was angry with Claire, I was angry with Coleen, I was angry at the world in general, but most of all I was angry with myself. I was angry at the way I'd wrecked my life. I remember going around wanting to pick a fight because I wanted someone to beat the shit out of me, because if that happened then people would feel sorry for me rather than despise me.

You have to remember I was going on stage every night performing *Boogie Nights*, which was semi-autobiographical. One of my lines was: 'Ah, you know what birds are like, treat 'em mean and keep 'em keen.' I felt sick every time I had to say it. In another scene Debs says to my character, Roddy: 'All you do is think about yourself, you are ready to forsake all your friends and family, for what, your name in lights?' Journalists would interview me in every town along the tour and they'd always ask if it reflected my life off screen in any way. I'd always deny it and say it was just a show, but the truth is that was exactly the state of my life.

I'd drink anything and everything. A typical night would start with a large Jack Daniels simply to give me the confidence to go on stage. Then I'd have several glasses of champagne in the interval. And then I began to rely on it. There'd be champagne in the dressing room after the show, because whoever else was in town that week would come along to share a drink with me. It could be anyone from the latest boy band to Hale and Pace. The problem was I wasn't very comfortable around my peers. They'd expect me to be cracking gags with a smile on my face and the only way I could manage that by then was with several drinks inside. A group of us from the cast had rented a big house on the outskirts of Blackpool and when we arrived back there I'd hit the Jack Daniels. I could easily get through a bottle in a night. I'd drink myself to sleep; it was the only way I could blot things out.

Things all came to a head when Coleen filed for divorce. I'd begged her not to do it and asked her to wait because it might not work out with Claire. Quite rightly she said it had been two years and she wasn't prepared to wait any longer – she'd moved on. Her lawyers kept sending me letters, but I wasn't prepared to accept that things had reached that point, so whenever they arrived I threw them in the bin. One night, as I was sitting in my dressing room waiting to go on stage, there was a knock at my door. I was told there was a man waiting for me down at the stage door and that it was urgent. I went down and found him and he handed me a brown envelope. I opened it up and inside were divorce papers. I raced up to the dressing room and phoned Coleen in a fury asking why she'd done that to me. She said she'd been forced to because I wouldn't listen to her and one of us had to move things forward.

That day the Capital Radio DJ Steve Penk had given out my mobile phone number on air. He's a good mate of mine and he'd done it for a laugh, asking listeners to phone me. Not surprisingly I'd been bombarded with calls all day. It rang non-stop; at one stage I had 174 missed calls. His joke couldn't have come at a worse time.

That night I went back to the house feeling so low. Like most nights there was a party in full swing, but I just walked straight past them and went up to my room. Everything inside me shut down.

I believe everybody is capable of suicide; only very few choose to do it. I've always thought it was a sign of weakness, but at that moment I remember thinking: 'How can I finish this?' I was in so much pain I just wanted something to take it away. Even Claire seemed to have given up on me; she was at the end of her tether. What had I become? I had truly hit rock bottom. I'd try to tell Claire how miserable I felt, but she'd say: 'Oh, just go and sit in a corner and drink your Jack Daniels and feel sorry for yourself.' She was running out of patience and I don't blame her.

That night was the worst ever. Inside I was dying a million deaths. I was so ashamed of myself and started to sob uncontrollably. I knew then I needed help, but I certainly wasn't going to ask the rest of the cast. I was the star of the show and they looked up to me. I couldn't let them know I was human after all.

At two o'clock in the morning, not knowing what I was doing or where I was going, I walked out. All I had on were a pair of tracksuit bottoms, an old jumper, my long coat and a hat. And I just carried on walking and walking. I went to a place called Stanley Park and I lay down on the grass and sobbed. It was the end of September and a really windy night, but I was shaking so much I didn't feel the cold. I was in a terrible state. I had pins and needles all over my body, my head was pounding and I was retching. Was I on the verge of a nervous breakdown? Even to this day, I have no idea. All I know is that I wanted the pain inside to stop. I've never been a religious person, but if there was a God, boy did I need Him now. I sobbed and prayed until I was so exhausted I could barely move.

I had to speak to Coleen; she was the only one who would understand what I was going through. I reached her on the mobile. She knew straightaway what a state I was in, but she was away and told me to call her sister Maureen. Bear in mind most of the Nolans had little time for me by now because of the way I'd treated Coleen, but Maureen, to her credit, told me to come to her house, even though it was three in the morning. She only lived a few minutes away so I went straight round and when she opened the door I just fell into her arms and sobbed my heart out. We went through to the sitting room and I talked and cried for hours and eventually fell asleep on the couch. At 10 o'clock the following morning Maureen called a cab and took me straight to the Nolans' family doctor. By now the whole family knew what had happened and they were all phoning to see how I was. All I can remember is begging Coleen not to tell the boys because as far as they were concerned their dad was invincible, and here I was, a wreck. I was unfit to call myself a father.

When I was shown into the doctor's room I looked in the mirror and saw someone that just wasn't me: I saw my dad. I'd been up for nearly 24 hours and my face was red and puffy and distorted. The doctor sat me down and asked me to tell him – on a scale of one to ten – how depressed I felt. I asked him how the scale worked. He said one meant you were having a bad day. Two meant you were having a run of bad days but you knew you were going to get through it. He worked his way up to eight, which he said meant you couldn't see light at the end of the tunnel and everything seemed to be falling apart around you. At this point I started crying. He asked me if he should stop and I said: 'No, it's not that, I've just realised I think I'm at 11.' The doctor was immediately concerned: 'Very few people will sit here and cry and admit to 11. Most people cry and admit to six or seven. You really need help and you need it now.'

He called an ambulance and I was taken straight to the BUPA Fylde Coast Hospital. As soon as I arrived I started to feel better. It was as if someone had taken the weight off my shoulders. All of a sudden it was out of my hands and someone else was going to sort things out. Maureen phoned Claire, but I was told that apart from Claire I couldn't see anyone and I couldn't take any phone calls. I was put in a private room and a statement was put out to the press that I'd been experiencing chest pains and breathing difficulties caused by a back injury. Meanwhile my understudy in *Boogie Nights* took over.

I was put on a drip because I couldn't eat and I still couldn't stop crying. I was gone, my body had shut down on me and I just lay there in this hospital bed. Nurses would come in and say: 'Oh, you're Shane Richie, I love you, can I have tickets for *Boogie Nights*?' which didn't help, because I just didn't want to be Shane Richie anymore. I hated everything I'd done, everything I stood for and everything I'd become. I just hated being me.

Doctors and psychiatrists and counsellors would be in and out all day, but I was miles away. I was put on strong anti-depressants and given drugs to sleep and I didn't leave the room for four days. No one ever said it was a psychiatric ward, but I was under 24-hour surveillance and while I was there they ran a barrage of tests. The psychiatrist would bring in pictures of shapes and ask me what I saw in them. I remember one was a landscape picture. They asked me what I saw and then told me to imagine I was in the picture.

'What are you doing in the fields, Mr Richie?'

'I'm driving.'

'Really? Why do you not want to walk in the fields then? Do you feel restricted?'

'No, it's just that I own a car.'

He got a bit annoyed at that point and said I wasn't taking it seriously. And he was right.

I remember another doctor asking: 'Did you have any problems in your childhood?'

'No, it was a great childhood, fantastic. I loved every minute of it,' I told him.

It was a lie, but I didn't want them to know. The problem was I didn't want to open up to anyone at that point. That's how pig-headed I'd become. I'd let my guard down in front of Maureen and a couple of the nurses, but I just didn't want anyone else to see any weakness in me. After four days I started to lie even more. The doctors checked me over and said: 'You seem fine now, Mr Richie, perhaps all you needed was a bit of rest,' and I jumped at this. 'Yes, that was it. That was all I needed, just a bit of rest.' But it wasn't true. What I needed was to sort my head out, but I convinced them I was well enough to leave and was discharged.

By now the press had found out where I was, but at this stage I couldn't face being photographed, so Claire drove to the hospital in my car and Goz came out wearing my coat and climbed in with her. They drove off and out of nowhere journalists and photographers started springing out from behind trees and parked cars and racing after them. I stood in the shadows watching and when everyone had gone I walked out of the hospital and back to the digs. That night I was back on stage. Not surprisingly the photographers were waiting for me and the following day the *News of the World* ran a picture of me turning up at the Opera House looking a wreck. I was unshaven, my face was red and blotchy and I was wearing dark glasses to conceal the state of my eyes. A reporter asked me if the rumours were true that I'd suffered a collapse. 'A few days in hospital and then back on stage again? I wish it was a collapse,' I joked. If only they'd known the truth.

I'd been given some anti-depressants when I left the hospital. Looking back I realise that all they did was help me forget about my problems, they didn't sort them out, but at the time they seemed the perfect answer to blotting out the pain. When *Boogie Nights* left Blackpool the tour continued through the rest of the year. The fact that we were never in one place for more than a week made it easy for me to get my hands on whatever I wanted. In each new town I'd go to the local doctor and say the tablets weren't working or I'd lost them – rubbish like that – and they'd give me another pack. I remember going to a doctor in Swansea and asking him for Prozac. He asked if I'd taken them before and I pretended I had. And what the doctors wouldn't prescribe I could get on tour anyway. When you're starring in a show and constantly surrounded by musicians and hangers-on you can get anything you want. People are afraid to say no. Come on, I'm Shane Richie, I can blag anything. I tried everything during that tour – Valium, Temazepam, Prozac. I was a space cadet. I'd take more than I should or mix them up, anything to stop the pain. And for a brief moment I felt invincible and was back to being jolly. I never worried about it. If I was caught taking drugs at least they were prescribed. I'd be able to say a doctor gave them to me. Being around musicians there were a lot of people smoking dope, which I tried to help me sleep, but very rarely. Sitting around discussing why *Songs From the Key of Life* was the best Stevie Wonder album ever until five in the morning wasn't my idea of a good time. I wanted to be out, in clubs, having a good time and feeling lively.

At that time I couldn't bear to be alone. I'd hire cinemas at £1,000 a time so that after the show I could go along and watch a film with the rest of the cast – anything so I didn't have to be on my own. I remember in Swansea even hiring a swimming pool for £2,000. I paid for the staff to stay on and keep it open for me and we had it from 11pm to three in the morning.

Things were no better when I was back home. Now I knew my marriage was over I had to make it work with Claire, and I really wanted to, otherwise everything I'd done was for nothing, but it was hard and I ended up treating Claire very badly. The problem was that I didn't want to be on my own with her because by now I felt we had nothing in common. She'd fallen in love with the Shane Richie she'd met in Manchester – the party animal, the man that had everything, Mr Popular – but that wasn't me. I wanted my old life back. I wanted Coleen. I wanted my boys. I wanted to do the school run, I wanted to help them with their homework and tuck them into bed at night. I wanted to be the dad they'd always wanted and the husband Coleen had always deserved.

To cope and to help me forget what I'd done, I surrounded myself with friends and my house became like a lonelyhearts club. I was seeing less and less of Goz – he didn't like what I was turning into and it was putting a strain on our friendship. But there were other friends. Spongo had just split up with his wife and he moved in, and another old friend, Barry Upton, a record producer, came to stay too. It became open house – friends of friends would turn up and stay for days on end. For a while I loved it, but the musicians I knew were late-night people and they drank everything and smoked anything and things just spiralled downwards with Claire. I'd start rows with her over nothing because deep down I wanted her to finish it. Then I could claim I'd tried to make it work, but that she'd given up me. How she stayed for so long I'll never know. I guess she must have loved me. The problem was I was worthy of no one's love then.

I was drinking more and more. Claire would do everything she could to try to stop me, but it was very hard because I was so determined. In the evening she'd say: 'Right, I'm going to fix up some drinks, we'll have a Diet Coke,' and I'd plead with her to put in a little bit of Jack Daniels. She'd say, 'OK, but only a tiny bit,' and then when she sat down I'd pretend I needed some more ice and I'd go back to the fridge and top it up with JD.

I remember the lowest I got was pleading with the owner of my local off-licence to open up. He closed at ten and I turned up at five past. I saw him through the door and banged on it until he came and then begged him to serve me. He said he would, but only if I gave him two signed pictures. I was so desperate I walked all the way back to the house, picked up two pictures and then went back out again. After all that he had no Jack Daniels so I ended up buying half a dozen bottles of flavoured vodkas. After that I always made sure I had plenty of JD hidden about the place. The house is so big you can hide anything anywhere; there are hidden staircases and a cellar and various rooms off the cellar. I'd make excuses: 'I've just got to pop down to the cellar to get something.' I had bottles of Jack Daniels everywhere – behind the jukebox, under a pile of *Planet of the Apes* magazines, in the car, in the garage, in my sports bag – and miniature bottles in jacket pockets and drawers. There was Jack Daniels in every dressing room of every venue

I played – it was on my rider. I'd mention it in every interview I did, and the company would end up sending me crates of the stuff. Claire was pulling her hair out and one day she suggested we should get rid of all the booze in the house. I went along with it and even pointed out where some of the bottles were hidden, but I knew all along that however many bottles she got rid of, there would still be a JD somewhere.

It wasn't all bad with Claire. When she got me away from my mates we were capable of having some fantastic times together. That November we flew to Barbados and ended up having a great holiday. But I was still paranoid and I changed my whole appearance while I was out there because I couldn't stand the idea of being recognised or photographed by the press. We went to the local hairdresser, Claire had her hair braided and I even went so far as to have dreadlocks all the way down my back. Claire looked beautiful, but I looked like Animal from The Muppets. I didn't care as long as the disguise worked. I remember standing having a drink at a beach bar with the football manager Ron Atkinson and his lovely wife Maggie, and he'd no idea who I was, even though I'd been on a TV show with him just a few weeks earlier. I loved not being me for a while.

CHAPTER 17

'Didn't you used to be Shane Richie?'

After all the flak I'd been getting in the press it was strange to open up a paper and see myself described as a hero. I was still touring with *Boogie Nights* and was driving home from a show late one night in November 1999. I pulled into my local garage to pick up the usual tube of Pringles and a pie when I noticed a guy obviously the worse for wear, trying to fill his car with petrol. What he seemed oblivious to was the fact that his bonnet was on fire.

I shouted: 'Oi, mate!'

'What?' he slurred.

'Your car's on fire.'

'No, it's alright, it's just over-heating.'

He then staggered to the bonnet and lifted it open. It was like a scene from *Apocalypse Now*. The flames shot ten feet into the air. I raced across and pulled him away. Next thing I know the bloke behind the till is running towards the fire with a bucket of water. Now I've never been a great one for physics, but correct me if I'm wrong here – bucket of water and electrical fire? I don't think so.

With one hand I was trying to keep the drunk from getting back into his car and with the other I was trying to stop the attendant, whose English wasn't that great, from chucking a huge bucket of water into the engine.

'What the bleedin' 'ell you doing, mate?'

'What? Don't tell me please, I'm in charge.'

Now I can speak a bit of Hindi. But not enough to explain that you shouldn't throw water onto an electrical fire.

'Turn off the power to the pumps,' I told him.

'How many times I must tell you please, go away.'

'Listen, mate…'

'No listen mate me, I bloody do this long time, you hold bucket water, I turn off pump.'

I couldn't believe I was standing there arguing with this bloke and his entire petrol station was about to go up in flames. We eventually shut down the station and I stood at the entrance waving other cars away, still in my stage make-up. The police and the fire brigade turned up and I explained to them what had happened. The attendant was having none of it. He had his side of the story and funnily enough there was no mention of his bucket of water anywhere. After an hour or so chatting with the Old Bill and the fireman I was able to go home. And you know what? The attendant still made me pay for my pie and Pringles. There's gratitude.

A couple of days later I opened up the *Daily Mirror* to see a story describing me as 'Blaze Hero Shane'. As if that wasn't enough I got a call the following day from Michael Burke's office. He was the presenter of *999* on BBC1, which re-enacted amazing rescues, and they wanted me to take part and act out the petrol station rescue. I turned them down. I know I wanted to be an actor, but I wasn't that desperate!

I wasn't particularly excited about Christmas that year. I booked into a hotel in Blackpool with Claire and we spent the day with my boys. We had a lovely time, but when my boys weren't there we weren't getting on. When Millennium Night came round I wasn't feeling much better. I'd been invited to a million and one parties, but instead I opted for a quiet one with Claire, my mum and dad, my friend Lisa Maxwell and her fella Paul. I remember everyone making resolutions. They were going to give up smoking, drinking or lose weight. All I wanted was to be happy and turn my life around. It certainly needed it. I knew how bad things had got when I was considered for presenting a one-off Channel 5 TV show. A few days later Stan phoned me.

'Sorry Shane, they like the idea, but they've found someone else.' Out of curiosity I asked him who it was.

'Are you sure you want to know?'

'Yeah, tell me.'

'They've got a TV weathergirl instead.'

Nice one. Instead I ended up working as a team captain on *Night Fever* singing karaoke songs on Channel 5 because nobody else wanted me. It was good fun, but it wasn't taking my career anywhere.

My affair, my drinking and my party lifestyle had given me such a reputation that new producers wouldn't touch me. Meanwhile, producers I'd worked with in the past had stopped taking my phone calls. At best they'd tell me that old chestnut 'Let's do lunch', but the lunch would never happen. TV executives, journalists and directors who'd constantly wined and dined me at London's best restaurants now wouldn't even meet my eye at showbiz dos. I was fully aware how I was perceived.

Strangers would come up to me at parties and say: 'Didn't you used to be Shane Richie?' There was even a joke doing the rounds.

'Knock, knock.'

'Who's there?'

'Shane.'

'Shane who?'

'That's showbusiness!'

It bothered me less than I thought it would. Because my personal life was in such a mess, I was caring less and less that my professional life was the same. All of a sudden I was nothing. I'd become a caricature. The reality TV thing was just starting and I was considered a bit cheesy. But through it all, I never once lost faith. I never thought that was the end of my career and I never believed that people didn't want to see me on television. I knew that I had to re-invent myself and that one day it would happen all over again.

For the past couple of years, on Stan's advice, I'd worked hard to build up a show-reel. By taking small parts in films I could gradually build up a video of my work as an actor to show TV executives what I was capable of. It was a case of starting at the bottom again and slowly building my way back up.

It had started in August 1997 when I was asked to appear alongside Greta Scacchi and Sean Pertwee in a Channel 4 movie version of *Macbeth*. They offered me the role of the porter. It wasn't a big part, but it was integral to the plot. That's what I used to tell people anyway! I wasn't stupid, I knew they only wanted me in it because it would get them some publicity and attract another type of audience – tabloid readers – the director had never even heard of me. I remember being terrified on my first day. I walked in and I saw all these proper actors looking at me and then looking at each other as if to say, 'Isn't that the bloke from the Daz ads?' Here we go again. But it was a start.

The same year I'd travelled to Monaco. I'd gone out there with Goz, Spud and Charlie from Daytona to watch the Grand Prix. When I realised the film festival was on in Cannes at the same time, I'd got myself suited and booted and gone along. In for a penny, in for a pound. One night I talked my way into a private party on board a luxury yacht moored in the harbour. I still loved a blag. While standing at the bar sipping free champagne I ended up chatting to a guy called Chris Barfoot, whose girlfriend was a big fan of me in *Boogie Nights*. He was putting together a short film called *Dead Clean* with the actor Andrew Sachs and asked if I'd play a Greek assassin. It ended up winning an award for Best Short Film in Houston, Texas, although no one saw it in Britain. In 1999 director Howard Ford, who was a friend of Chris Barfoot, was making a British thriller called *Distant Shadow* and he asked me to appear as an accountant called Paul who gets killed. You don't get paid for these films, maybe a couple of hundred pounds a week to cover your expenses, but the truth is I'd have done them for nothing, just for the experience.

Once we'd got the show-reel together Stan started to send it round a few TV companies, one of which made *The Bill*. They called back to say they were interested and would I come in. I turned up and it felt like I was only there for the novelty factor. All the secretaries were hiding behind their doors, whispering 'Ooh look, it's Shane Richie,' and I ended up signing dozens of autographs. The same thing happened with a load of other dramas. I don't think any of them were really considering me; they just wanted me in so they could say, 'You'll never guess who we had in today – Shane Richie.'

Eventually my show-reel fell into the hands of a casting director, Louis Hammond, who did take me seriously. He was working on a spin-off of *The Bill* called *Burnside*, which would star Chris Ellison. In January 2000 I got a call to say he liked what I'd done. I went in to read for them and ended up being offered the part of a grass called Tony Shotton. This was a proper TV role and I jumped at it. Filming would begin in April, which was perfect – my last tour of *Boogie Nights* was scheduled to end in March.

By now I was toured out with *Boogie Nights*. I'd done it every which way: physically I was wrecked and mentally I was shot. We bowed out at the Hexagon Theatre in Reading, Berkshire on 11 March – my 36th birthday. I began filming *Burnside* the following month.

The producers wanted to change my whole look and I suggested dying my hair peroxide blonde, which they jumped at. My character appeared throughout the whole series and I got the chance to work with some great actors, including Cristian Solimeno and Ricky Groves. At lunchtimes we'd sit on the crew bus and chat about what we were off to do next. Cristian said he was about to film a new TV drama called *Footballers' Wives*. I wished him luck. Ricky said he'd just landed a part in *EastEnders* as a mechanic called Garry Hobbs. 'Oh mate,' I said, 'I really envy you. I'd love to do something like that. Good luck and keep in touch.'

After I'd finished filming I was approached about all sorts of TV shows. I was asked to host the Lottery show and there was talk of me presenting *The Generation Game* and a new Saturday night show like Ian Wright's *Friends Like These*. But I turned them all down. I really didn't have anything against them – some were great shows – I just felt that if I did them I'd have been going backwards. I'd done *Burnside* and I wanted to wait until that was screened and see what happened. I was prepared to gamble it all to be taken seriously as an actor.

Burnside eventually went out on ITV that summer. I waited with bated breath. The reviews were good, the viewing figures were OK. But guess what? Nothing happened. Zilch. For some reason it didn't really capture the public's imagination and it ended after one series. By this time, Stan was tearing his hair out. He warned me that if I kept turning game and variety shows down they'd stop asking me, and they did. And after a while nobody was asking me to do anything. The only other TV show I did that year was one in which they took celebrities and put them into other jobs. I ended up being a London tour bus guide. I enjoyed it, but it was just another of those cheap television shows, it didn't lead to anything.

Nothing that had happened in my life could have prepared me for what was to happen in June. I'd started to notice that Coleen was becoming more and more unhappy living in London. Now we weren't together she felt she had no reason to stay. She sat me down one afternoon and told me that she and the boys were moving to Blackpool, to be closer to her family. Something inside me died. I pleaded with her to stay. It had been hard enough when the boys moved out to live just a couple of miles up the road. Now they were going to be 250 miles away. The thought of them going was killing me. The simple things I'd taken for granted – school runs, sports days, helping with their homework, trips to the movies and of course Sunday football – all this would be gone.

Coleen had put her house in London up for sale and had arranged to stay with one of her sisters until she could buy a place of her own in Blackpool. A removal van came on a Saturday and took their furniture and they were due to follow the next day. I went round on the Saturday night to say my goodbyes. It was the hardest thing I've ever done in my entire life. Words cannot describe how I felt. These boys were the two most precious things in my life. I loved them unconditionally and now they were going. I hugged them tight and never wanted to let them go. I did my best not to cry in front of them, but it was hard. I told them how much I loved them and how sorry I was for everything that had happened. Coleen was great; she made light of the whole situation because she could see I was losing it. The boys meanwhile were really excited about living so close to the beach and all their cousins. They had loads to look forward to and I told them I'd visit weekends and that I'd always be there for them. I was determined not to be a Sunday father. As I hugged Coleen goodbye I knew she was still concerned about me. 'Shane, please sort yourself out,' she said. I knew she was right; I couldn't go on like this.

The following month she called to tell me she'd met a musician, Ray Fensome, who coincidentally had been a drinking pal of mine the previous year when I was in Blackpool. She said it was serious and asked me how I felt. At that point I trusted nobody – certainly not a musician. As far as I was concerned, she was still my wife and Ray was my mate, what was she playing at?

To add to my misery, Claire walked out on me. I'd blamed her for Coleen taking my boys to Blackpool. I'd throw it in her face every chance I got. 'If it hadn't been for you, they'd still be here,' I'd tell her. Of course I was wrong, I was just in so much pain I was lashing out and she was the closest to me, so she got it full on.

I couldn't bear being on my own and after a week I called and asked her to come back. She said she'd only come back if I got rid of all the people living in my house. I'd have done anything for her at that stage and I sat down with Barry and Paul and explained the situation. It was hard for me to see them go; they'd been such great mates and we'd listened to each other's problems, but luckily they understood and packed their bags and Claire moved back in.

I'm not the tidiest person to live with and Paul knew I was looking for somebody to help out, so before he left he recommended a lovely lady by the name of Carol, who used to clean his flat. She proved to be a godsend and was always there to pick up the pieces, whether it was the house trashed from a party, or me trashed in the hallway. If she found me in that state she'd wake me up and make me go up to bed. Friends would phone and she'd always cover for me and tell them I was out. She quickly became a very good friend.

My main problem was that there was nothing to distract me – there was nothing in the diary for the rest of the year. I didn't want to do *Boogie Nights* again and I certainly wasn't going to go back to *Grease*, but I missed a live audience. I sat down in my office with Stan and Jon Conway and told them I fancied doing my own tour. They agreed, but said that to make money we'd have to keep it simple; all I'd need with me was a duo and a speciality act to open the first half. I refused. I said I wanted a band. What's more, people were used to seeing me in *Grease*, with a full-scale production, so it couldn't just be any band. A five-piece group and they had to be the best musicians, with the best sound system and the best lighting. I wanted a director and a producer and a choreographer and good support acts. Singer Steve Serlin, who'd played Terry in *Boogie Nights*, would do ten minutes and funky soul trio The Divas would do 40 minutes – that would make up the first act. Then I'd go out and do a couple of hours for the second act – songs and stand-up.

We called the tour 'Shane Richie Live In Concert' and we kicked off the first of 42 nights in August. It was a chance to try out some new material, and inevitably I ended up talking about my personal life. There was a line I used to do: 'Me and Coleen weren't compatible; she was Pisces and I was a wanker,' that used to get a great reaction. The audiences seemed to like it when I was having a go at myself. Most venues sold out, but it wasn't always a success. I wasn't on TV now and perhaps people had had enough of reading about a love-rat, and as a result I had my share of playing to half-empty auditoriums. I'd turn up at some venues and there'd be such a small number of die-hard fans that I could address them by name. My opening line on those nights was always the same: 'It's nice to see such a huge crowd here tonight, even though a lot of you seem to have come dressed as empty chairs.' Publicly I'd never let it get me down.

During the tour I'd do guest spots on any radio show that would have me, plus the odd regional TV show. The interviewers would say, 'Well, you've had a fabulous career'. And it was always in the past tense. Despite the tour, I was dead in the water. I was a jobbing entertainer talking about his former career. At the end of October, when the tour finished, I found I owed £15,000. I'd spent a fortune on merchandise and staging the show and it hadn't made a penny.

I'd only been back at the house a couple of days when I received a message to call Coleen urgently. During my tour I'd been speaking to her practically every day and at several venues my boys had been with me, and I knew from my conversations with them how serious things were getting with Ray. I still hadn't expected this.

'Shane, I need to tell you something.'

For some reason I knew exactly what she was going to say.

'Go on.'

'I'm pregnant.'

'Oh, ok.'

I couldn't think of anything else to say. I didn't know how I felt. It was only after I put the phone down that it hit me. I was happy for her, but I was gutted. Up until then I'd always believed there was still a chance we could get back together. Coleen had never ever suggested it was on the cards, but in my heart of hearts I believed it. But now she was having a baby with Ray, my dream was finally over.

In November that year I went with my boys and Spongo and his kids, Chris and Nick, to New York. We had the best time. We went skating in Central Park, we went to see shows on Broadway, we flew around Manhattan in a helicopter. This was when I was at my happiest. I was a father again. It was with a heavy heart that I flew back to Britain and reality. I'd only got panto to look forward to and in all honesty I was dreading it. I was due to play Hook in *Peter Pan* in Southend. It was a big mistake because all my terrible memories came flooding back. The last time I'd been there was when I was in *Boogie Nights* and I'd lied to Coleen. The other thing that got to me was that previously I'd been in panto and played Peter Pan, but they said I was too old at 36 and had to play Hook. Looking back I shouldn't have done it. I needed to stop working and have a rest, but the problem was that when I stopped I began wallowing in self-pity, so despite my reservations I took it.

The truth is I'm not a big fan of panto because I don't believe you have to be that good to be in it. Sportsmen and reality TV stars – they're people who've probably never set foot on stage in their life, but because of their profile producers think they're worthy of the money they're paid. I don't. I've got too many friends who've slogged their guts out for years and would wipe the floor with these people, but they don't get the chance.

The rehearsals for the panto took place at the Old Vic in London and while I was there I could see actors rehearsing *Othello* and *The Iceman Cometh*. I was in awe of them. Here I was, playing Hook. Someone said to me: 'Yeah, but don't forget, Shane, you could do that and none of them could come and do this.' I said: 'That's fine, but at the moment they're not letting me do that. Why am I not up there doing *Hamlet*?' I was on a real downer. I had absolutely nothing in the diary other than panto and yet another tour of *Boogie Nights*.

It was at that time that I realised life didn't have to be that way. One day I was driving to rehearsals with Goz and Terry Morrison. We were listening to Tommy Boyd on Talk Radio and he had a caller on who was saying that people who had no ties should live life to the full – climb Everest, sail a ship, ride a Harley around America. I asked Terry: 'If you had no ties and nobody could stop you doing whatever you wanted, what would you do, Tel?' Terry replied that he would love to sail around the world. I asked him what was stopping him and he said he had a family.

He said: 'What would you love to do?'

I said: 'I'd love to ride a Harley across America.'

He said: 'What's stopping you?'

I said: 'Well…' and then I paused. It dawned on me, I had no ties. I wanted to say that the only thing preventing me was my family, but the truth was there was nothing to stop me. When that realisation hit me I was in pieces. My boys came from a broken home and there was no family. At the same time it meant I could do what I wanted, and that scared the hell out of me.

I'd never ridden a motorbike before but the very next day I picked up the *Yellow Pages* and found a motorbike school just up the road from me in Greenford. I called them up. 'In nine days we'll have taught you to ride a bike and on the tenth day you'll have passed your test,' the guy on the other end of the phone promised me. I phone Goz and told him that I wanted him to drive Harleys with me across America. He was incredulous. 'What about Claire?' he asked. 'What *about* Claire?' I said. 'That should have finished a long time ago. What's stopping us, Goz? Nothing stopped us when we were at Pontins and there's nothing stopping us now. It's over with Coleen, my boys are at school and Claire and me are holding on by the skin of our teeth. Goz, mate, I ain't got nothing.'

For the first time it dawned on Goz, too, that he was in the same boat. He'd been engaged for six years, but that had ended two years earlier and, like me, he was just treading water. We were two grown men in our mid-thirties with nothing in our lives but freedom. We had no one to answer to and that was a bitter pill to swallow. Even so I called Coleen and asked her permission. She was still my point of reference.

All of a sudden I stopped drinking; I had something to focus on now. For the next nine days I was out of bed at 6.30 in the morning, up the A40, driving a bike in the freezing cold, then off to Southend for two shows. My test was booked for the tenth day – a Friday. We finished panto on the Saturday, late in January 2000 and Goz had booked two single flights to Phoenix, Arizona, leaving on the Monday.

I knew I was cutting it a bit fine with the flights booked for two days after the test, so I was ready to do a blag and had a dodgy licence lined up in case I failed. It was easy enough to do – a friend of a friend knew someone who could get hold of them. Nothing was going to get in the way of me driving this Harley around America.

When I passed the test I hugged the startled examiner. 'You don't know what this means to me mate, you may have just saved my life.' The panto finished, I said my goodbyes and spent the Sunday packing. By now Claire had spoken to Coleen about my decision to go away and Coleen had pointed out that this was the best thing for me. Claire was doing bits and pieces on TV at this point so she was focused on her own thing anyway, and she didn't seem to mind.

My mate George Lyle – the guy I'd met in LA – had landed a new job in Phoenix and he would be our base for a couple of nights, but after that it would just be me, Goz, two Harleys and the open road for six whole weeks. We'd drive into the middle of nowhere, where nobody knew my name. Out there perhaps I'd work out exactly where I'd gone wrong in my life. How I'd screwed up my career, my marriage and lost everything that ever mattered to me. Out there I would try to sort my head out. Find some answers. I didn't know whether I'd succeed, but there had to be a chance. Out there, there was at least hope.

CHAPTER EIGHTEEN

Easy Rider

''Ere, Shane, what's wrong?'

We were 35,000 feet above the Atlantic and I was gazing out of the plane window over the sea in my own little world. Just an hour earlier, having finished the in-flight meal, I'd been pouring over the map of Arizona excitedly with Goz. Now, for no good reason, a black cloud had suddenly descended and I couldn't help but think about the mess I was leaving behind. Goz understood and he didn't let me stay down for long, but I must have driven him crazy during that ten-hour flight to Phoenix.

When we landed at the airport in January 2001, George Lyle was there to meet us. I hadn't seen him since we were knocking back tequila slammers on the balcony of his LA apartment overlooking Manhattan Beach while I was struggling to come to terms with my new tattoo for Colin on my backside. But the minute we walked into Arrivals I spotted him. It wasn't difficult. He was standing there holding a bottle of Jack Daniels and two of the finest Cuban cigars, dressed as Krusty the Clown. In his hand was a sign saying 'Mr Richie and Mr Goz'. He had party written right across his forehead. Bless him. I didn't have the heart to tell him that wasn't what I was there for. For once I didn't want to party and I didn't want to drink. This trip was about something else.

George was worth a few quid and had a fantastic bachelor pad on a golf course in Scottsdale, just outside Phoenix. We spent the next couple of days there getting acclimatised. Several times a day I'd ring Coleen and my boys and of course Claire. They'd ask if I was having a good time and I'd make out I was, but all I'd done was take my problems to another place. I felt down, miserable and angry. Angry at Stan for what had happened to my career, angry with Claire for forcing me to break up my marriage and angry with Coleen for letting me go. I was angry at everything and everybody. Everyone was to blame but me.

After three days we set off to pick up our bikes. Now to hire two Harleys for six weeks is pretty expensive. They were asking $200 a day. There was no way we could afford that and we had the blag worked out before we left the UK. I knew how big the BBC was worldwide, so I brought out some BBC stickers and we stuck one on a digital camera we had with us. I'd made up some BBC headed notepaper with a stencil and sat down with Goz to compose a letter that explained I was Shane Richie and I was currently making my own video diary for the BBC, with my assistant Chris Gosling. I showed this to the Harley Davidson hire shop and the bearded guy with his bandana said:

'Well, are we going to get a mention there boys?'

'Bloody right you are!'

The guy beamed. 'Please have the Harleys for nothing. You take care of the insurance – and enjoy the ride.'

They were beautiful bikes. Like something straight out of a movie. Mine was a Heritage Softtail and Goz had the Fat Boy. All we needed now was a route. The idea originally was to drive right across the States, but that would have cost a fortune and I didn't want to be away from my boys for so long, so we decided we'd do 3,000 miles, taking in Arizona, Nevada and California and ending in Los Angeles. How we were going to get there was the adventure – we had no set plan.

My old friend Paul Berg came down from Portland, Oregon to wave us off and at 8.30am the following morning we loaded up the bikes, said our goodbyes and were away. The adventure was nearly over before it had begun. We were literally 100 yards from the door when Goz realised he'd forgotten something and turned round. Now the thing about a Harley is you need a wide berth to turn these babies round and Goz was trying to do it on a sixpence. Before I knew it he was lying flat on his back with the Harley at his feet. I nearly fell off, myself, laughing. We pulled ourselves together and set off again – in our minds like Butch Cassidy and the Sundance Kid. Sadly, we probably looked more like Hinge and Brackett.

After that we took it fairly easy because the bikes were heavy machines and took some getting used to, but within a couple of hours we'd reached the desert. We were literally in the middle of nowhere. We turned off the engines, climbed off the bikes and stood there and stared at each other in this eerie silence. Was this how it was going to be for the next six weeks? The difference between a bike and a car is that in a car you have plenty of things to distract yourself. You can chat to each other, listen to the radio, use your phone, light a cigarette. Now I had nothing to occupy my mind other than my own thoughts. I'm not sure whether I was nervous or excited. Either way, I was going to have to face up to what I'd done in my life.

The first day we rode 170 miles and boy, did my bum know it. We ended up that night at a little place called Prescott. We checked into a cheap motel, where we shared a room to keep down the costs. It was tiny – two single beds and a TV in the corner – does that sound familiar? We were back at Pontins. We got up the next morning at 5.30am, cleaned the bikes and had breakfast at Denny's – a diner, which is an American institution. It soon became our regular morning ritual. We'd have eggs, sausage and muffin and then stock up on supplies for the bike – bottles of water, chewing gum and cigarettes. Then we'd make a leisurely start. We had a very laid-back approach to it. I always said that if I wasn't able to light up a cigarette on the bike then we were going too fast.

As we rode along I found that other Harley riders would wave to me. It was always quite subtle. A little wave with the left hand held down at the side of the leg. For a while I thought I was being recognised. It was only when we got into conversation with someone in a diner that they explained it was simply a sign of respect for the Harley! Damn.

After just a couple of days I found myself starting to loosen up and enjoy my own company. And once we'd got used to the bikes we realised they rode themselves. I'd ride along with no hands on the handlebars, smoking a cigarette; we were in our element.

We decided we'd stick to the back roads because we thought it would be more interesting riding through small towns and villages off the beaten track. We pulled up at one spot – Cottonwood, population 260

– and the roar of two Harleys seemed to bring out the whole town. By this time we looked like real Harley riders. I had leather chaps on my jeans and a leather jacket. Forget Butch and Sundance, by now we were Dennis Hopper and Peter Fonda. (Though in reality I probably looked like one of the singers in the Village People). We walked into the town's tiny bar.

'What canna get you boys?' the guy asked with a real drawl. It was like something out of a cowboy film, all we needed now was two guys chewing straw and strumming banjos in the corner. We both started giggling.

'You found som'en funny boys?' the guy growled.

'No mate, not at all.'

At the sound of our accents the guy's face lit up.

'Where you boys from, you Australian?'

'No mate, we're from London.'

'You from London? Gid outta here!'

He shouted to the rest of the bar. 'Here boys, we got us two bikers in here from England!'

He turned back to us, looked me straight in the eye and said: 'You met the Queen?'

Everybody always asked this. It was always the Queen, The Beatles or Benny Hill. By now I was sick of it.

'Yes, I've met the Queen, mate.'

'Hey, everybody, he's met the Queen!'

He turned to me again. 'We lurve the Queen. Next time y'all meet with Her Majesty y'all tell her Bob from Cottonwood sends his lurve. Hey,' he said excitedly. 'Y'all met the Beatles?'

I couldn't resist.

'Yeh, Paul McCartney's my second cousin.'

'Is that right? That's a beautiful thing. We lurve Paul McCartney, we lurve The Beatles out here. Y'all make sure you send my best to Paul when you gid back t'England.'

He never asked me about Benny Hill. Shame that, because I actually had met Benny Hill.

We didn't have to pay for a single drink all afternoon and when we left, the whole bar emptied to wave us off. 'Y'all have a safe time now and don't ya forget, yer ever in these parts again, y'all come and see yer Uncle Bob now.' The great thing was they didn't know me from Adam. I could have told them I was anything from a plumber to a rocket scientist. It was an exhilarating feeling of freedom.

As the journey progressed we soon realised that even the cheap motels weren't quite as cheap as we'd anticipated. To get by we were going to need another blag. Rather than stopping at cheap motels I began calling decent hotels the day before we arrived, pretending I was phoning from England.

'Hello, this is Mr Jones from the BBC. I'm just calling to let you know that one of our artists, Shane Richie and his assistant Chris Gosling are making a documentary and will be passing your way.'

Some of them wouldn't be at all impressed.

'BBC my ass, you pay the full price or you gid outta here.'

More often than not though they'd jump over backwards to help. 'Yes sir, well you're more than welcome to two nights in our hotel. We've got a lovely room for you. Enjoy all the facilities and everything is complimentary of course.'

We turned up on our bikes the next day with our BBC stickers on the boxes on the back and took full advantage of their hospitality. Not that we were tearing it up. Far from it. Most nights we'd get into our room around seven o'clock and we'd have great intentions of going to the local bar, but once we got off the bikes we were usually too tired. We'd end up grabbing a bite to eat, mapping out where we'd been, doing a quick piece for the video diary and then crashing out at 10 o'clock.

Although we mainly stuck to small towns, there were some tourist spots we just couldn't resist. One of these was the Grand Canyon. After a week on the road, we rolled up at a place called Bright Angel, which is on the north side of the ridge. The plan was to find a motel nearby, have an early night and then get up at the crack of dawn to see the sun rise over the canyon. The next morning when we woke it was pitch-black and freezing. I wasn't surprised: the weather had been getting worse for days. I was already wearing three T-shirts, a fleece, my leather jacket, two pairs of socks, a hood, my helmet and two pairs of gloves.

And I was still bloody cold. But as we were about to set off the motel owner warned us that not only was it bitterly cold, with a wind chill of −5, but there was also a thin sheet of black ice on the roads. I was petrified about driving in those conditions and persuaded Goz to abandon the bikes at the motel and get the tour bus instead. We turned up at the bus depot and at that time in the morning we were the only tourists there. We set off – just the tour guide and the two of us – and eventually arrived at the side of the canyon.

What a view. It made me feel so small and insignificant. The best was yet to come though and when the sun finally appeared above the rocks it was an inspiring sight. So inspiring I suddenly needed to call everyone I loved.

I called Coleen and my boys. They were excited to hear from me, but boys being boys it wasn't long before they were asking me what I was going to bring back for them. I laughed and told them I'd bring back as much as I could fit on the back of the bike. But the truth was that what I really wanted to take back was a different person. I wanted to take them back their dad. I'd left for America a confused and angry man. But the hours on the bike were giving me time alone to think. I was being forced to confront what I'd done. It was painful at times and I still hadn't quite worked out what had gone wrong or how I could put things right, but I knew I was heading in the right direction.

Then I called my mum and dad. My dad was still waiting for a kidney and liver transplant and was in a bad way. He'd been on dialysis for a few years now and it was wearing my mum out. The thought of them both all those miles away made me choke up and I felt a desperate urge to speak to them and tell them how much they meant to me. My dad answered the phone.

'Dad, it's Shane.'

'Ah, how are'ya, where are'ya?'

Dad could never remember where I was from one month to the next.

'Dad, I'm in America, on the side of the Grand Canyon, watching the sunrise. It's an incredible sight and it's made me think about things. I know why things were the way they were between us, but I just want to tell you that I love you.'

There was a brief silence.

'You're in America? Can you get me any plimsolls?'

He put my mum on.

'Shane, where de feck are 'ya?'

'I'm at the Grand Canyon.'

'De Grand what?'

'The Grand Canyon, in America.'

'Ah Jayzus, ya back dere are ya? Hang on son, ya father's shouting something. What's dat, Harry? Oh yes, Shane, he says can he have a size ten.'

After two weeks of cold and rain, Goz and I decided that it was time to ride towards the sun. We were ready for some good weather. We decided to take our usual back roads to find it and set off with California firmly in our sights. We'd been riding for an hour along open roads with fields either side when we came to a sign: 'Sheriff's chain gang at work, do not stop'.

Talk about red rag to a bull. We hadn't seen a soul for hours. It wouldn't hurt to take a quick peek, would it? Within seconds of turning off the engines, a helicopter appeared from nowhere in the distance. It came closer and closer and landed in the field next to us. Out climbed two huge policemen with shades and shotguns and started walking towards us. Oh no, I could see the good cop, bad cop routine about to start.

'Goz, don't make no sudden movements,' I muttered. We'd had a warm welcome wherever we went until now, but I had a feeling these guys weren't coming over for a chat about the Queen, The Beatles and Benny Hill.

'Boys, step away from the bikes.'

We slunk away from the bikes like two naughty schoolboys.

The biggest, or should I say the fattest, of the two came right up to me and put his face inches from mine.

'Hey, can you read, boy?' he drawled.

'Sorry mate?'

'I said, can you read, boy?'

'Er, yes.'

'What d'ya think the sign back there said?'

'I'm sorry, we were probably going a bit too fast to read it,' I bluffed.

At this point the younger and by far the spottier of the two stepped forward and asked for our ID. At the sight of it his face lit up.

'So, y'all from England then?'

Oh please don't start asking me about Benny Hill…

Luckily, when they realised we were British they seemed to loosen up a bit.

'The reason why we stopped you guys was because every so often we'll get bikes come through here that'll stop and try to bust out some of their friends from the chain gang,' the bigger one explained.

'What chain gang?' I asked.

He walked us to the other side of the road where, 15ft below in a ravine, there was a row of prisoners chained together, all chipping away at rocks.

'So what happens if someone does try a rescue?' I asked.

'Well, we have to pop 'em in the ass,' he said, grabbing hold of his gun.

We didn't hang around much after that.

Goz and I had been singing the song 'Get Your Kicks on Route 66' for days now. The road was legendary and there was so much folklore surrounding it. Even before we left England it was the one road we said we had to ride down. After weeks we eventually reached it.

Get your kicks on Route 66? What the hell was Chuck Berry thinking of when he wrote this? Get your kicks? We couldn't even get a cup of coffee. It was a bit like meeting The Nolans and finding out that no one was actually in the mood for dancing. Nothing actually happens on Route 66. In the past it was one of the main routes across America, but not anymore. Today it's just an open road, with rocks either side. With little to see or do we put our feet down and chalked up 230 miles, eventually pulling off the road in a place called Loughlin. We'd been told that it was a bit of a party town, with casinos and bars, but in actual fact it was full of OAPs. The average age was dead. If Blackpool was the British equivalent of Las Vegas, then Loughlin was Margate. But after a few beers we didn't care. We hit the casino and I just had to do it, I had to have a bet. It was the odd $50 here and the odd $50 there. Six beers later I'd lost the best part of $400. And what's worse, almost the keys to my Harley!

The following day, about half an hour into the journey, Goz pulled over and told me we'd taken a wrong turn. The only way to get back on track was to ride for 15 miles on the freeway. So far I'd always refused to ride on the freeways. I wasn't comfortable enough on the bike and I also felt it would be too much like being stuck on the M25; all we'd see were cars either side of us. I reluctantly agreed. After 30 miles Goz pulled over again. He'd just worked out he'd read the map wrong. We were actually going to be stuck on it for another 130 miles. I was so angry.

The road was so open that every time a truck passed I was getting blown all over the place. Goz found it funny, which just made me even madder. I lost it with him. For the first time on the trip I wanted to go home. It had stopped being fun. I climbed back on the bike and rode off again. After another 70 miles we pulled over at a truckers' stop in the middle of the Mojave Desert. I'd cooled off by now and offered to buy Goz some lunch. There was a place that sold burgers and soft drinks and I took off my helmet and joined the queue. I reached the front and asked for two cheeseburgers and two Diet Cokes. It was then that I heard a voice pipe up from behind me. 'Bloody hell, you're that Shane Richie ain't cha? I saw you in *Boogie Nights*, you were bloody fantastic.' The lad was from the East End of London and was touring America with a mate of his. It was strange. Since I'd been on the bike I'd forgotten who I was and now I had to put on a front again. I wasn't sure how I felt.

One thing the trip did was bring Goz and I even closer together. We'd always been best mates, but I wasn't always great at listening to other people's problems and that included Goz. I was listening now though. Some nights we'd have a bite to eat, go back to the room at nine o'clock at night and just sit and talk for hours; we didn't even put the television on.

As we got closer and closer to LA things were slowly starting to make sense. In the past I'd have a drink or take anti-depressants to forget about things. I'd always say 'I'll deal with that tomorrow.' On the bike there was no escape. I'd had time to reflect on my childhood, my relationships with my mum and dad, Coleen and my boys and of course Claire. I was still calling my boys every day, but I found I was talking to Claire less and less. I still loved her but it was gradually dawning on me that we couldn't carry on the way we were.

With all this going on in my mind, it was inevitable that things were going to come to a head and they did. It was after a morning riding through some of the most beautiful sights I've ever seen. We'd been through orange groves, mountains, fields and lovely little villages. It was idyllic. I followed behind Goz as usual and after a couple of hours he pulled over so we could have a break and stretch our legs. He'd chosen a beautiful spot, at the side of a mountain and right next to a sign – 134 miles to San Francisco. I sat down at the side of the road with my head in my hands and just cried. It was like someone had opened the floodgates.

Suddenly everything had fallen into place. I'd been so busy blaming everyone else – I'd blamed Coleen for letting me go to Manchester, I'd blamed Stan for letting my career go down the pan, and for making me do jobs I didn't like, simply for the money, I'd blamed Claire for getting involved with a married man, I'd blamed Spongo for letting me drink too much and at one point I'd even blamed Goz for letting his best mate end up like this. Yet sitting at the side of the road I realised the only person to blame was me. It was that simple. Coleen had done nothing wrong; Stan and Claire and Spongo and Goz – none of them had done anything wrong. All they'd done was stay by my side through thick and thin. I was the only one who had made a mess of things. I sat there trembling for almost an hour. Every now and then a car would pass by and slow down to see if everything was all right. I wasn't making much sense, but I tried to explain how I felt to Goz – that everything was my fault, that I was in control of everything I did. I was the one who decided if I wanted to drink or not. I was the one who decided whether or not to go to a nightclub and whether or not to sleep with a stranger. I was the one who'd lied and cheated, who'd had an affair and taken the decisions about my career. All of it was my doing. I'd caused this mess. No one else. All of a sudden Billy Connolly's words came back to me: 'The true strength of a man is how he rises after he falls.' Those words had never seemed more apt. As soon as I'd calmed down enough to speak I phoned Coleen. She asked if I was all right.

'No, but I will be.'

I wanted to tell her there and then how sorry I was for all the hurt I'd caused her, but that would have to wait. I needed to do it face to face; no more being a coward. I climbed back on the bike and straightened my back. All of a sudden I cared about how I looked again. The old Shane Richie was coming through and it felt really good. I was on the way to becoming the man I'd always wanted to be – someone brave enough to own up to their mistakes, someone who takes charge of their own life and stops trying to blame other people. For the rest of the stay I had a real spring in my step. I was looking forward to the future. I certainly wasn't going to forget what I'd done, but I was ready to move on.

Next stop was Oakland and I was on such a high. On the outskirts of the town we quickly realised that we were lost. We came to some traffic lights and pulled over at the side of the road. As Goz studied the map I could see, over his shoulder, groups of lads appearing from round corners. It reminded me of Stonebridge where I grew up; when strangers came to town we knew straightaway. As we tried to find our bearings a trucker stopped, wound down his window and said:

'Hey, you two guys, are you locals?' Of course he knew we weren't.

'No mate, we're just a bit lost,' I told him.

'Gid yer asses on yer bikes and gid the hell outta here now.'

What we hadn't realised was that we'd driven into the Mexican 'hood. We got straight back on our bikes and rode for half an hour without stopping. When we pulled in to a café and told the owner what had happened he said we'd had a lucky escape. A couple more minutes and those lads would have been all over us. We'd have been dragged off and the bikes would have been nicked, stripped and then dumped at the side of the road. We'd had a lucky escape.

The next day we reached San Francisco. We checked in to a little hotel in the Bay area and rode straight down to the Golden Gate Bridge, where we spent the afternoon posing on our bikes and taking pictures of each other. We were going to have a right old time in Frisco. That night we started off in an Irish bar in the Bay area and they recommended a great Scottish bar nearby. We had a couple of hours there and when they closed they mentioned a private club around the corner. Please don't let it be a Welsh bar, I thought. We made our way round there, walked in and ordered two beers. An elderly Chinese lady appeared from nowhere.

'You like massage?'

'Sorry, love?'

'Very nice massage.'

Now while I was in *Grease* I used to visit a Chinese masseur at least once a week. She'd release the pressure in my back and I'd leave feeling refreshed and invigorated. Loads of dancers from the cast swore by her. After three weeks on a Harley I thought this sounded like heaven.

'Thanks a lot darling, that'd be great, I've just been on a Harley for the last three weeks.'

The bit about the Harley fell on deaf ears.

'Ah, you want nice special massage.'

She took me into a little room off the bar and told me to go and have a shower before the massage. I turned on the shower and fiddled with the controls but there was only one temperature – freezing. As the icy water hit my body I sobered up quickly. What was I playing at? Here I was stark naked in the middle of the night in the back room of a bar. It started to dawn on me: there was no way I was going to get a legitimate 'this will release the pressure, Mr Richie' massage in a place like this. This was more 'I love you long time, $5 please'. Before I had chance to think what to do next, the shower door opened and in walked the same little old lady, only this time wearing nothing but a see-through negligee. Bless her.

'Sorry, love, this isn't what I had in mind,' I stuttered, trying my best to maintain eye contact. I've seen people take bad news better. The smile dropped from her face. She bent down, which trust me wasn't a pretty sight, picked up a bucket of cold water standing next to the shower and threw it right at me.

'No, you must pay money,' she shouted angrily. 'You come in, you order massage.' There was no point arguing. I emptied out my pockets and managed to come up with $50, which I handed to her. I pulled my clothes back on and with my hair still dripping wet, went back into the bar to find Goz. I looked around and saw him emerging from another room, with a dirty big grin on his face, followed by a beautiful girl.

'OK, thank you very much, that'll be $150,' the girl said to him.

Goz turned to me. 'I've got $100 left Shane, lend me your $50 will you?'

I explained that I'd spend my last $50. I was too embarrassed to tell him what I'd spent it on.

'Sorry, love, I've only got $100,' Goz told her apologetically and gave her his best smile. It didn't work. The woman angrily reached under the bar and pressed a bell. From nowhere a huge beer-bellied Mexican guy appeared.

'You must pay up the money now, English boys.'

'Pay money for what? I've just given that little old lady over there $50 for the privilege of having a bucket of cold water thrown over me. And anyway we ain't got anymore money.'

He was having none of it. After a lot of argy-bargy he ordered us to take off our watches and jewellery and leave them behind as bounty while we went to find a cash machine. We eventually came back, picked up our jewellery and settled our bill. Well, Goz's bill. Before we had a chance to leave, the little old Chinese lady appeared from nowhere again and tapped me on the shoulder.

'You come back for more?'

Don't even think about it, darling.

Over the next couple of days we did all the usual tourist stuff, including Alcatraz and the trams, before deciding to do a bit of filming down at the university, which had a beautiful landscaped area down by the Golden Gate Bridge. It was pretty hot, so I rode down to it wearing just my boots, a pair of shorts, a skimpy little T-shirt and my bandana. We thought it was a private road so for a laugh when we got there I stripped off naked, apart from my boots, tied my bandana around my bits and rode up and down, while Goz killed himself laughing. Of course I'd totally forgotten that San Francisco was the gay capital of the world and what I didn't know was that this wasn't a private road at all. Guys started appearing from all over the place. 'Hey, cheeky boy, how ya doing? You wanna ride that bike over this way and come spend the day with me?' That would have been enough to send most blokes running for the hills, but not me. I love an audience – any audience – and I just hammed it up even more. We only scarpered when we heard that someone had called the police. The last thing I needed was to be in the papers – 'Shane Richie arrested naked on Harley in gay capital of world'.

We left San Francisco after two days for the last leg of the journey home – 380 miles down the Pacific Highway into Los Angeles. We stopped several times along the way to take in the stunning views of the Pacific Ocean – Santa Cruz, Monterey, Carmel, Pismo Beach, Guadalupe, Santa Barbara, Ventura, Santa Monica and finally into LA. By the time we reached LA we'd clocked up close to 3,000 miles. We'd had the time of our lives. We said goodbye to our Harleys at the airport like we were saying goodbye to two old friends.

I was going home a changed man. Now I had a different problem to deal with – the guilt and how I was going to make amends for my mistakes when I got back. But the cloud that had been hanging over me had finally gone. I'd worked out what had gone wrong and it was time now to turn my life around once and for all.

CHAPTER NINETEEN

Labour of love

When I returned from America in late February 2001 things were no better with Claire. Although I'd cut back on the drinking and was in a more positive frame of mind, despite my best intentions to make a fresh start, my career was still going nowhere. Her career meanwhile was on the up. She was getting more and more work as an actress. It meant I was hard work to live with, and not surprisingly, she left me again. Our relationship was becoming like a yo-yo and each time I was making promises that ultimately I couldn't keep. I kept telling her I'd change and that I'd treat her better, and I would for a while but then it would drift back.

I convinced her to come back, because I still wanted to make it work. I had to, otherwise all the lying and cheating and pain would have been for nothing. She said she would as long as I got some help. I reluctantly agreed. It wasn't really my thing, but Claire found me a counsellor in Hampstead, North London. She was obviously English, but she'd given herself a spiritual Indian name. I should have clocked there and then what I was walking into. First of all, she didn't have a consulting room. It was her front room. Chintz curtains and settee; the lot. When I walked in the place was lit with hundreds of scented candles and there was strange music in the background, which sounded like whales mating. In a faint whisper the woman told me that in order to relax I had to concentrate on my breathing, letting out the bad air and breathing in the good. This went on for several minutes before she asked me to lie down on the floor. Not another singing lesson! She was still talking in this quiet voice about my breathing when out of the blue she suddenly whispered, 'I loved you in *Boogie Nights*. Is it about you?'

The whales were still going for it in the background, the candles were flickering away and she was gazing down at me intently.

'Well, it's semi-autobiographical,' I whispered back.

'The bit I like best is when you sing "Sorry Seems to Be the Hardest Word".'

'Thank you very much.'

She disappeared from the room and re-appeared wearing a hat with beads dangling down from it. She sounded like a set of wind chimes in a gale. Then she lay down on the floor next to me and put her hands on my stomach. She was quite an attractive woman and I was convinced now that something was going to happen. She told me she could feel pain and energy coming from me and that my aura had been dented. I remember thinking that if she carried on moving her hand much lower my aura definitely wouldn't be dented for much longer.

All the time she continued whispering questions about *Boogie Nights*. Who'd written it? What was my favourite song? Where was I appearing in it next? And still her hand was moving up and down my stomach. I was supposed to be lying there relaxing and all she could talk about was *Boogie Nights*, which I was trying to forget. This went on for about an hour and then she suddenly jumped up, turned off the whales, blew out the candles and said in a booming voice: 'Right, thank you very much, that'll be £70.' £70 to lie on the floor for an hour and have my stomach stroked? All I wanted now was a little Chinese woman to appear and chuck a bucket of water over me for $50. And I thought I was the blagger. Claire called me afterwards and asked how I got on. I told her it was wonderful and that I was releasing my demons, or some old psychobabble like that.

Claire and I were apart for three weeks before she came back and for a while I thought we stood a chance. In March I was invited over to Pittsburgh. They were putting on their version of *Boogie Nights* and as one of the producers and the star of the British production they wanted me and Jon Conway there on the opening night. While watching rehearsals I was introduced to the young American actor who was playing Roddy O'Neil, who of course was based on me. I noticed that he was missing something. I was soon to find just how much he was missing. Roddy, like me, is very tactile and this young American couldn't seem to get it. I called him over.

He skipped towards me with his hand firmly on his hip.

'Well hiya, Shane.'

Oh no, here we go. I explained to him that Roddy is very tactile with his friends.

'Well, how d'ya mean by tactile, darling?'

I proceeded to show him what I meant and put my arm around his neck and playfully ruffled his hair. The bloody thing came off in my hand. He was only wearing a syrup.

So not only had they thought the best person to play me would rather be playing Debs, but he was also as bald as a coot. You live and learn.

At the same time a six-months pregnant Coleen and Ray were on holiday in Orlando with the rest of the Nolan family. I spoke to Coleen and she suggested I fly Claire out and join them. Claire thought it was a great idea, it was a way of moving forward; I wasn't so sure. So much had happened between us all that I was convinced it was going to be awkward. How could we sit around the pool and act as if we were two ordinary couples on holiday together?

Coleen booked a room for us at the same hotel and we were given the room right next door to her and Ray. Could this get any worse? And what was I supposed to do during the day? Sit by the pool with my wife who was six months pregnant by another man and my girlfriend who was now getting broody herself?

To my amazement, when I arrived it all seemed so natural. Coleen's sisters immediately took to Claire, Ray was so laid-back it all seemed to wash over him and the more time I spent with him the more I grew to like him. I realised Coleen had made a good choice and if I'm honest I envied their relationship. We ended up having a fabulous time. Coleen and Claire would have girly days out shopping, Ray and I would sit and have a beer by the pool and my boys seemed to love having us all around. Of course Coleen's sisters and brothers-in-law found the whole thing hilarious and would make cracks and ask how the hell I'd pulled this one off. But I hadn't. It was all down to Coleen and her dignity and courage that this bizarre set-up was working.

In May I was invited to audition for *Chitty Chitty Bang Bang*, which was going to open in the West End. I walked in and sitting in the waiting-room were Bradley Walsh, Bobby Davro and a host of other household names. I met the director and for a moment I really thought the part was mine, but in the end he decided I was a bit too Cockney. I always thought that was the point – the dad was meant to be that way – but apparently not. They went for Michael Ball instead.

As nothing was happening Goz and I decided it was time to go back to basics – back to the holiday camps. Just the two of us and a mini disc. For three months, from June to August in the summer of 2001, I did seven nights a week, touring Haven and Butlins camps from Scotland to Cornwall, from Wales to Great Yarmouth – all the places I'd worked 12 years previously. I'd go on at nine o'clock at night in front of 1,500 people and 700 of them seemed to be kids doing knee slides across the ballroom floor in front of me. It was demoralising. Was this really how my career was going to end? Back where it had started? Sometimes, if I could be bothered, I'd sing – they wanted to hear the old classics from *Grease* and *Boogie Nights*, but most nights I'd stick to stand-up. It hurt, but bills had to be paid. Following that, Butlins Bognor invited me back to appear as their special cabaret in July. Why not? They were using a lot of people they considered has-beens at the time and I was just another name on that list.

By this time Coleen had given birth to a little baby girl, Ciara, and also landed the job of hosting ITV's *This Morning*. It meant she needed to come backwards and forwards to meetings in London before the job started in September. I talked her into using my house, which of course used to be ours, as her base. The whole family came down with her and while they were staying I put Ray to good use and he became my musical director at Butlins every Saturday night. At last I could put the mini disc away and sing with a live band.

It soon became clear that Coleen couldn't commute backwards and forwards from Blackpool to London forever. She was going to need to move back to London with my boys. I suggested that she, Ray, Shane, Jake and Ciara all move in with Claire and me. Why wouldn't they stay at the place that had been their home? Other people found it weird, but to me there was nothing strange or unnatural about it. Surely it was better for Shane and Jake to see their mum and dad getting on together, rather than arguing in front of them. Ray was secure enough about his relationship with Coleen and as for me, I'd finally got what I wanted: my boys back under the same roof.

Friends would pop round in the evening and when Coleen opened the door their jaws would drop – had we got back together? They'd come in and there would be Coleen and Ray cuddled up on one couch and Claire and me with our arms around each other on the other. Dinner times were strange. While my boys were outside playing football with their mates we'd all look at each other not quite knowing who was going to make the first move about making dinner. Claire was a great cook and she'd do exotic dishes from around the world, but Coleen's speciality was bangers and mash. Occasionally I'd do the cooking. Of course I never knew where anything was. From the kitchen I'd shout through to the living room ''Ere, darling, where's the potato masher?'

Coleen and Claire would answer at the same time: 'In the cupboard under the sink.'

To her credit Claire was supportive about the whole plan. She could see I was desperate to have my boys around me. But what did upset her was the amount of time I spent chatting to Coleen. In the evenings Ray would eventually go to bed, Claire would go up too and I'd tell her I'd follow in a minute, but then I'd just sit and talk for hours with Coleen. We spoke about Claire, but more importantly about our boys.

By now Coleen and I were going through our divorce. We'd both been advised by friends to get the best and most expensive showbiz lawyers, but at the same time we wanted to sort it out as amicably as we could. Unfortunately that's not what the lawyers wanted. My lawyer would say, 'You know she's entitled to half and we've got to defend it,' and I'd say, 'No, she's entitled to whatever she wants.' They'd give us each secret instructions and then we'd promptly sit down and discuss them with each other. The lawyers were furious when they found out and insisted that all business was conducted solely through them.

One of the first things they asked us to do was list all our belongings and their value. I was even asked to itemise every single piece of *Planet of the Apes* memorabilia and how much it was worth. Now a ragged old *Planet of the Apes* comic from the 1970s was probably worth 2p. To Coleen it was worth even less. To me it was priceless. Coleen meanwhile had to walk around the house listing everything that was hers, even down to her underwear drawer. We both hated it. To make matters worse my memory wasn't that great, so I didn't list half of what was in the house. This list would then be sent to Coleen and she'd tell her lawyer that I'd missed off the grand piano, the juke boxes and the cinema equipment. Of course every time I missed something off the lawyers would have to prepare a new affidavit. They were £500 a time and we ended up doing four of them. Money was flying out of the window. When we finally did end up in court Coleen and I sat there giggling at opposite sides of the room, flicking bits of paper at each other. Our lawyers meanwhile were stony faced and barely able to speak to each other. It was pathetic.

Although I'd gone back to the holiday camps it was simply to make money, and deep down inside I was adamant now about what I wanted to do. I wanted to be taken seriously as an actor. No more variety shows, no more game shows or panel games, just straight acting. In the late summer of 2001 I got my chance.

A writer-director called Malcolm Needs got in touch with my office and said he was working on a small film, set in 1939 in an East End jazz club. He had some producers on board who had between £80,000 and £120,000, they already had a set at the old Brick Lane musical hall in the East End of London and they wanted to know if I'd be interested in appearing in it. When we met we got on like a house on fire. Malcolm explained the story. It would start in the present day with a young lad who shares a flat with his girlfriend and best mate. He's been left a derelict building in Shoreditch in his grandmother's will and when he goes into the basement he sees there was once a club in there. The film then cuts back to the 1930s with me playing Thomas Hickman who ran the club. It sounded a great dark story, full of incest, affairs and betrayal and I was happy to do it for next to nothing because I thought it was the perfect chance to re-invent myself.

Spongo meanwhile was having personal problems and needed

somewhere to stay. How could I turn him down? He moved back into the manor. He liked the idea that this film was going to be a labour of love, so he said he'd help get a bunch of musicians in. Little did I know that one of the guys was going to be Elton John. Spongo knew him and apparently Elton loved that era and his aunty had loved me in *Lucky Numbers* so he said he'd be happy to do a cover song for us for the soundtrack. He didn't want a fee, he was happy to do it for a slice of the film profits. In the end it didn't even cost us a taxi fare. He walked round to the studio from his house in Holland Park, sang the song 'Making Whoopee' and then walked home. Wow! We'd not shot anything yet and already we'd got Elton John on board. Now I was really fired up. We then managed to get Cleo Laine's daughter, Jackie Dankworth, to play the nightclub singer for a nominal fee.

Now the producers started panicking. How were they going to afford to buy the equipment for the film? They needed cameras; they needed period costumes and props for the sets. I contacted Marcia Stanton, who dressed me for all my shows and she said she'd help with the costumes. Big Mark had his own security firm and said he'd provide security and drivers. Meanwhile more great names were coming on board. The singer Dane Bowers was another mate of mine and he jumped at the chance to play a nightclub crooner. We got Adam Ross, a good actor and the younger brother of Jonathan and Paul, to play the young guy and I persuaded the producers to give Claire the part of his girlfriend. We then got Brian Bovell, who starred in *Gimme Gimme Gimme* with Kathy Burke, to play Adam's best friend. Another friend of Spongo's was the actor John Standing and he agreed to come and play the solicitor. We also managed to get Lance Ellington, Ray Ellington's son, to play his own dad.

It was a wonderful cast, but every time we came back with another name, the producers were more and more edgy. They thought the whole project was running away from us and getting far too big and costly and that we should pull it back a bit. Pull it back? Anyone who's ever met me knows that's not my way.

Next on the list we needed an actress to play my wife. I was quite keen on us using Sally Anne Triplett, who'd played Rizzo opposite me in

Grease, but Malcolm felt it was better to get someone who was known solely as an actress, who would bring out my performance. I was gutted, but he said it was better to cast someone I didn't know, because we didn't want it to seem as if I were simply surrounding myself with friends. We found a young woman who'd just done *Gosford Park*, called Natasha Wightman. She came to read for Malcolm and me in our tiny offices in the East End and she blew us away. She'd been out of the country for quite a while and didn't know I was Mr Game Show. 'I hear you did a Daz advert,' she said after the audition. 'What? Oh, yes, but that was ages back,' I said and changed the subject!

We then needed someone to play my sidekick, William. I was desperate for Tony Hadley, the former lead singer in Spandau Ballet, to get the part. Tony was a mate and was having the same problem as me at the time, in that he'd become pigeon-holed, so I felt for him. We tried out a scene at my house and he was phenomenal; he put so much into his character. I went back to Malcolm and said we had to use him, but Malcolm returned to the argument about the dangers of surrounding myself with old mates. Tony was disappointed, but he understood. Instead we found an impressive young actor called Joe Shaw, who'd done various bits and pieces. It turned out he was Martin Shaw's son and he used to sit and entertain us with stories about his dad in *The Professionals*. We then roped in Glenn Murphy from *London's Burning* to play a heavy, and a fabulous actor called Jonathan Coy to play Karl, a sleazy official from the War Office.

The most difficult job was to find someone to play the nightclub singer, Butterfly – the leading lady. Malcolm came back to my place one night and we sat down and made a wish list. He was thinking artistic, but I was thinking publicity. Who would get this film noticed and talked about?

No. 1: Victoria Beckham. Why not? I knew her personal assistant. I rang the girl and she put it to Victoria, who loved the idea, but said at that moment she'd rather concentrate on her singing career.

No. 2: Kylie. She was up for it, but had a promotional tour to do. If we could move the dates she was on board. We couldn't. We had a strict eight-week shooting schedule that started in October. It was set in stone.

No. 3: Samantha Janus. She wasn't keen. I think she wanted to re-invent herself too and didn't want to be associated with Shane Richie anymore. It was nothing personal, we were still great mates, but after we'd been together in *Grease* for so long, she thought it might be a bit cheesy to team up again.

No. 4: Martine McCutcheon. She wanted to do it, but she was having problems with *My Fair Lady* at the time. She'd had time off with throat problems and she knew if she was seen singing in a movie it would really wind up Cameron Mackintosh.

No. 5: Amanda Holden. She was also keen, but was about to start a new series called *Cutting It* and her bosses at Granada wouldn't let her out.

We were only a couple of weeks away from pre-production and getting quite anxious when Malcolm called me at home one day.

'Shane, I think I've got us a leading lady,' he said excitedly.

'Who is it?'

'No, I need to see you face to face.'

He came round and told me to sit down.

'Shane, we've got someone who I think will make this film.' He could hardly contain himself.

'Who's that then?'

'Joely Richardson. She wants to do it.'

I couldn't believe our luck. She wasn't going to do it for nothing, but she liked the fact that it was a British film and she'd get the chance to sing. I think she wanted to re-invent herself slightly too. The only problem was that her management weren't too sure about her appearing alongside Shane Richie.

When the producers heard this they told Malcolm that they'd need to re-cast my part and give me a smaller role. I was happy to step down, but Spongo said: 'Hang on. It's Shane and I who've got you Elton and all these other singers.' And Malcolm told them that if I wasn't the lead, he wasn't doing it anymore. I owe him a big favour for sticking by me like that. The producers told Joely that I'd been with the film since the beginning and that if she didn't want to appear with me they'd have to find someone else. She went away and thought about it and came back and said she was still interested. Was I flattered? Her last leading man was some bloke called Mel Gibson in *The Patriot* and now it was going to be me.

Around that time I compèred a charity event for a school for kids with learning difficulties in High Wycombe, Buckinghamshire. The kids were *Grease*-mad and I went along and presented the prizes. While I was there I met a guy who was the managing director of a company that rented out cameras and lights. At the end of the night he gave me his card and told me that if there was ever anything he could do for me, I should get in touch. Literally two days later Malcolm sat me down and said we needed to get hold of cameras and lights. What's more, we'd need to blag them because we didn't have much money. I couldn't believe it; it must have been fate. I dug out this guy's card and called him and true to his word he gave us the cameras and lights for next to nothing.

Money was now getting a bit tight, we only had £120,000 maximum, so to appease the producers I said I'd put in a few quid myself. I came up with £15,000, which would cover day-to-day stuff, such as food for the crew and taxis. The producers told me to keep receipts and I'd get the money back at the end when we sold the film.

A week later the £15,000 had been spent.

'Don't worry Shane, you'll get it back when we've sold the film,' I was told again. Fair enough. We needed another £2,000 just to get through the next couple of days so I emptied out my building society account. Two days later that had gone.

'Don't worry Shane, you'll get it back when we've sold the film,' I was reassured yet again. I called Stan. I was due to appear in panto that Christmas. Could Qdos sub me £15,000 of the money I'd get from the panto? Not surprisingly Stan asked if I knew what I was doing. Bear in mind I'd set the panto money aside for my divorce.

'Yeah, yeah,' I said impatiently. Now, all of a sudden, the film owed me £32,000. This carried on and on until I'd been subbed all my panto money – all £130,000 of it. Spongo, meanwhile, who had been due to go away with Robbie Williams, pulled out of the tour and cleared out his bank account. My mates and extras were chipping in £200 here, £100 there.

It still wasn't enough. Two weeks into filming the producers suddenly called a meeting with Malcolm and I and said they couldn't afford to go any more.

'But I'm skint, I can't put in anymore,' I told them. They apologised profusely and said that if anyone wanted to take the film over they'd be more than welcome, but it would need to be in the next 24 hours otherwise they'd have to shut everything down. People weren't going to wait – they had other schedules. Joely was about to do a play with her mum in the West End; she only had these few weeks set aside. If there was any chance I was going to re-launch my career it was in a film starring opposite Joely Richardson. And this wasn't just my dream. By now so many people had invested so much time and money in this project. I couldn't let it go.

That afternoon I met my financial advisor, Kate Buxton. I know what you're thinking now – what on earth was I doing with a financial advisor? I'd never listened to a single piece of advice about money in my life. Kate still hadn't forgiven me for buying the *Planet of the Apes* wagon. Now I wanted to buy a film that hadn't even been finished yet. To my delight, rather than talk me out of it, she was as up for it as me.

'Right,' she said. 'We're going to form a company. Who else is in on this?'

No one. Just me.

Thankfully Kate wasn't going to let me do this on my own. She wanted to be a part of it too. Now we needed a name. We tossed around the idea of Bluecoat Productions after my days at Pontins, but in the end decided to name it after my mum whose maiden name was Meighan – Mother Meighan Productions. The next day I went off to Coutts Bank and re-mortgaged my house for close to £500,000.

Without a doubt it was the most stupid thing I've ever done. Friends had warned me that I might not even make my money back. They told me that other people might come in at the end and I'd just be another investor, but I was adamant that this wasn't going to happen. It was my production company and my film. I believed in it and I was prepared to risk everything I'd got to make it work. And besides, once the film was in the can, I was promised that it would be mine and I could sell it on and make my money back.

We went back to work and of course I was now the producer, which meant I was the one doing the hiring and firing. I hated the firing, but it had to be done because it was my money now. The hiring was much better and I even ended up giving the part of a musician and waiter to Ray, who along with Coleen and the boys was still living with me. Sadly, not for much longer…

The irony was that I got on well with Coleen, but things were slowly deteriorating with Claire and at times the atmosphere was hellish. I'd walk into a room and she'd walk out and vice versa. Coleen and Ray were well aware of this and I think they found it a bit awkward. In November they found their own place two miles away. I was distraught when they told me they were moving out. I'd already said goodbye to the boys once and now I had to do it all over again, but at least this time they were only going to be up the road. They left on a Friday and as I stood and watched them empty out their bedrooms that morning it broke my heart. I had to go to work at lunchtime and by the time I returned in the evening they'd gone. I walked in feeling desolate, to find Claire sitting crying on the couch.

'What's the matter?' I asked her.

'I'm going tomorrow,' she told me.

'What?'

'It's over. I can't do this anymore.'

I later found out she'd had it planned for weeks. She'd told Coleen; she'd even told the gardener. Everyone seemed to know except me. What's more, she'd waited until she'd virtually finished filming her part in the movie before telling me. For a long time mates had warned me that she was using me and I never believed them. At that point I finally did. The following morning her mum and brother turned up with a removal van and loaded all her possessions and everything we'd ever bought together.

While they packed I sat down at the lake at the bottom of my garden with Spongo. I felt desolate. It wasn't just that Claire was leaving me, it was that I'd suddenly realised that this was how Coleen must have felt when I left her and I hated myself for it. I'd kidded myself that she'd coped, but the truth was she'd had years of anti-depressants and counselling before she was able to move on and find happiness again. It suddenly dawned on me just how much I'd hurt her.

The worst thing was I didn't know why I'd done it. At the time I convinced myself it was great with Claire. It wasn't great; it was just different. I now realised that it was Coleen and I who were great together. I'd always felt that if you were going to leave your wife you should leave her for somebody you wanted to spend the rest of your life with, and I hadn't. Nobody had made me feel as good about myself as Coleen did. I told Spongo that if I had all the money in the world right then I'd have invented a time machine and gone back and changed what had happened. And I really meant it. That way I could have avoided hurting Claire as well. She was a fun-loving girl when I met her, but I'd broken her spirit and her confidence.

To cope with my pain I threw myself back into work. It was my only salvation. Rehearsals had begun for panto, so by the day I was working on *Jack and the Beanstalk* and by night I was filming *Shoreditch*. Love was the last thing on my mind, so it made me laugh to read reports in the papers that I was having a fling with Joely Richardson. Paparazzi started hanging around and word leaked out that we'd filmed a love scene. We certainly got on well and I hope there was a chemistry on screen, but that was all there ever was to it. The truth was I still wanted to patch things up with Claire. I'd try to talk to her on the set and ask her what I could do to make it better between us, but she'd just tell me again and again that it was over.

My mates were worried about me. Spongo, Goz and Big Mark would all come to stay. They joked that they were on 24-hour watch. They were convinced that now I was on my own again I'd either get depressed or be out every night tearing it up, getting drunk and bringing strange women back to the house. But I didn't. I had no interest in that lifestyle anymore. I'd changed. I think I changed the day Claire walked out. If she didn't want me I'd rather be on my own and concentrate on trying to find myself again. I wanted to find the person I used to be; the man that Coleen and Claire had fallen in love with.

The film finished, having cost me close to £700,000 of my own money and I was promised that come the New Year it would be sold and I'd get all my money back. In December I went off to the Wimbledon Theatre in south London to play Jack. It was with a heavy heart. I'd never liked panto that much and as far as I was concerned there were only two positive things about it. The first was that I'd get to spend some time with Jake, who I'd got a part playing Harry Potting Shed. The second was the £130,000 cheque at the end of it, which had already been spent on the film. As far as I was concerned I would get nothing else out of it. How wrong could I be?

CHAPTER TWENTY

Love, happiness and Alfie Moon

I started panto as a single man. For the first time since my days as a Pontins Bluecoat I was on my own. The difference between then and now? This time I didn't want to make the most of the situation. I could have been out every night in a different club, drinking and picking up girls, but I didn't. I went the other way. I cut right back on the drink, I had some early nights and I actually found I was starting to enjoy the panto.

The opening night was in December and usual we held an opening night party in the dressing room with the local mayor, the producer and the director, all the cast and a few of my friends. I was just about to change out of my costume and start to greet them all when my mobile went. It was Goz.

'Where are you mate?'

'I'm in the foyer of the theatre, can you come down now?'

'Goz, I'm busy mate, I've people up here with me.'

'Shane, it's really important. I need you to come down now.'

'What is it?'

'My daughter's here.'

'What daughter?'

'Exactly.'

What neither of us knew was back in the 1980s when he was working at the holiday camps, Goz had fathered a child, who he'd never seen. My heart skipped a beat. I could only imagine what he was feeling.

I dashed downstairs and there standing in the foyer was Goz's double. It was like looking at a 15 year-old female version of Goz. I looked at Goz and could see his hands were shaking, he was so nervous he had no idea what to say.

It was time for me to help him out.

'Hello, my name's Shane,' I said to the girl.

'Hello, my name's Lauren,' she said.

'So, when's your Dad taking you to the zoo then?'

If in doubt, crack a gag!

I'm glad to say they have a great relationship now. Goz has the daughter he's always wanted and hopefully Lauren has got the Dad she always wanted.

On 16 December a group of mates from *Boogie Nights* came along to see the show and afterwards they persuaded me to go to the pub with them for a drink. I'm not really a pub person and as I'd been climbing up and down a beanstalk trying to kill a polystyrene giant all day, I wasn't really up for it. I'd just come off stage, I hadn't taken my make-up off properly and I looked a wreck. I reluctantly said I'd go for just the one.

As I stood and chatted to my mates they introduced me to a friend of theirs by the name of Christie Goddard. It was like the old cliché of your legs going from underneath you. She had the most beautiful eyes, the blondest hair and a lovely way about her. She knocked me for six. I fancied her straightaway and from that moment I knew I wasn't going to be on my own for much longer. We were like magnets. We started chatting and we must have seemed so rude because we just sloped off from everyone else and sat on our own in a corner for two hours. Other people tried to come across and say hello, but I couldn't take my eyes off Christie.

And in those two hours I forgot about everything else in my life. I discovered she was a great listener, very honest and so grown-up; even though she was 15 years younger than me she was an old head on young shoulders. And what was great for me about the whole evening was that I was single. I could talk to her without lying or feeling guilty. I didn't have to hide anything. It was such a relief. In that short time we talked about everything.

Christie told me that three days later she was due to start in panto herself, playing Cinderella in Croydon. At the end of the evening I asked for her phone number and told her that I'd send her flowers for her opening night. She laughed and said she knew what blokes were like. She'd take my number instead and see if I actually sent them. Then she'd call. Although we'd got on well I think she was wary. She had her own life and friends and although she didn't know a lot about me, she knew enough to know that she didn't want to be just another girl going out with Shane Richie. I really admired that about her.

At the end of the night I drove off with Goz and said to him: 'I've just met somebody I think I'm going to spend the rest of my life with.' I had butterflies in my stomach and walked around with a huge grin on my face for the next three days.

True to my word I ordered the largest bouquet of the most beautiful flowers I could find. As it was her opening night I knew all her friends and family would send heaps of flowers, so I organised for mine to be delivered a couple of hours after the show started, so she'd get them in the interval. That night I was walking through Wimbledon on my way to the theatre when my mobile rang. It was Christie.

'Mr Richie, I don't appear to have received any flowers yet.'

'What you talking about?'

'I thought you were going to send me flowers.'

'I thought you weren't going to phone me until you got them.'

'I just wanted to prove you wrong.'

'Well ring me back with your apology later,' I told her and hung up.

Two hours later she rang with a huge apology. The flowers had arrived in the interval as arranged and she loved them. I asked her if she'd meet me that night – she said she had her opening night party, but would see me the next day. I couldn't wait. I had her mobile phone number now so I sent her a text message saying, 'I miss you and I don't even know you.' And it was true.

We spent a lot of the next day talking to each other on the phone and that night Christie turned up at the Wimbledon Theatre to meet me. I looked a prat dressed up as Jack, with my loud T-shirt, baseball boots and silly make-up. Of course I had Jake with me, so after the show the only place I could take her was back to my house. And that was our first date – the three of sitting at home eating pizza and having a laugh. I suppose what it did do was make totally clear from the start that I came as a package – it was me and my boys. And luckily Christie had no problem with that. In fact I think it only brought us closer because she was a real family girl herself.

Five days later, on Christmas Eve, just eight days after we'd first been introduced, I knew I was in love and I had to tell her. That afternoon we met in my dressing room after the show and exchanged cards and presents. Here was my moment. I held her face in my hands and gazed straight into her eyes.

'Christie, there's something you need to know…I love you.'

'And I love you too, Shane.'

I kissed her tenderly on the lips and held on to her like I never wanted to let her go. I had absolutely no doubt about how I felt. This was the real thing. She was gracious, kind and loving, but more than that she made me feel good about myself. And I hadn't felt like that for a very long time.

That evening I bombed up to Blackpool with Jake to spend Christmas Day with Coleen, Ray, Shane and the family. I slept with my boys in their bedroom and the next morning we did all the Christmas stuff, hiding the presents and videoing the boys opening them. Later that morning Shane and Jake went off to have fun with their cousins and suddenly there was just me, Coleen and Ray. They'd invited me to stay for Christmas dinner, but it just didn't feel right. Coleen and Ray had a new baby now. It was their first Christmas with her. This wasn't where I belonged anymore and I made up my mind to drive back to London and spend the rest of the day by myself. It didn't bother me. I was perfectly happy to be on my own.

Then my mobile rang. It was Christie calling to wish me Happy Christmas. When I told her what I planned to do she was horrified. She told me I couldn't spend Christmas Day on my own and that I should come over for dinner with her family.

'Christie, I've only just met you,' I said. 'I can't come round and meet your family for the first time on Christmas Day.'

She shouted across to her mum, who said she'd be delighted to have me there. I hung up and asked Coleen if she'd mind if I went. I needed her blessing. She gave me a big hug.

'Shane, if it makes you happy then you get yourself back to London and go and be with Christie.'

It was 230 miles back to London and every ten minutes Christie would be on the phone and we'd tell each other how much we loved and missed each other. I couldn't wait to get there. I went home first and had a quick shower while singing at the top of my voice; it had been a long time since I last did that. I put on my best suit and went round to their house near Reigate in Surrey. I was pretty nervous, but excited at the same time. I walked in and met her mum, Jackie and her dad, Phil and her three sisters, Ashley, Kelley and Shelley. Kelley's boyfriend, Justin, was there too and it was really strange. It was like being back at the holiday camps and making brand new friends with a family on Christmas Day. They were really close and I envied them so much. I was made to feel so welcome and pretty soon I was scoffing their home-cooked dinner as if it was my own home. But after a while I noticed that Jackie couldn't make eye contact with me. Every time I looked across at her, she'd look down at her plate. She'd seen and read enough about me to know exactly who was sitting at her table. I later found out that from the conversations she'd had with Christie she knew this was the real thing and that I was the man who would be taking their daughter away from them.

That evening Christie came back to my place and we stayed up talking until the small hours. In front of the log fire we made love for the first time. I was so in love, nothing could spoil this day. Feeling sleepy, we got the quilt from my bed and slept in front of the burning logs. From that night on, she never went home. She made me feel so happy and made me feel like the man I'd always wanted to be. We couldn't bear to be away from each other, not even for a day.

The funny thing was, I still wanted Coleen's approval. Coleen and Ray had been invited to a Christmas party hosted by John Leslie a few days later and I was going to be there with Christie. I called Coleen the day before and said that I hoped she'd like Christie when she met her. Not surprisingly Christie was a bit upset when she found out what I'd done. Why did I need my ex-wife's approval on a new girlfriend? It was hard to explain but after all those years together Coleen was still my point of reference. I still needed her approval and trusted her judgement.

That New Year's Eve was one of the best I'd had for years – surrounded by people I wanted to be with, rather than people I felt I should be with. Professionally I was still nowhere, but personally I was going somewhere I wanted to be.

Then Stan broke the terrible news that he was going to call it a day. He'd been in the business for close to 40 years. Not only was he my personal manager, agent and close friend, but also I loved him like a father. He'd picked me up when I was down and guided my career like I was his own son. I found it hard to accept that he wouldn't be involved in my life anymore.

So here I was starting 2002 with no manager, no career, nothing at all in the diary and even less in the bank. What's more my company, Mother Meighan, was worth nothing. I'd been promised that *Shoreditch* was mine to sell on, but I discovered that wasn't the case. Somebody else owned the rights to the film and wasn't prepared to hand them over to me, even though I'd given every penny and more. I'd trusted the wrong people. I'd been done. Even those you think are close to you can shaft you. It was now down to the lawyers to sort this mess out, which meant spending even more money I didn't have.

Now when you're a big star on television everyone wants to know you, and that includes the banks. When you're not, they can be your worst enemy. I'd been with my bank for 15 years and held virtually every single account with them. When I was at the height of my fame their executives would take me to lunch and get me to perform at their corporate dos where they could show me off to their friends. I'd get them tickets for my shows and could talk to them day or night. Now all of a sudden I owed them £500,000 and was falling behind on my mortgage and they wouldn't take my calls. They got lawyers in and said they were going to serve a repossession order on me to take my house. Even their lawyers wouldn't take my calls; I had to get my own lawyer to speak to their lawyer. I had a lawyer for the film. I had a lawyer for the divorce and I now I had to have another lawyer to talk to my bank. I had more lawyers than Michael Winner's had free dinners.

On top of that I owed £50,000 to my credit card company. When I'd taken out the card the previous year they said: 'Shane Richie! We'll give you a £50,000 limit.' And I blew it on the movie.

I was in dire straights and had to call in favour after favour. Big Mark lent me £50,000 and my insurance broker, David Heath, even insured my car and paid for it himself. The lowest point came when, for the first time ever, I had to borrow money from my mum. I needed £3,000 to clear some bills. It was a lot of money to my mum but she didn't even bat an eye when I asked her. Here's a woman who lives in a council house in Wembley and works as a cleaner, having to lend money to her 37-year-old son who used to be a millionaire. I felt I'd let her down terribly.

Then Christie lent me £5,000. That was awful, as I hadn't known her very long. She knew I needed help when my Jeep was repossessed. I got a phone call one morning asking if I was going to be in all day. I said I was and asked why.

'You've defaulted on your payments for your car, we're coming to pick it up.'

I'd bought it brand new and had it customised with blacked-out windows, leather seats and a state-of-the-art sound system. It was £800 a month and it was £800 I didn't have. After that I drove Christie's car for a while and then her mum let me borrow her motor until I could find a deal on a rental car.

During the years when the money was pouring in, friends kept telling me to put some aside for a rainy day. How I wished I'd listened. The rainy day was here and I had absolutely no reserves to bail myself out.

In February Christie and I went on holiday to Jamaica. I'd won it in a charity raffle. I actually had a bit of luck for a change. We had a fantastic time. For the first time since Coleen I'd found a relationship that was based on honesty. It was pure. There were no secrets or lies. I could tell her everything and anything and I did. I was so happy with her that it put my money and career troubles into perspective. Had I won the Lottery at that point I think I could quite happily have cleared my debts, sold up and walked away from the business and gone abroad with Christie to live happily ever after.

I returned from Jamaica to the news that my dad was to be admitted to hospital for his liver and kidney transplant. It was sad to see this big strong man lying in a hospital bed looking so frail and vulnerable, but thankfully the operation was a success and my dad was told that as long as he stayed away from the drink there was no reason he couldn't live a long and healthy life.

In March came some bad news. Coleen's job at *This Morning* had gone belly up. I was gutted for her. I thought she was doing a great job. Ray wanted to work in London so she decided she would stick it out, rather than go back to Blackpool and I said I would try to help pay for her to stay here, but I was holding on by my fingertips, keeping the bailiffs away weekly. Realistically there was no way I could pay two mortgages. I'd been stitched up on the film. It made me so angry because the money I should have got back would have kept both our heads above the water.

To make matters worse there was absolutely no money coming in. With Stan gone I was in limbo. I was still with Qdos, but nobody in the office really knew what to do with me. There was talk of a show on Sky television, but the producers opted for one of the contestants from *Big Brother* instead. That's showbiz. Jon Conway was even talking about putting me back on the road with *Boogie Nights*, but I was having none of it. As far I was concerned *Boogie Nights* was part of the past; I needed to move on and besides, there was no way I wanted to be away from Christie.

It was then that Phil Dale stepped in. I'd known Phil for around 15 years, though we'd never really been formally introduced, and we had a mutual respect for each other. He was responsible for re-inventing Errol Brown's career with *The Full Monty* and he was fairly rock and roll – he reminded me of a young Stan. Stan always used to say to me, 'If you're going to bring down city hall, bring it down from the inside.' And that summed up Phil. He was a loner. He had a girlfriend, but no children and he seemed a bit of a playboy. What I really liked about him was that he seemed to live and breathe the business. He was now a director of

Qdos and during one of my endless meetings in their office he turned to Jon and said: 'Let me take the boy on. I'd like to manage him. He's ready again and I think he's got a fantastic future.'

He said it with such conviction that I believed him. Agents come and go, but I needed something more personal and Phil was the man to do it.

Of course I expected instant results. I'd call him every day and every day he'd say: 'Nothing at the moment, Shane, I'm making phone calls.'

'Phone calls for what?' I'd say impatiently and he'd explain that he was ringing casting directors. Phil looked after Paul Usher who was in *The Bill* and Tricia Penrose who was in *Heartbeat*, so he had some ins with TV executives.

I desperately needed to make some money. I looked at some strange things and at one time I was doing more pilots than a British Airways stewardess. In one show, thankfully never commissioned, I threw a dart at a map of the UK. Wherever it landed we'd get the phone book for that town and pick a number at random. We'd call and invite them into the studio, I'd ask them some questions and they'd get the chance to win a few thousand pounds. It was like *Parkinson* meets *Bullseye*. I'd do these pilots and they'd go forward to the BBC or ITV who'd say: 'Yes, we like it, but we're not sure about Shane.'

There was talk of me taking over in *Heartbeat* and at one point there were even plans to re-make *Budgie* with me as the lead, but nothing came of it. I could easily have given up, but Phil told me to persevere – it would happen eventually.

He was right. One day, out of the blue, he rang to tell me he'd landed me a casting for *The Bill*.

'Yeah, that would be good Phil, put me down. I'll play a copper, stay a couple of years, re-invent myself as an actor and take it from there.'

'Don't jump the gun, Shane, just go along for a meeting,' Phil told me. Louis Hammond, who'd hired me for *Burnside*, was there. I read for him and was offered a part. It wasn't a copper, it was a much smaller role, but as far as I was concerned it was a start: they wanted me. Phil turned it down though. He said it was too small a part and wasn't right for me. I was nervous, but I decided to trust his judgement.

A few weeks later I was offered a part in an ITV soap called *Night and Day*. It had a great cast including Lesley Joseph, Joe McGann, Lysette Anthony and Glynis Barber. The soap had been going a few months and it wasn't getting great reviews but I just needed to get in front of a camera again and show I was capable of doing it. I didn't have a car, so I'd get up in the morning, give Christie a kiss and set off to catch the train to Bow in East London where it was being filmed. I was only supposed to do a couple of episodes, but while I was there they discovered the show wasn't going to be re-commissioned and so my character suddenly had to tie up all the loose ends. I went from playing a sycophantic lover to a killer, to a child abductor to a mass murderer. And all in the space of four weeks!

Around that time Phil told me he'd received a cast breakdown from *EastEnders*. When the show is looking for a new character they approach the major agencies with details of the sort of actor or actress they're looking for.

They were looking for a 6ft tall cheeky Londoner to play a fireman by the name of Tom.

'This is you, Shane,' Phil told me. 'You can do this.'

'Don't be daft, Phil, they're not gonna want to see me.'

'Let's see what I can do.'

He made a call while I waited in his office and before he came off the line the smile on his face said it all. I'd only gone and got an audition for *EastEnders*.

The night before I couldn't sleep and went over everything I thought they could possibly ask me. Phil had already warned me they had reservations about my baggage and I rehearsed my answers to their possible questions over and over again in my head.

I went along to the *EastEnders* studios at Elstree and met the Executive Producer Louise Berridge and Julia Crampsie, Head of Casting, and I immediately felt at home. They asked me to read for them. They set up a video camera on a tripod, pretty much like the one you'd have at home, and handed me a script. Julia pretended to be Sharon Watts while I was Tom. It lasted about 15 minutes, trying it in different ways. Some with an accent, some without, standing up, sitting down, slow and fast; I'd have done it naked if they'd asked me.

After I'd finished reading we sat and chatted for 20 minutes and they asked what I'd been up to recently. Bloody hell, where should I start? I told them stories from *Grease* and how I'd just finished producing a film with myself and Joely called *Shoreditch*. Louise seemed to like the idea that I was taking control of my life and taking my career seriously.

I left Elstree and phoned Phil immediately.

'Phil, have you heard anything?'

'Shane, you've only just left.'

'OK, but let me know won't ya.'

In the meantime Phil asked me to try to get together a short clip from *Shoreditch*. It was easier said than done. Although the film was in the can, it was also in the hands of the lawyers. I either needed someone to come in and buy the whole thing from me, or to find another investor to help me to finish it by paying for post-production. This meant editing, dubbing the sound and generally putting together the finishing touches. But no one wanted to touch it. What? Shane Richie? The bloke who did the game shows? So what if Joely Richardson's in it? You should have got a bigger star than him. That was the reaction. Even though it wasn't finished I managed to get a friend to help put together a three-minute trailer and Phil biked it off to Louise at Elstree. The part of Thomas Hickman was so different from Shane Richie and hopefully she would see that I could play someone other than the Cockney wideboy.

A couple of days later *EastEnders* called and said they'd like me to go back and do a screen test for the part of Tom in a studio. Things were slowly creeping forward. When I got there they seemed pleased to see me again and after a little chat, they gave me the script and said they were going to break for lunch. After lunch we'd go into the Queen Vic to do some filming.

The Queen Vic?

'Yeah, no worries,' I said with a smile. 'See you after lunch then.'

I went straight to the toilets and threw up. I came out and phoned Christie straightaway. 'You're never going to believe this, babe, they only want me to screen test in the Queen Vic.'

Meanwhile there were 24 messages from Phil wanting to know what had happened. I phoned and told him and then my mum called.

'Mum, I can't talk, I'm just about to go into the Queen Vic.'

'What de feck are ya doing there?'

'Mum, I've got no time to explain. Talk to you later. Love ya.'

I called Coleen and my boys and everyone was rooting for me.

I went back inside and they brought two of the cast members along, Gary Beadle, who plays Paul Trueman and Kim Metcalfe who plays Sam Butcher. I did a scene with each of them; with Paul I had to square up to him when I came off the phone and with Kim I had to flirt while she was behind the bar. I was bloody petrified but I did my best not to show it. I ended up loving every second of it, I was in my element.

When I got home I sat down with Christie and excitedly re-enacted my whole day, scene by scene, line by line, like a little boy coming home from his first day at school. And then I sat and waited by the phone again. A couple of days later *The Bill* got back in touch with Phil. They wanted me to read for the part of an undercover copper. Phil had been right turning down the smaller part. I put *EastEnders* to the back of my mind and went along.

Of course all these auditions weren't paying the bills, but I didn't care. I'd have quite happily done auditions for the next six months if I thought it was going to put my career in the right direction. The bank didn't feel the same way though. In April I received a letter instructing me to appear in court. I owed more than £1 million on the house, I'd just ploughed nearly £700,000 into the movie and now I was £120,000 behind on my mortgage. The bank couldn't hold on anymore – they were winding things up. I went to court and somehow managed to persuade them to give me six months breathing space on my mortgage. In those six months I desperately needed to find myself some work and some money.

In the middle of all this, Phil received a phone call from *EastEnders*. It was bad news. They hadn't felt I was right for that character. In the end they'd gone for another actor, an Irishman by the name of Colm O Maonlai, but they wanted me to go along and do some workshops instead. Now I'd done enough workshops to last me a lifetime and I knew they didn't necessarily lead to a job, but I had nothing else to do so I went. I felt pretty confident. Workshop is all about improvisation.

I'm not saying I'm the master of improv, but I've never had a problem thinking on my feet. The day I was in they'd brought in a group of actors who were all much younger than me. They gave us a situation where we were a group of brothers; one of the brothers was turning 18 and they asked how we would celebrate. It would have been so easy to take over and do gag after gag, but I held back and listened. I didn't ramble and I chose my moments. It worked and several times I was called back for more workshops. In one of them I even did an improv with a girl called Scarlett Johnson, who eventually landed a part in the show herself, as Vicki Fowler.

At home, meanwhile, Christie and I were bang in love. For the first time in a long time I would wake up in the morning and look forward to the rest of the day. I was blissfully happy. Christie met my boys and they both adored her. Jake fell in love with her and Shane, who is actually closer to her age than I am, said to me: 'Dad, you do realise when I'm 16 I'll be steaming in on your girlfriend.' Cheers Shane, make me feel better, big boy. He's got a great sense of humour. No idea where he gets it from.

Around this time there was more talk of me presenting *The Generation Game*. This time they were a bit more serious. Phil said it was up to me. He said that if I did *The Generation Game*, then *Shoreditch* and all these auditions and workshops would be for nothing. On the other hand it would be a chance to get back on top and earn bundles of money.

There was no way. I'd come this far and I didn't want to go back there. I'd done the game show thing, I had to move forward. That's not to say I would never do it again. Because as Stan used to say, 'Never say never'.

By now the bank had frozen all my assets and shut down all my accounts. But it wasn't about the money anymore. I'd been there and had the money and the big cars and I'd been unhappy. We decided to stick with what we were doing. Then *The Bill* rang back. They wanted me for the part of the undercover copper. I sat down with Phil and we discussed what to do.

Phil immediately called *EastEnders*. *The Bill* had made an offer and we wondered what the situation was. They were very polite, but said that at this stage they couldn't offer me anything definite. To my amazement Phil still suggested I turn *The Bill* down.

'Phil, are you mad? It's too big a gamble.'

'Trust me, Shane.'

Ironically, while my career was still stalling, both my boys were racing ahead. Through a friend of a friend, Jake had landed a small part playing an orphan in a film about J M Barrie, called *Neverland*. It was filmed in Richmond, Surrey and starred Dustin Hoffman and Johnny Depp. It was a paid role and ironically I was paid too - £50 a day for being his chaperone! I wasn't proud – it came in handy and I took it. At the same time Shane was just signing a deal to join Blackpool Football Club. At least two members of the Richie family were earning anyway!

In early June Christie's parents asked us to join them and their daughter Ashley in a villa they'd rented for a week in Majorca. I was a bit unsure about going away when I was struggling so much financially, but Christie said she'd pay for the flights. I was glad we went. There was a great atmosphere out there and I bumped into quite a few people I knew – cabaret acts and comics I'd worked with, who'd hung their boots up in Britain and were making a decent living for themselves out in Majorca. All of a sudden I had an idea. If the bank repossessed my house I could come out and make a few quid working the hotels and bars. Christie was quite happy about it. It sounded like a nice new lifestyle. I'd had the fame and everything that goes with it. Now I was in love and that was more important.

The island was buzzing at the time because we were slap bang in the middle of the World Cup. The day England were due to play Argentina, Christie's dad Phil and I found a pub where there were loads of lads I knew. We sank several beers between us and watched David Beckham's goal knock out Argentina. That afternoon we left the pub on a high and made our way back to the villa where the girls were cooking a barbecue. I was giggling and singing, 'Beckham, Beckham, la la la la la' as I danced around the garden. I'd pretty much stopped drinking by then, so it hadn't taken a lot to make me legless. Eventually I went inside and picked up my mobile. There were 19 missed calls. They were all from Phil. He's a big Man United supporter like me and I assumed he'd been ringing because Beckham had scored and he'd been watching the game as well.

I called him back.

'Phil, it's Shane, how are you?'

'I'm fine, how are you?'

Of course I couldn't stop giggling. 'I'm great.'

'Shane, I want you to remember this day for the rest of your life.'

'Bloody right an' all. Beckham knocking the Argies out of the World Cup, come on son!'

At this point Christie started videoing me. I have a tendency to walk around when I'm on the phone and there I was weaving up and down the side of the pool with a beer in one hand and the phone in the other. She thought it looked hilarious and would be funny to show me later.

'No, Shane, I've got news for you.'

He sounded so serious that I stopped and looked up at Christie and frowned.

'What is it, Phil?'

'*EastEnders* want you.'

I could hardly speak. I looked across at Christie with tears welling up in my eyes. By now she was convinced it was bad news.

'Phil, hang on a moment.'

I put my hand over the phone.

Christie shouted across: 'What's the matter, babe?'

'*EastEnders* want me!'

I shouted across to Jackie and Phil and Ashley and everyone started yelling and jumping around.

Meanwhile Phil was trying to talk to me.

'No Shane, hold on, there's more, there's more.'

'What do you mean there's more?'

'Listen carefully, they want you. Not only that, you're coming in as a new character called Alfie.'

I wasn't too keen on the name, but it grew on me very quickly. I'd have quite happily been called Nancy if it meant a part in *EastEnders*.

'What am I then? Am I running a stall on the market, am I working in the café?'

'No, Shane, in your first episode you're coming in and you're taking over the Queen Vic.'

At that point it felt like David Beckham had come running out of the bushes and kicked me right in the nuts. I could hardly breathe. I started to laugh and cry all at once.

'I wish you were here, Phil, so I could give you a big hug.'

'Hang on Shane, there's a but…'

'What is it?'

'You can't tell anyone for three months.'

It was a small price to pay. I put the phone down and ran straight across the lawn and threw my arms around Christie. She knew the pain I'd been through, she'd seen what had happened to my career and she'd heard people say, 'Didn't you use to be Shane Richie?' but now I was coming back.

When we returned to Britain I immediately told the boys and Coleen and swore them to secrecy. I thought I'd leave it a while before I told my mum and dad, because as much as my mum thinks she can keep a secret I knew she would have been straight down to Woolies to tell her friends that her son was going into *EastEnders*.

I then went in to see Louise Berridge and Julia Crampsie. My house is about half an hour's drive from Elstree and I was so elated I could have run all the way there. Louise introduced me to a guy called Tony Jordan. Tony was a writer and a series consultant, which meant that he liaised with the writers, story editors and Louise on potential storylines. He was also the man responsible for Sharongate, The Slaters, Who Shot Phil – and now my character.

Of course I wanted to know everything about Alfie.

'He's been in prison for five years.'

'Well, what for?'

'We can't tell you that at the moment, Shane.'

They told me that Alfie would turn up at Walford Station by accident after being thrown off the Underground there. He would make his way through the Square and by the end of the episode he'd have convinced Peggy Mitchell he was the new manager of the Queen Vic, Chris Wright.

We then discussed a surname. I quite liked the name Carter, as a tribute to Michael Caine and also I thought Alfie Carter had a nice ring to it. They said they'd think about it, but rang me the next day to say they'd decided on Alfie Moon. Alfie I'd got used to by now, but Moon? I couldn't think of anything worse. Needless to say I kept my opinions to myself, I hadn't even signed the contract yet.

The next decision was Alfie's style. We went for jeans and cowboy boots and I suggested lairy shirts. He'd been in prison for five years and wouldn't be quite up to date with fashion, but still wouldn't look totally out of place. I also suggested a long black leather coat, which proved a big mistake. A few years previously while on holiday in New York I'd bought a long black leather coat. It was before my money troubles and it had cost me the best part of $3,000. It was my pride and joy. Now there was no way I could ever wear it again because it would always be associated with Alfie Moon.

They told me I'd have a much younger brother called Spencer and a grandmother I'd call Nana Moon. I was impressed; they'd got it all planned out. Louise told me she'd known I wasn't right for the part of Tom the fireman the minute she'd seen me. She said she'd seen something else – a brand new character. I was so honoured. They had created Alfie Moon for me. It wasn't put out there for an open audition, it wasn't put out there for other actors; Alfie was created just for me.

By the middle of June the story had leaked out into the press. Overnight my life changed.

'What? I can now talk to the bank? The bank manager wants to speak to me again?'

Then the company that took away my car called offering me another car. And how about this, folks: *Shoreditch*, which had been lying on a dusty shelf in an office in Soho was now back on track again. A private investor had approached me. He thought it was a great idea that Shane Richie was starring alongside Joely Richardson in a film and wanted to put in some money to help finish the film.

That's how it works. When you're down the bastards want to kick you, when you're up they want to put you on their shoulders.

Sadly the TV company that had brought Ooleen down to London

had now turned their back on her. I really felt for her. Producers come and go, but Coleen is a real talent and she deserved better than that. She hadn't been able to pick up enough work and in July she told me she was moving back to Blackpool permanently with Ray, Ciara and my boys. Please, not again. The only consolation in it all was that my new job would enable me to spend more time with them. There wouldn't be the endless nights away on tour in god-forsaken places. I was finally about to get some consistency and purpose in my life.

In August I was invited to Elstree to watch an *EastEnders* episode being filmed and to be officially shown round. Of course I'd been there before with Anthea Turner. When the tour reached the Fowlers' house I held my breath and stole a glance at the fridge. My graffiti had been removed and I wasn't about to put it back.

The episode they were filming that day was Little Mo and Trevor caught inside the Slater's burning house with Tom the fireman dying heroically as he went in to rescue them. What an ironic coincidence. It could so easily have been me. It was Halloween and all the cast were there, dressed up in crazy outfits and masks. I already knew some of them – Barbara Windsor (Peggy Mitchell), Dean Gaffney (Robbie Jackson), Wendy Richard (Pauline Fowler), Shaun Williamson (Barry Evans) and Adam Woodyatt (Ian Beale). Funnily enough when Adam was 16 we'd been part of the same crowd for a while and I was the one who'd introduced him to nightclubs – he's never let me forget it since. All these years on he was showing me around Albert Square; it had come full circle.

I was taken to the room that would be my dressing room. On the door there was already a sign – Shane Richie, Borough of Walford. I looked up at it and swallowed hard; I felt so proud. The dressing rooms at *EastEnders* are a bit like a Travelodge – long corridors with rooms either side. Next door to me was Shaun and opposite was Pam St Clement, who plays Pat Evans. Also on my corridor was Natalie Cassidy, who plays Sonia Jackson and of course Jessie Wallace, who plays Kat Slater, who would go on to become the love of Alfie's life.

Now don't think for one moment that a BBC dressing room is glamorous. Far from it. It reminded me of where I'd started – in a Pontins chalet. Just the bare essentials: a chair that folds out into a bed, a sink, a loo, a shower and a fridge. But I didn't care; it was mine.

I finally signed the contract and was given my first scripts. Eight episodes arrived in the post at once. How on earth was I going to learn all this? I immediately phoned Barbara Windsor, who would go on to become Alfie's 'Duchess'.

'Sweetheart, don't panic, just one at a time, love. Sit down each night, darlin', and spend two hours looking at what you've gotta do tomorra. You'll be fine.'

Two hours reading? I couldn't even sit still for half an hour. But I knew Barbara was right. I needed discipline in my life. I needed to make this work.

I started recording my first episodes in September – ironically the same month as my divorce came through. As I stood behind the bar of the Queen Vic for the first time my hands literally shook. I suddenly realised how far my journey had taken me. *Toad of Toad Hall*, the Belisha beacon, the Donkey Derby and Glamorous Granny, Jersey's very own Mahatma Coat, those endless nights at pubs, clubs and holiday camps, the lead in *Grease*, game show after game show, the Daz ads, my opening night in *Boogie Nights*, *Shoreditch*, the hearts I'd broken on the way, the money I'd lost. And now I could put it all behind me. I'd been given a fresh start.

On 21 November 2002 Alfie made his first appearance on screen.

What viewers didn't see in that first episode as I walked out of Walford station was the crew standing at the side of the cameras with a huge box of Daz. 'Oi, Richie, is this yours?' they shouted. I knew immediately I was at home.

The reception I received from the press and viewers was overwhelming. Who'd have predicted women under the age of 40 would be uttering the words, 'I fancy Shane Richie' and not getting laughed at?

So how do I feel? At times confused, at times honoured, but most of the time like a kid in a sweet shop. Never again will I be complacent; never again will I take anything for granted and every time I turn on my television at 8pm on a Monday night and hear the *EastEnders* music start up, I remind myself how lucky I've been and more importantly how lucky I am.

No one knows what the future holds, but one thing's for sure, right now this is where I belong.

Index

3-2-1 130
999 226

Abbott, Russ 111
adoption plans 172, 200
alcohol 84, 203, 215–7, 222–3
America 66–70, 134–9, 237–50
Armour, Liz 34
Aunty Kathleen 28
Aunty Mary 21, 197–8

Baddiel, David 127
Ball, Bobby 113, 122 *see also* Cannon
    and Ball
Ball, Michael 254
Barlow, Gary 100
Barrymore, Michael 131
Bay City Rollers 20–1
Beach Boys, The 182
Beckham, David 187, 278
Berg, Paul 134, 238
Berridge, Louise 280, 281
Big Breakfast, The 180
Big Mark 155, 173, 177, 257, 263, 271
Black and White Minstrel Shows 52
Blackpool 128, 189, 215–16, 230, 268,
    278, 282
Bluecoats 11, 29–30, 38–40, 47–9, 52,
    59, 82, 85–6 *see also* Pontins
Boogie Nights 34, 199, 201, 212
    in Blackpool 215–16
    in Bromley 196–7
    in Southend 203
Bournemouth 108
Bowen, Jim 124
Boyzone 182
Brean Sands 58, 59–65
Bromley 196–7
brothers
    Dean 16–17, 20, 37, 183
    Ricky 122–4
Bruce, Ken 72, 75
Burke, Michael 226

Burnside 229
Butlins
    Bognor 120, 122, 254
    Somerset 99
Buxton, Kate 261

Caesar's Palace 97
Camber Sands 118
Canberra, returns from Falklands War 72–3
Cannon and Ball 106, 108, 109, 111, 121,
    155
Carroll, Lee 77
Carrott, Jasper 79–80
cars 151, 171, 186–7, 271
Carson, Frank 97
casting agents 138–9
Caught in the Act 141–2
Children's Royal Variety Show 162
Children's Society, The 200
Chitty Chitty Bang Bang 254
Christie, Steve 108, 116
Christmases 28–9, 57–8, 65–6, 99, 119,
    147, 190–1, 198–9, 226, 268–9
Class Enemy 58, 67
coach tours 72, 82–3
Cold Feet 182
Coleen *see* Nolan, Coleen
Collins, Phil 127
Comedians, The 79
Comedy Club, Silver Dollar 134
Conley, Brian 94, 108, 111, 147, 148, 160,
    183
Connolly, Billy 212, 246
Conway, Jon 9, 144, 231, 252, 272
Cosgrove, Johnny 97
Crampsie, Julia 9, 280
Cross, Lisa 41, 53, 88, 196
Cruise, Tom 208
Cryer, Maddie 133

Dale, Phil 9, 272–3, 279
Dallas, Stan 9, 120, 148–51, 155, 198, 231
    known as 'The Colonel' 157–8

moves to Qdos 196
retires 270
Dankworth, Jackie 257
Davro, Bobby 109, 111, 254
Daz adverts 167–70
Dead Clean 228
Deayton, Angus 79
debts 93, 270–1, 276
depression 218–20
Des O'Connor Tonight 130
Distant Shadow 228
Divas, The 232
Dixon, Mike 152
Donovan, Jason 160
drink problems 84, 203, 215–7, 222–3
drugs 35, 49, 132–3
Dye, Barry 9, 78, 89–90, 99, 119–20
Dying Rooms, The 172

EastEnders 11, 100–1, 153, 229, 274–83
Enfield, Harry 145
Eternal 182
Evans, Chris 79

Falklands 119, 121
tour 131
father (Harry) 16–17, 21, 24–5, 123–4,
197, 242–3, 272
drink problems 27–30, 90, 104–5
Fensome, Ray 231, 253
Fenwick, Perry 28
Ferguson, Sarah 179
Footballers' Wives 229
Fuengirola 80
Fun Funkyteers 52, 54

games 60
Gary T 118
gigolo 50–1
Goddard, Christie 266–271, 277
family 269, 278–9
Going Live 100, 142
Gosling, Chris *see* Goz
Goz 9, 66, 91–2, 132, 152
Bluecoat 58, 60, 117–18
Shane's PA 125, 146, 161, 163–82, 254
Best Man 128
lives with Shane 185
and Claire 190
in America 234–50
meets daughter 265–6
Grand Canyon 241–3

Grange Hill 35
Grease 79, 147–156, 177–84, 193
in Manchester 185–192
lead role 157–9, 159–63
Grumbleweeds 111

Hammond, Louis 229, 273
Hanger 17 153
Harlesden, NW London 17–19, 22, 31–2
Working Men's Club 26–7
Harris, Keith 111
hen nights 90–1
Henry, Lenny 79, 86–7, 142
Hillingdon 141
Hoffman, Dustin 162
homeless 55–7
Hopkins, Anthony 127

Ian, David 147, 148, 151, 161
Idol, Billy 136–7
Inside the Firm 193

Jack and the Beanstalk 263–4
Jameson Tonight 126, 130
Jameson, Derek 126–7
Janus, Samantha 177, 209, 259
Jersey 93, 97–8, 103–5, 106–8
banned from 143
John, Elton 257

Kray, Reggie 173–7

Lambrianou, Tony 193
Laugh Factory, the 136
Law, Annette 133
Les Dennis Show, The 130
Leslie, John 177, 269
Lewis, Frank 59, 66
Liptons supermarket 37
Little Canada 70–3, 85–9
Live from the Palladium 120
Longthorne, Joe 131
Los Angeles 66–70, 135
Love Me Do 195
Lucky Numbers 159, 160, 163–4, 180
Lulu 182
Lyle, George 135–7, 235, 237

Macbeth 228
Majorca 278
Manchester 185–192
Manning, Bernard 92–3

Marcus, Diane 32–3
Marie, Rose 125
Mathis, Johnny 130
Maxwell, Lisa 203, 209, 226
McLachlan, Craig 152, 153, 159
Me and My Girl 147
method acting 67–8
Miller, Mick 98
Mills, Bob 127, 155
Moir, Jim 142
Moonshine Youth Theatre 33–4
Morocco 83
Morrison, Terry 196, 234
mother (Elizabeth) 16–25, 31–2, 36, 42–6,
    53–4, 66–7, 81–2, 158–9, 197,
    242–3
Mother Meighan Productions 261, 270
motorbikes 234–5
Murphy, Stephen *see* Spud

Needs, Malcolm 256
Neverland 278
Newcastle 121
News of the World 131, 201
Newsround 23
Newton John, Olivia 178
Nielsen, Brigette 127
Night and Day 274
Night Fever 227
Noddy Train 63–4
Noel Edmonds Saturday Roadshow 130
Nolan, Brian 106, 109, 115
Nolan, Coleen 9, 105–6, 109, 111–22,
    127–8, 197
  babies 122–5, 141, 146–7, 233
  wedding plans 127–9
  marriage blessed 189
  discovers affair 198–9, 204
  end of marriage 210–11
  new relationships 214, 215, 231
  files for divorce 216–17
  moves to Blackpool 230, 282
  hosts *This Morning* 254
  loses job at *This Morning* 272
Nolan, Maureen 124, 128, 218
North, Chris 94, 97

Oliver 27
Oregon 134
Orlando, Florida 130
Osmond, Donny 20
Outhwaite, Tamzin 154

Pakefield 47–53
Paramount City 133
Pebble Mill 130
Penk, Steve 217
Peter Pan 233
Peter Pan, The New Adventures of 144–5
Phillips, Arlene 148–9, 150, 153
pilot shows 181, 273
Planet of the Apes 21
  memorabilia 171, 255–6
Please Sir 19
Plymouth 54–7
Pontins 11, 29–30, 38–40, 41–5
  Brean Sands 58, 59–65
  Camber Sands 118
  Jersey 94
  Little Canada 70–3, 85–9
  Pakefield 47–53
  Torremolinos 75–84
Princess Diana 178–9

Qdos 196, 197, 272–3

racism 23
rambles 71–2
Ray, Dick 97–8, 132
Read, Bridie 39–40, 42–3
Rice, Callum *see* Spike
Richardson, Joely 259, 261
Richie, Lionel 88
Richie, Shane, *see* Roche, Shane
Roche, Jake 146, 264, 278
Roche, Shane
  education *see* schools
  films *see Dead Clean; Distant Shadow;*
    Macbeth; Shoreditch
  holiday camp work *see* Butlins;
    Pontins
  pantomime *see Jack and the*
    Beanstalk; Peter Pan
  relationships see Cross, Lisa; Goddard,
    Christie; Nolan, Coleen; Rodgers,
    Dawn; Tyler, Claire
  stage shows see *Boogie Nights; Class*
    Enemy; Grease
  television shows see *Big Breakfast;*
    Burnside; Caught in the Act;
    EastEnders; Going Live; Jameson
    Tonight; Lucky Numbers; Night
    and Day; Night Fever; Paramount
    City; Run the Risk; Shane Richie
    Experience; Summertime Special;

The Bill; Up to Something; Win, Lose or Draw; You Gotta Be Joking

Roche, Shane Jr 121, 125–6, 134, 187, 201, 277, 278

Rodgers, Dawn 105, 106–8, 115–16, 120

Ross, Jonathan 145, 159

Rowlands, Pauline 32–3

Run the Risk 142–3

Salmon, Micky 44, 117, 132, 164–5

scar 64

Schofield, Philip 160

schools
    Barbara Speaks Stage School 25
    Cardinal Hinsley 22–3
    Stonebridge Junior and Infants 19
    Willesden High 23, 32

Scunthorpe Youth Theatre 41

Seinfeld 136

Serlin, Steve 232

Shane Richie Experience, The 180–2, 184, 195

Shane Richie: The Album 180

Shaw, Tracy 187–8, 191

Shoreditch 256–63, 275, 281

Some Mothers Do 'Ave 'Em 20

Sonia 161

Southend 203

Spiers, Judy 130

Spike 117, 132, 154, 165

Spong, Paul (Spongo) 199, 222, 233, 256, 263

Spud 117, 132, 154, 165, 228

stag nights 101–3, 128

stage names 76, 86–7

Status Quo 182

Stevenson, Jeff 77, 132

Stewart, Rod 79

Stigwood, Robert 147, 149, 150, 158

Sting 154

Stringfellow, Peter 127

strippers, male 90–1

Summertime Special 117, 120, 131

Sundown, The 37–8

Sutton, Mark *see* Big Mark

Sweet and Simple 77

Sweet, The 20

Take That 100

Tank Tops and Tarts 196

tattoos 136–7

The Bill 228, 273, 276, 277–8

The Sun 163

Thicker than Water 182

This is Your Life 182–3

This Morning 254, 272

Tiswas 86

Toad of Toad Hall 19

Torremolinos 75–84

tours 90, 99–101, 232
    Falklands 119, 121
    holiday camps 254

Triplett, Sally Anne 152–3

Turner, Anthea 153

Tyler, Claire 188–94, 198–206, 210–17, 220–3, 231, 251–3, 262–3

Up to Something 130

Wagner, Jamie 103–4

Wagner, Paul 9, 93–4, 98, 120, 143, 182

Walker, Mick 77, 79

Walsh, Bradley 254

Warwick, Dionne 130

Willesden & Brent Chronicle 19, 92, 131

Williams, Barry 89

Williams, Robbie 180, 260

Williams, Robin 145–6

Wilson, Lee 79–80

Win, Lose or Draw 155–6, 159

Windsor, Barbara 126, 282

windsurfing 88

World Cup 2002 278

World Malibu Dance Championships, The 105

You Gotta Be Joking 133

Zany, Micky 131, 182